Federalism on Trial

Federalism on Trial

State Attorneys General and National Policymaking in Contemporary America

PAUL NOLETTE

UNIVERSITY PRESS OF KANSAS

To Cindy

Published by the University Press of Kansas (Lawrence, Kansas 66045), which was organized by the Kansas Board of Regents and is operated and funded by Emporia State University, Fort Hays State University, Kansas State University, Pittsburg State University, the University of Kansas, and Wichita State University

Library of Congress Cataloging-in-Publication Data

Nolette, Paul, author.
Federalism on trial : state attorneys general and national policymaking in contemporary America / Paul Nolette.
pages cm
Includes bibliographical references and index.
ISBN 978-0-7006-2089-0 (cloth : alk. paper)
ISBN 978-0-7006-2090-6 (ebook)
1. Exclusive and concurrent legislative powers—United States. 2. Federal government—United States. 3. Attorneys general—United States—States. 4. Actions and defenses—United States. 5. Subsidiarity—United States. 6. Competent authority—United States. I. Title.
KF4600.N65 2015
320.60973—dc23

2014040564

British Library Cataloguing-in-Publication Data is available.

Printed in the United States of America
10 9 8 7 6 5 4 3 2 1

The paper used in this publication is recycled and contains 30 percent postconsumer waste. It is acid free and meets the minimum requirements of the American National Standard for Permanence of Paper for Printed Library Materials Z39.48–1992.

CONTENTS

PREFACE

I don't smoke, but tobacco served as the inspiration for this book. My interest in state attorneys general (AGs) began with research into the multi-billion-dollar Master Settlement Agreement in 1998 between the tobacco industry and most of the nation's AGs. What I found fascinating about the settlement was the way in which it served as a form of national regulation of one of America's largest industries while simultaneously bypassing the typical channels of national policymaking in Washington, DC. This prompted me to ask what AGs had been up to since the tobacco settlement. The answer, I soon discovered, was a lot. While the Master Settlement Agreement was unusual for its sheer size—it remains the largest civil settlement in American history—AGs have become increasingly aggressive in using coordinated litigation strategies to exert influence in national policy. As this book details, AGs have used the legal process as a form of national policymaking in several major areas of American public policy—activity that has exhibited greater partisan divisions among the AGs themselves and prompted many other private litigants and groups to collaborate with AGs to accomplish policy goals.

I hope to convince readers of three main propositions in the pages that follow. The first is that AGs are more than simply, as the joke goes, aspiring governors. Instead, AGs have been and continue to be an important and underappreciated force in contemporary American political development. Their litigation campaigns—and they are indeed best described as campaigns, consisting of individual skirmishes as part of a long-term battle for political influence—have gone beyond simply enforcing the law and have instead crucially shaped the contours of national policy. Second, the rise of contemporary AG activism helps illustrate an aspect of American federalism that receives far too little attention in both contemporary scholarship and in political rhetoric. While advocacy of federalism and states' rights is so often associated with a parallel commitment to a weaker national government, the activity in this book illustrates how the activism of state-level actors can lead to expanded governmental power at all levels, including the central state. My third main argument is that the emergence of AG activism as a form of national policymaking intersects with several fundamental questions about democracy in America. On the one hand, AG litigation promises to be an avenue for policy development at a time of significant political deadlock in our national policymaking institutions, thereby providing an outlet for public demands for policy change. On the other hand, the AGs' peculiar form of policymaking raises some significant difficulties, not the least of which is that policy goals achieved through litigation often fail to adequately balance competing interests and are developed in highly technical forums obstructed from public view. It is my hope that this book serves to generate more interest in AGs' role in American politics and focus more attention on the positives and negatives of this distinctive form of national policymaking—especially as Congress and the courts continue to encourage AG activism.

Many individuals and institutions helped bring this book to fruition. At Boston College, I could have hardly imagined a more supportive mentor than Shep Melnick. I learned countless things from Shep, but perhaps the most valuable lesson was that many of the most interesting and consequential developments in American law and politics happen outside of the US Supreme Court and its constitutional jurisdiction. His encouragement to explore the complex relationships of law and politics outside of the most familiar contexts led me to write this book and will remain with me throughout my career. Michael Greve first introduced me to the politics of state attorneys general and was immensely helpful at various stages of this project. Even as he juggled a remarkable number of projects of his own, he provided me with so many incisive comments on draft chapters, and so quickly, that it puzzles me to this day how he did it. Special thanks as well to Ken Kersch and Marc Landy, both of whom provided several excellent comments on early draft chapters and encouraged me to think more about the origins of the modern institution of the AG. Ken and Marc were also superb mentors whose contributions to my scholarly career extend well beyond this book alone. Several others at BC also provided invaluable assistance during the early stages of this project, including Kay Schlozman, Christopher Kelly, Peter Skerry, Dan Geary, Hillary Thompson, Alison Smith, Carol Fialkosky, and Shirley Gee.

My gratitude also goes out to many at Marquette University who have helped in various ways to make this book a reality. I have been lucky to have outstanding colleagues in the political science department at Marquette, all of whom provided a great deal of personal and intellectual support throughout the development of this project. I would especially like to thank Julia Azari and Amber Wichowsky for their willingness to read several draft chapters and provide insightful comments. I also received helpful comments throughout this research from many other colleagues, including McGee

Young, Duane Swank, Ryan Hanley, Barrett McCormick, Jeff Drope, Dongwook Kim, and Lowell Barrington. Several others at Marquette also provided encouragement throughout the project, including Sameena Mulla, Heather Hlavka, and Sam Harshner. A number of talented graduate students provided research assistance at various stages, including Shannon McLean, Jason Mumma, Katelyn Lucas, Mashal Amjad, Molly Giese, Shana Scogin, Diana Oprinescu, Siyue Liu, and Liliya Yakova. The staff of the Marquette libraries also assisted at various points in my research. Special thanks to Marva Coward at the Marquette Law School library, who helped me access a particularly difficult to obtain source of information. Finally, Marquette University provided generous institutional support throughout this project, including a grant in the summer of 2012 that helped me complete the data collection for this book.

Many others also enriched this project throughout its development. I presented research on AGs at various academic conferences, and I received helpful comments from Kevin McMahon, Dale Krane, Dave Robertson, Paul Brace, Karl Trautman, Tom Burke, Richard Flanagan, Paul Parker, Eric Kasper, Kenneth Manning, and Seval Yildirim. I am also grateful for enlightening conversations about my research with numerous additional scholars, including Chuck Epp, Catherine Albiston, Martha Derthick, John Dinan, Paul Herron, Carol Weissert, Michael Solimine, Cynthia Bowling, Robert Agranoff, Jeb Barnes, Aaron Ley, and Phillip Wallach. Dan Schweitzer at the National Association of Attorneys General generously provided key information concerning AG amicus curiae brief filings, and my conversations with several other practitioners in the world of state attorneys general were helpful throughout my research.

I am also extremely grateful to the editorial staff at the University Press of Kansas. Chuck Myers was an exceptional editor who provided many constructive comments on my chapters and made the process from draft manuscript to completed book smooth. Thanks as well to Larisa Martin, Michael Kehoe, and others at the press who have assisted throughout the production process, as well as the anonymous reviewers who provided many excellent comments and suggestions.

I also owe a debt of gratitude to my parents, Kathy and Ron Nolette, who have long provided support and, more recently, numerous comments on this book. Finally, I would like to thank my wife and best friend, Cindy. She has been a constant source of encouragement and support, and I dedicate this book to her.

CHAPTER ONE

STATE LITIGATION AND THE STRUCTURE OF CONTEMPORARY AMERICAN POLICY

On January 1, 1999, when I got this office, I suddenly became an enormous fan of the new federalism. I suddenly said, "States' rights are a beautiful thing." States' rights are the future, and we want to do everything we can to promote them.
Eliot Spitzer, former attorney general of New York

Before a personal scandal precipitated his dramatic fall, Eliot Spitzer was one of corporate America's most feared regulators. Yet his influence on national regulation stemmed not from a political position in Washington, DC, but from his role as his state's chief prosecutor. As New York's state attorney general from 1999 to 2006, Spitzer conducted litigation campaigns against Wall Street firms, gun manufacturers, energy producers, and other prominent national industries. Joined by several of his fellow attorneys general from across the country, Spitzer also led lawsuits aiming to force the George W. Bush administration to address environmental hazards such as acid rain and climate change. These actions were necessary, he claimed, because of the federal government's failure to protect consumers and the environment. By battling national corporations and federal regulators under the banner of a new states' rights, Spitzer aimed to use litigation to pursue national policy goals Congress and federal agencies had declined to adopt.

Eliot Spitzer's rise to national prominence was part of a growing trend in American politics. Beginning in the last decades of the twentieth century, state litigation has taken on an expanded role in national policymaking. State attorneys general (AGs), the actors responsible for nearly all state litigation, have increasingly collaborated across state lines on investigations and lawsuits against major corporations and the federal government alike. Just before Spitzer took office, for example, forty-six of the nation's AGs completed a $206 billion settlement with leading tobacco firms in what remains the largest civil settlement in American history. This settlement, which followed the failure of comprehensive tobacco regulation in Congress, established a host of new tobacco advertising regulations, industry lobbying restrictions, and new de facto taxes on cigarettes.[1] More recently, the 2008 foreclosure crisis prompted a coordinated AG investigation of several of America's largest banks, which concluded with a $26 billion settlement in 2012 imposing new regulations on the American lending industry not otherwise required under federal law.[2] Meanwhile, AGs have made aggressive use of lawsuits against the federal government to challenge several federal policies. For example, the constitutional challenges to President Barack Obama's signature domestic achievement, the Affordable Care Act, began with coordinated groups of AGs filing suit just minutes after the bill became law.

The emergence of this activity may initially appear as simply the latest example of states playing a central role in American political development. Many ideas born at the state level have found their way into national policy, from labor laws in the Progressive Era to welfare reform in the 1990s. Moreover, tensions between state and federal power have long been central to the American experience. "The question of the relation of the states to the federal government," as Woodrow Wilson remarked in his classic *Constitutional Government in the United States,* "is the cardinal question of our constitutional system."[3]

Yet the activity examined in this book, I suggest, is different. Although states have long served as laboratories for democracy as well as sources of political conflict, the rise of state litigation as a force in contemporary national policymaking represents a new and significant development in American federalism. Rather than merely influencing national policy through the diffusion of political innovations, AGs have increasingly used the legal process to dictate the terms of national policy. This complicates the standard conception of intergovernmental conflict, which typically focuses on state efforts to protect their interests against a federal government encroaching upon their prerogatives. Instead, this new form of politics raises precisely the opposite problem—state policy preferences effectively trumping those of the federal government.

Further complicating the familiar narrative of "the states versus the federal government" is that "the states" in this story are not a monolithic group. Armed with nearly complete control over determining their states' position in litigation, AGs have defined the state interests they are tasked with representing in increasingly divergent terms. Reflecting broader trends of political polarization and conflicts over policy, AGs have used their position to ally with like-minded advocacy groups and partisan interests to pursue ideological policy goals. This in turn has led to greater conflict between AGs and other state institutions as well as among the AGs themselves. These conflicts have become increasingly important in American politics because coordinated state litigation is different from the policymaking tools available to other state actors—and, as I argue, has become a particularly powerful method of national policymaking.

The Origins of Contemporary State Litigation

What explains how and why state litigation has become such an important part of policymaking in the United States? What are the consequences for American politics? Is this new assertion of states' rights really a "beautiful thing," as Spitzer suggests? In the following chapters, I examine the causes and consequences of state litigation's emergence as a new dimension of American federalism. Anchoring my analysis is the notion that "new policies create a new politics."[4] This idea has drawn attention from scholars of American political development who have explored how policy regimes, once established, generate feedback effects setting new political forces in motion.[5] Theda Skocpol's work on early social policy development in the United States, for example, illustrated how the expansion of Civil War pensions in the late nineteenth century created negative feedback effects, making adoption of a European-style welfare state more difficult.[6] Jacob Hacker demonstrated how American welfare politics has been profoundly shaped by regulatory and tax policies encouraging the development of private social benefits.[7] These examples are a reminder that, as Paul Pierson put it, "social life unfolds over time."[8] Understanding developments in contemporary politics requires attention to how prior policies set these new politics in motion.

Building on these insights, my analysis illustrates how earlier decisions by federal policymakers contributed to the rise of state litigation as a challenge to national policy. Most fundamentally, state litigation's status as an increasingly powerful aspect of national policymaking is a product of the peculiar structure of new social policy regimes constructed by state and federal lawmakers in the 1960s and 1970s. These policy regimes adopted broad, national objectives—such as cleaner air, wider access to health care, and greater protections for consumers in the marketplace—while reflecting both the horizontal and vertical fragmentation of power in the American state. The policies manifested America's horizontal fragmentation, which separates power across governing institutions, by carving out a major role for the judiciary in the policy process. In particular, new social policies adopted a framework of adversarial legalism by making litigation a crucial component of the enforcement and implementation of new regulatory requirements.[9] The new social policy also reflected America's vertical fragmentation, which separates powers between federal and state governments, by making states a major component in the operation of national policy. Federal environmental, health care, and consumer protection statutes adopted new forms of cooperative federalism in which federal and state actors shared responsibilities for the implementation of national policy goals. The federal government encouraged actors on the state level, including AGs, to administer and enforce these broad new areas of social policy.

The incorporation of a distinctive brand of cooperative federalism and adversarial legalism in federal policy provided fertile ground for entrepreneurial AGs to take advantage of their position as state litigators. Yet federal support for the rise of modern state litigation did not end there. Beginning in the 1970s, federal policymaking institutions specifically empowered AGs in a variety of ways. Congress provided federal grants for AGs, bolstering their ability to initiate large-scale litigation campaigns. Federal courts, along with Congress, have steadily expanded AGs' jurisdiction by granting these state actors greater ability to bring lawsuits across a range of policy areas. Meanwhile, federal agencies expanded resources available to state litigators by sharing resources and information with the states in efforts to streamline enforcement efforts. In some cases, examined later in this book, federal agencies even supported AG lawsuits against the federal government as a way to expand the regulatory state. Already armed with a great deal of institutional autonomy as the chief legal representatives of their states, AGs have benefited from this federal support to bring an increasing number of coordinated lawsuits—which, ironically, have served as a significant challenge to federal policy itself. Over time, these coordinated efforts to reshape national policy have made state litigation a major venue for broader battles over politics and regulation in America.

From Veto Points to Opportunity Points

The outgrowth of state litigation from the structure of contemporary American policy challenges the notion that the American system of separation of powers stymies, rather than encourages, national public policy development. The common view is that the vertical division of powers between the national and state governments, especially when combined with the horizontal division of powers among branches of governments, fragments policy to such a degree that it presents major obstacles to the establishment of new national policies.[10] Except during those rare critical moments when a political party can achieve unified control of federal policymaking institutions, the numerous veto points available to opponents of policy development result in little more than gridlock and inaction.[11]

This book, however, illustrates a different aspect of the operation of the structure of contemporary American government. Although horizontal and vertical fragmentation can indeed produce veto points leading to more difficult national policymaking, institutional fragmentation simultaneously opens up new opportunity points for national policymaking. It can spur "unorthodox lawmaking," Barbara Sinclair's term for new procedures and processes that aim to accomplish policy goals through unconventional and often innovative lawmaking strategies.[12] Fragmentation can also enable a wider range of policy-seeking actors, such as the AGs, to gain entry into the national policymaking system. By taking advantage of the horizontal and vertical fragmentation inherent in contemporary American policy, these actors have ironically derived the ability to forge centralized, national policies.

Although the rise of this new style of politics has served as a way to overcome the many veto points embedded in the American policymaking system, it raises new normative concerns about the proper role of this form of policymaking in a democracy. Several scholars have noted the increasing judicialization of American politics, in which the complex and technical arena of law and courts has become a crucial battleground for political competition.[13] State litigation is a prime example of this type of political contestation, becoming increasingly important in creating national regulatory policy yet occurring in venues largely shielded from the normal democratic process. Unlike policymaking in legislatures or administrative agencies in which the public has the opportunity to follow the process via C-Span or notice-and-comment rule-making hearings, the AGs' national policymaking is conducted largely behind closed doors. Out-of-court settlements involving billions of dollars and establishing new regulations require only the approval of a single judge, if at all, to go into effect. Lawsuits against administrative agencies proceed in highly technical legal forums, serving to muddy the waters of electoral accountability by complicating the ability of lawmakers to achieve a proper balance of government regulation and economic efficiency.

I will return to these normative concerns throughout this book. First, I turn to the broader relationship between state litigation and the two aspects of American separation of powers, adversarial legalism and cooperative federalism, that have given rise to this new form of policymaking. In doing so, I note how this book contributes to our understanding of the politics of litigation as well as the operation of federalism in contemporary American politics.

State Litigation in a Sea of Adversarial Legalism

Observers of American politics have long recognized the peculiarly legalistic nature of American politics and society. The American republic, it is said, is "one of laws and not of men," and the law has structured relations since the founding of the republic. Alexis de Tocqueville famously noted the influence of law in the United States in 1835, stating, "There is almost no political question in the United States that is not resolved sooner or later into a judicial question."[14] Others point to American society's status as "profoundly rooted in law" as a key element of American exceptionalism.[15]

However, although law has a long and distinctive history in American politics, something has changed in the past few decades. Since the middle of the twentieth century, courts and litigation have become much more important in resolving complex questions of public policy.[16] The "juridification" of American policy, as Gordon Silverstein has argued, has entailed the increasing substitution of ordinary politics with judicial decisions and legal formality.[17] Part of this juridification has been constitutional, with a variety of groups pursuing rights-based claims that built on the classic model of public interest litigation developed by the NAACP's success in *Brown v. Board of Education*.[18] Much of it, however, has been spurred by statutory changes, as Congress has built a litigation state by opening the courthouse doors for litigants to enforce key elements of federal policy.[19]

The construction of this litigation state has been built on Americans' reliance on what Robert Kagan calls "adversarial legalism."[20] This distinctive form of policymaking calls on adversarial features of law and courts to resolve complex questions of public policy. For example, the tort law system has grown to become a central method of compensation for victims of large-scale public health issues, and the American process of regulatory decision making allows many avenues for groups to challenge agency decisions in court. This system contrasts with the dominant methods of policy implementation in other industrialized democracies, which grant centralized, expert bureaucracies more autonomy to resolve issues of implementation.

Adversarial legalism—the distinctive American reliance on lawsuits in public policy—was a product of Americans' seemingly contradictory demands. On the one hand, Americans demanded "total justice," Lawrence Friedman's term for the society-wide call for the law to protect citizens from harms previously accepted as a normal part of modern life.[21] The public expected government to address a bevy of new quality-of-life issues including the environment, consumer protection, and health care.[22] At the same time, however, Americans retained a long-standing skepticism of concentrated political power. The more centralized political structures of Western Europe also faced calls for total justice, but the similar American demands were filtered through layers of institutional fragmentation built up because of this continuing distrust of concentrated power. How, then, were we to achieve the ambitious goal of providing Americans increased protections against the vicissitudes of modern life while avoiding too much centralization of the American state?

One answer was reliance on litigation to achieve social goals rather than placing the task wholly within centralized federal bureaucracies. Federal civil rights statutes, beginning with the Civil Rights Act of 1964, adopted private enforcement regimes empowering private litigators to enforce provisions of federal law.[23] This adversarial model of policy enforcement quickly became commonplace in federal statutes, including environmental statutes containing citizen suit provisions allowing individuals to sue polluters directly for violations of federal law.[24] Paralleling this development was a revolution in state-level tort and consumer law encouraging private parties to sue corporations for a variety of alleged harms. Large scale class-action litigation sought to use the courts to not only achieve compensation for victims but as an avenue to solve wider social problems.[25]

The exercise of adversarial legalism by private litigators generated considerable controversy, with concerns about an alleged "litigation explosion" in America prompting politicians such as George H. W. Bush to declare that Americans were "suing each other too much and caring for each other too little."[26] After expanding the private litigation state for decades, legislators and courts alike have more recently sought ways to make private litigation more difficult.[27] Yet even as legislatures and courts have trimmed America's reliance on private litigation, they have continued to strengthen the enforcement power of public prosecutors, particularly AGs. Congress has provided funding to AGs enabling them to expand their capability to handle complex legal investigations. State legislatures placed greater responsibilities on these actors to enforce broadly worded state consumer protection statutes against corporations. Federal legislation, such as the Dodd-Frank Wall Street Reform and Consumer Protection Act enacted in 2010, expanded AGs' ability to enforce federal law.[28] Meanwhile, courts have changed legal rules, making it easier for states to sue corporations and federal agencies.[29]

As the avenues for state prosecution have expanded, AGs have increasingly filled the role played by interest group litigators and private class action attorneys, both of whom have found it more difficult to access the courts. AGs have relied on adversarial legalism to achieve compensation for victims of alleged fraud, challenge agency rule making, and alter corporate behavior in ways increasingly resembling the private elements of America's litigation state. However, despite the often politically charged nature of their litigation, AGs have avoided becoming enmeshed in the broader political controversy over litigation in American society. By engaging in an "acceptable" and less controversial form of adversarial legalism, AGs have become a more attractive avenue for interest groups, plaintiffs' lawyers, and political parties seeking their own financial and policy interests.

One of the broader themes of this book is that modern state litigation illustrates a different way in which law is used to exert power in the American state. Too often in contemporary scholarship on law and courts, the examination of the role of law in America focuses on the formal actions of judges, and particularly those on the US Supreme Court. This characteristic hovers over much of the debate over whether seeking social and political change through the law is merely a "hollow hope."[30] Yet other scholars, especially those in the law and society tradition, have noted that the reach of the law goes well beyond formal judicial decision making. Much of what is important in legal development occurs not because of formal court decisions but because of contentious bargaining in the shadow of the law.[31] As Charles Epp has explained in the context of efforts to reform police practices and reduce sexual harassment in the workplace, the threat of legal liability is a powerful lever to produce compliance with new norms even in the absence of formal judicial action.[32]

This dynamic has been central to much of the litigation by AGs. My narrative examines how AGs have attempted to use the law to force political change, but courts and judges often play only a supporting role. The bulk of the AGs' litigation is resolved via out-of-court agreements before formally entering the court system, with little, if any, judicial oversight. Nevertheless, because the threat of active litigation remains ever present in the background, defendants are willing to sign settlements containing regulatory standards not otherwise required by existing law. Piece by piece, these settlements represent a patchwork national regulatory regime created outside of the typical national policymaking process. This form of policymaking has proven especially resilient because it leverages the power of the law while simultaneously insulating new policy creation from further oversight by judicial, legislative, or administrative institutions.

State Litigation and the Reshaping of American Federalism

AGs are not just litigators, taking advantage of the sea of adversarial legalism that has emerged in the latter half of the twentieth century. They are also state actors who have benefited from important changes in American federalism during the same period. As Daniel Elazar noted, the post–New Deal period represented a transition from a dual federalism in which state and federal governments operated in separate policy spheres to a cooperative federalism in which both worked together to achieve common goals.[33] According to one oft-cited metaphor, American federalism has increasingly resembled a marble cake, in which functions of local, state, and federal governments mingle together, as opposed to a layer cake, in which governmental functions are strictly separate from one another.[34]

As federal policies grew rapidly after the era of the New Deal, federal policymakers increasingly looked to the states to help implement these new programs. This was especially true in the 1960s and 1970s, when federal policy enlisted states as partners in administering programs aiming to solve large-scale social problems including racism, pollution, and poverty. Clean air and water statutes adopted during the environmental decade of the 1970s, for example, articulated national goals but placed much of the responsibility for implementation on state governments. Medicaid, the health care system for lower-income Americans, likewise adopted a cooperative federalism model by splitting funding between the federal and state governments while giving administrative responsibilities for the program to the states.

The increased role of the states in policy implementation had profound impacts on the shape of federalism in the United States, with many suggesting that the rise of cooperative federalism posed challenges to the vitality of state authority. When in 1969 constitutional scholar Philip Kurland bluntly declared that "federalism is dead," he had in mind the ways in which the federal government was increasingly dictating the shape of national policy and squeezing out the traditional role of the states.[35] John Kincaid argued that cooperative federalism was morphing into coercive federalism as Congress increasingly preempted state authority and attached various strings to states' receipt of federal money.[36] By the 1990s, the Supreme Court—the institution that Kurland accused of playing a central role in killing federalism—became increasingly concerned with cooperative federalism's role in allowing the federal government to commandeer state officials into carrying out federal objectives at the expense of traditional state autonomy.[37]

Yet the suggestion that cooperative federalism would lead to the demise of federalism overlooked the way in which marble cake federalism has also served to empower states by providing them additional avenues through which to affect federal programs. Taking note of the ways in which federal programs since the 1960s entailed a "great expansion in the use and activity of subnational governments," Samuel H. Beer noted that states "in consequence find themselves in a stronger position to make demands on the central government."[38] By inviting states into the national policymaking process, federal policy opened the door for entrepreneurial state actors to have a hand in shaping the contours of that process. Although the federal government maintained leverage over the states by means of threatening preemption and attaching strings to federal grants, states maintained leverage over the federal government because federal policy depended on them to carry out federal objectives.

Meanwhile, Congress, federal agencies, and the courts provided AGs specifically with additional resources bolstering their capacity to enforce new national policy regimes. This included grants to AGs allowing them to expand their operations as well as the ability to directly enforce federal law. The incorporation of AGs into the national policy process allowed federal policymakers to achieve enforcement goals without the necessity of creating large new federal bureaucracies. At the same time, however, it bolstered an entrepreneurial set of actors who have taken advantage of the invitation to influence national policy to both complement and complicate the goals of federal policy. Another of this book's main themes is that the rise of coordinated AG activity, which has emerged as both adversarial legalism and cooperative federalism became crucial aspects of national policy implementation, requires a reevaluation of common conceptions of the federal–state relationship.

For one, the AGs' activities run contrary to the familiar view that a vigorous commitment to states' rights serves as a limit on national power. This view of federalism has a long lineage in American politics. In his famous argument in *Federalist* No. 51, James Madison argued that federalism worked with separation of powers to provide a "double security" for the liberties of the people. The commitment to maintaining separate spheres of authority in state and federal governments, themselves both fragmented further into different branches, would help ensure that "the different governments will control each other, at the same time that each will be controlled by itself."[39] Alexander Hamilton similarly portrayed federalism in terms of limiting governmental power, suggesting in *Federalist* No. 28 that the "general government will at all times stand ready to check the usurpations of state governments, and these will have the same dispositions toward the general government."[40]

These founding-era conceptions of the federal–state relationship have infused much subsequent scholarly analysis as well as popular rhetoric concerning federalism. Several scholars have argued that by fragmenting power and creating additional veto points, federalism both in America and in other federal states contributes to weaker central state development.[41] Some scholars, particularly those from the public choice tradition, celebrate decentralization for its ability to constrain government growth.[42] Meanwhile, American political movements advocating a vigorous commitment to states' rights have been most frequently associated with political conservatives. President Ronald Reagan argued for a shift of governmental functions to the states because "the Federal Government is overloaded . . . having assumed more responsibilities than it can properly manage."[43] In the 1990s, conservatives in Congress and on the Supreme Court proposed devolution and dual federalism as ways to limit the reach of the national government.[44] The rise of the conservative Tea Party movement during the first term of Barack Obama's presidency also reflected a conservative commitment to federalism as a way to cabin the power of the federal government.[45]

However, the notion that federalism serves as a constraint on governmental power by allowing each level of government to "check the usurpations" of the other belies much of how contemporary AGs have used their position in the federal system. Rather than resisting the growth of a national regulatory state that threatens to expand federal power at the expense of the states, AGs have more frequently used coordinated litigation to promote the expansion of national regulation. By working together across state lines, AGs have developed new national policies conflicting with and even replacing regulatory policy choices adopted by the federal government. AGs have often made this goal explicit, as when Eliot Spitzer claimed his litigation against Wall Street was a way to accomplish what federal regulatory agencies could not or would not do: place new regulatory oversight over the financial industry's practices. The case studies in this book likewise illustrate how AGs used litigation to expand the national regulatory state across two of the most contentious and economically far-reaching areas of national policy: health care and the environment.

Although the AGs' version of states' rights bears little resemblance to the common portrayal of federalism as playing primarily the role of constraining government power, it appears to mesh better with scholarly conceptions of federalism that emphasize the ways in which post–New Deal federalism empowers government at all levels. In a profound reinterpretation of the New Deal's effects on the federal–state relationship, Stephen Gardbaum observed that the New Deal period, so often assumed to be solely a story of increasing federal power, was actually a period in which the regulatory power of the states was "unshackled" concurrently with increases in national power.[46] Rather than representing a zero-sum game in which the federal government gained power at the expense of the states, after the New Deal "*both* federal and state governments were constitutionally enabled to regulate a large number of areas of social and economic life that previously they had both been prohibited from regulating."[47] Far from killing off federalism, the New Deal revolution fortified state power even as the reach of the central government expanded.

Several scholars have celebrated the potential for the contemporary federal–state relationship to empower government rather than to check it. Robert A. Schapiro, for example, emphasizes the benefits of a "polyphonic" conception of contemporary federalism that "consists of independent state and federal voices that interact together" to bring their powers to bear on common problems.[48] Having multiple, overlapping layers of authority is valuable, Schapiro argues, because of the way it promotes the values of plurality, dialogue, and redundancy.[49] The value of plurality argues that policymaking benefits from multiple approaches to similar policy problems, harkening back to Justice Louis Brandeis's argument that it is "one of the happy incidents of the federal system that a single courageous state may, if its citizens choose, serve as a laboratory; and try novel social and economic experiments without risk to the rest of the country."[50] Contemporary federalism also promotes dialogue between federal and state regulators, which can result in better and more comprehensive regulatory schemes through the exchange of ideas. Finally, the redundancy of overlapping regulation can prevent the existence of regulatory gaps because regulation at one level of government can address regulatory failures at another. Schapiro's work parallels similar arguments by scholars who have used an array of monikers to describe contemporary American federalism, including dynamic federalism,[51] empowerment federalism,[52] intersystemic governance,[53] iterative federalism,[54] and adaptive federalism.[55] Uniting all of them is a defense of a system of modern governance that provides an expansive role for the states to engage in regulatory policymaking alongside federal regulators.

The emergence of coordinated AG activism appears to fit well into this polyphonic conception of federalism as empowerment rather than federalism as constraint. However, unlike other state actors such as governors and legislators, AGs use a policymaking tool—adversarial legalism—that complicates the alleged benefits of this polyphonic system. Although one of the major purported benefits of state activism is the potential for policy experimentation and regulatory dialogue, the AGs' brand of federalism often results in precisely the opposite. Rather than promoting regulatory experimentation, AG litigation has served as a way to set single regulatory standards across the entire nation. Rather than complementing the federal regulatory regime through intergovernmental dialogue, AGs have used adversarial methods to close off debate rather than promote it by trumping existing national policy and replacing it with their own view of ideal policy. In doing so, the AGs' attempts to solve perceived regulatory problems within national policy regimes have created new complications.

Overview of the Book

The structure of modern American policy, which combined cooperative federalism and adversarial legalism, served to create a new politics in the form of nationally focused state litigation campaigns. This in turn has sparked a different operation of the vertical and horizontal separation of powers than commonly assumed. Rather than standing in the way of national, coordinated policy development, the fragmentation of the American system actually encouraged such development. At the same time, however, the rise of the AGs' coordinated activism has raised new problems by setting into motion a variety of unintended policy consequences. This book examines this activity by relying upon an original dataset of multistate litigation and a series of in-depth case studies.

Chapter 2 provides the background for the case studies that follow by examining the broader trends and goals of coordinated state litigation. I suggest that state litigation falls into three basic categories: (1) *policy-creating litigation* that seeks settlements with national corporations establishing new regulatory responsibilities not otherwise required by law, (2) *policy-forcing litigation* that challenges regulatory inaction by federal agencies, and (3) *policy-blocking litigation* that attempts to thwart regulatory actions by federal policymakers. Relying on an original data set of multistate litigation from 1980 to 2013, this chapter demonstrates that state litigation has increased dramatically over time. It also examines why this has occurred, including how various state and federal policies and actions of the AGs themselves have bolstered the ability of state litigators to serve as powerful actors in national policymaking.

Chapters 3 through 5 examine the role of AGs in the fast-growing area of multistate pharmaceutical litigation. Chapter 3 examines how AGs used policy-creating litigation to fundamentally alter the multi-billion-dollar prescription drug industry. AGs, often working together with federal prosecutors, private attorneys, and public interest groups, aimed to redefine health care fraud to include practices in which pharmaceutical firms had long been engaged and that Congress had countenanced as a way to ensure that health care providers would remain in Medicare and Medicaid. The success of this litigation prompted an overhaul of the national drug pricing regime and expanded government oversight of the pharmaceutical industry.

Chapter 4 involves another policy-creating litigation campaign that has changed the way in which pharmaceutical firms market prescription drugs. Particularly through the use of out-of-court settlements against drug companies, states achieved new national regulations on the pharmaceutical industry. This has included new restrictions on off-label marketing, disclosures of clinical testing results, and new requirements for direct-to-consumer advertising, all of which are effectively applicable nationally but are not required under federal law. As with pharmaceutical pricing, these lawsuits have successfully disrupted the existing balance of policy objectives maintained by federal policymakers in an area affecting a significant portion of the overall American economy.

Chapter 5 ties together several of the broader themes of the states' pharmaceutical litigation. By making cooperative federalism and adversarial legalism a key part of the underlying statutory structure of government health care programs, Congress carved out entrepreneurial space for state litigators to challenge federal health care policies. The growth of AG capacity, bolstered by federal funding and partnerships with the private bar, helped enable these actors to bring complex pharmaceutical litigation. The effect of these drug pricing and marketing lawsuits has been to destabilize previous compromises in Congress with wide implications for the entire health care industry. In the meantime, the settlements have served to supplement the AGs' own power by affording them greater oversight over drug companies. The success of these lawsuits suggest that the basic dynamic present in these litigation campaigns, in which state policy choices essentially trump federal regulatory compromises, will continue.

I move to a second policy area in chapters 6 through 8, which examine how state litigation serves as a tool to shape national environmental policy. Chapter 6 addresses how AGs took advantage of the structure of the Clean Air Act—which placed a twin emphasis on cooperative federalism and adversarial legalism—in successive waves of policy-forcing litigation to address the emerging issue of acid rain. A first wave of state litigation targeted the Reagan administration's deregulatory approach to air pollution control. Although this litigation achieved only modest success in court, it signaled the emergence of a new tool to challenge national policy. A second and much more successful wave of lawsuits challenged the George W. Bush administration's approach to acid rain. This litigation built on the states' experience with the tobacco settlement to force a series of multi-billion-dollar settlements requiring industry leaders to adhere to an interpretation of the Clean Air Act that had been rejected by the Bush administration. A concurrent strategy was to sue the Environmental Protection Agency in an attempt to force the agency to expand regulation of energy producers. These efforts resulted in several state victories effectively reversing the regulatory approach adopted by the federal government.

Chapter 7 explains how states used both policy-creating and policy-forcing litigation strategies to challenge the Bush administration's approach to climate change. Because Congress and the administration appeared unwilling to take action to reduce greenhouse gases contributing to climate change, AGs took to the courts to try and achieve a regulatory approach rejected by federal policymakers. One strategy involved suing polluters directly under innovative common-law theories in an attempt to reach regulatory settlements. This policy-creating litigation campaign eventually sputtered, but a second policy-forcing approach was much more successful. AGs argued that the Bush administration was legally obligated under the Clean Air Act to regulate carbon dioxide and other greenhouse gases, a strategy that achieved success in the US Supreme Court's decision of *Massachusetts v. EPA* (2007). This decision, widely considered the most important environmental ruling in the Court's history, was the result of a lengthy litigation strategy orchestrated by AGs together with a cadre of interest groups and political interests.

Chapter 8 suggests that several of the themes of the pharmaceutical litigation have also appeared in the environmental litigation. As in the pharmaceutical context, the AGs' environmental litigation developed as a result of the statutory structure of the federal air pollution control regime and greater litigation capacity for AGs. Although their strategies were not always successful, AGs' actions in this area have had far-reaching consequences. This litigation has destabilized the federal air pollution control regime by seeking policy goals incompatible with the statutory structure on which the lawsuits are based. Although advocates of stricter climate change regulation achieved in the courts what they were unable to achieve in the executive or legislative branches, it has come at the cost of regulatory certainty. These litigation campaigns also highlight the growing polarization among AGs and increased collaboration between AGs and interest groups, suggesting that state litigation is becoming an additional battleground for national political conflict outside of traditional policymaking institutions.

The last of my case study chapters turns to the changing nature of AG litigation during the Obama administration. I focus in chapter 9 on AGs' use of policy-blocking litigation, especially constitutional challenges to the Patient Protection and Affordable Care Act and litigation seeking to block new climate change regulations. Although these conservative state litigation campaigns have tended to seek constraints on the national regulatory state, they illustrate how state litigators are increasingly part of a larger web of national political conflict in which AGs act as a stand-in for the interests of individuals and political parties as opposed to traditional "state interests." Particularly important is the intensifying polarization among the AGs on party lines, a dynamic that has also appeared in the AGs' use of amicus curiae (friend of the court) briefs. AGs have also increasingly collaborated with a variety of outside interests, including private attorneys and public interest groups. In short, AG activism has become a more nationalized battleground for political conflict in which states serve as a method of legitimizing and mobilizing broader litigation campaigns.

The concluding chapter 10 returns to the theme that state litigation reveals American federalism operating in a manner different from commonly assumed. Beyond simply protecting state prerogatives from an overzealous federal government, coordinated state litigation also serves as a way to challenge and destabilize the federal policy regime while often expanding the regulatory reach of government. This nationally focused state litigation has been institutionalized as a powerful way for political actors—along with the interest groups and political parties with whom they are increasingly linked—to get a second chance at policy change after failing to succeed in Congress or in federal agencies. Ironically, however, federal policymakers have contributed to the institutionalization of this national policymaking rival by bolstering the capacity of state litigators and by maintaining the model of cooperative federalism and adversarial legalism in federal regulatory programs. This development, I argue, is problematic for several reasons. Even as state litigation has often complicated federal regulation, however, various incentives for all of the affected parties are likely to maintain state litigation as a significant part of the national policy landscape.

CHAPTER TWO

THE EMERGENCE OF MODERN STATE LITIGATION

Who do these people think they are?
Senator John McCain (R-AZ), referring to state attorneys general during the congressional debate over tobacco regulation

Speaking at the Delaware Democratic Party's annual Jefferson-Jackson dinner in 2009, Bill Clinton turned to Beau Biden, the sitting vice president's son and Delaware's state attorney general. "He's got the best job in politics," Clinton told the crowd. "You know, I was attorney general. That was my first elected job. You don't have to appoint or disappoint, like governors or presidents do. If you did anything really unpopular, you could just blame it on the Constitution."[1] A week earlier, he told a candidate for California attorney general much the same thing, remarking that the office was "probably the best job in politics" because it was less beholden to the state legislature compared to other statewide offices.[2]

Even affording the former president some leeway for exaggeration, one can see the basis for his remarks. State attorneys general (AGs) occupy an unusual position in state government, with most of them armed with virtually full control over litigation in the name of their state and considerable independence from other institutions in state government. Although AGs have existed since the creation of the American republic, predating even the federal Department of Justice by a hundred years, their role in the years since Clinton's tenure as Arkansas AG in the 1970s has changed considerably. AGs have used their position to take on a more prominent role in national politics, especially through increasing collaborations among themselves and other actors in national politics. Most importantly, they have aggressively used coordinated multistate litigation against the federal government and a host of private industries as a way to influence several national policies.

To provide a broader context for the case studies discussed later in the book, this chapter provides an overview of the emergence of multistate litigation in contemporary American politics. This activity has become much more common in recent years, and the results of AG coordination have had an increasingly consequential impact on national policy and regulation. Modern state litigation, I suggest, has sought to achieve one of three goals with respect to national policy: (1) to create policy by crafting settlements requiring national industries to comply with new regulations stricter than required under current law; (2) to force policy by suing federal agencies to require them to expand regulation; or (3) to block policy by challenging federal agencies' efforts at regulatory expansion.

Although the forms of multistate litigation differ, all three are an outgrowth of similar trends within the contemporary American national policy regime. As federal policymakers in the post–New Deal period increasingly incorporated states into the process of policy implementation and expanded the importance of litigation in this process, AGs were primed to take advantage. The rapid growth of institutional capacity in the AGs' offices, spurred by additional resources available to these actors in terms of additional attorneys and expanded jurisdiction, aided their ability to influence contemporary national policy. As the office of AG developed from a primarily state-focused institution to one that is increasingly involved in national policy, AGs have become an avenue for a broader network of policy actors to influence national policy. In an era in which national institutions have so often appeared paralyzed by numerous veto points and hyperpolarization, the growth of this emerging avenue of policy development has become increasingly important.

AGs and the Rise of Multistate Collaboration

AGs maintain an unusual role at the crossroads of law and politics. Unlike the US attorney general, who is clearly a member of the executive branch, the office does not clearly fit into traditional notions of the separation of powers.[3] In addition to serving as their jurisdiction's chief legal representative in all fifty states and six territories, AGs perform a number of important duties combining executive, legislative, and judicial functions. This includes conducting litigation in the name of the state, issuing quasi-judicial opinions clarifying the law for government officials and private entities, and acting as legislative advocates and policymakers in areas concerning the public interest.[4] Forty-three of the nation's AGs are elected statewide separately from the governor or other state institutions, providing most of them with considerable political independence.

Despite these institutional advantages, AGs for years remained relatively obscure political actors who focused mainly on their own state's interests. Although they used their legal tools to regulate business behavior before the New Deal, their role appeared to diminish after the initial development of the national administrative state.[5] Drew Ketterer, a former Maine attorney general, remarked that until the end of the twentieth century, "Nobody really knew who these people were."[6] As late as the 1970s, Alabama AG William J. Baxley described the state's attorney as "generally regarded as (1) a criminal prosecutor whose primary concern was the protection of the public from robbers, murderers, kidnappers, and the like and (2) an advocate for the state and its agencies."[7]

Beginning in the last two decades of the twentieth century, however, AGs have increasingly coordinated their efforts to intervene in national politics. Several scholars have focused on multistate collaboration in the Supreme Court, where the states have become the second most active litigator after the federal government.[8] In addition to appearing as parties in Supreme Court litigation, AGs have also been considerably more active in filing amicus curiae briefs on behalf of their states.[9] These filings frequently involve close collaboration among AGs, and evidence suggests that they have often been successful in influencing Supreme Court outcomes.[10] In addition to their activities in the Supreme Court, AGs have collaborated to influence other branches of the national government as well. Assisted by their main national organization, the National Association of Attorneys General, AGs have lobbied Congress and the executive branch for various changes to national policy.[11]

The most important way in which states have influenced national policy, however, is by collaborating on multistate legal actions against private corporations and the federal government. Although formally fashioned as coordinated law "enforcement," these efforts have increasingly become a way for AGs to create, force, and block new national policies. All three of these roles, described in more detail below, are considerably different from the traditional state-centered roles AGs have played as their states' chief legal representatives. AGs once served as advocates for the state and its agencies primarily through defensive litigation, defending the state against legal claims brought against it by individual or class action plaintiffs. Although this defensive litigation still forms a portion of the AGs' activities, their most consequential efforts since the 1980s have involved offensive litigation in which they represent their states as plaintiffs in increasingly large-scale coordinated litigation campaigns.

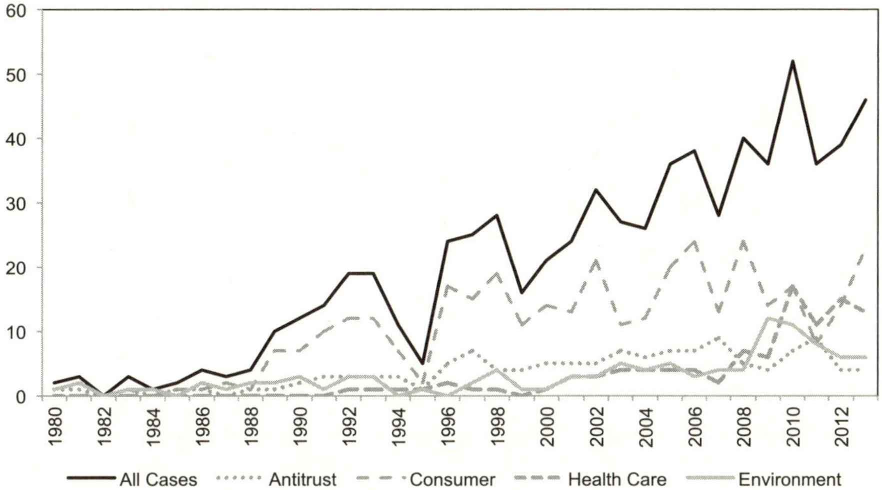

Figure 2.1. Multistate AG litigation, by number of cases resolved per year, 1980–2013. Source: Author's calculations.

I discuss several of these litigation campaigns in later chapters, but to provide the broader context for those campaigns, I cataloged all instances of coordinated AG litigation over a thirty-four year period from 1980 to 2013.[12] This search resulted in 686 unique cases across this period, virtually all of which have occurred across four broad areas of policy: antitrust enforcement, consumer protection, health care, and environmental policy. As figure 2.1 illustrates, litigation across all four areas has become much more common since the 1980s.

Multistate litigation, once unusual, has become considerably more common over time. From a consistently low number of one to four cases a year throughout the 1980s, the quantity of multistate cases reached double digits for the first time in 1989. After a decrease in both 1994 and 1995, the number of multistate cases gradually increased, reaching twenty for the first time in 1996, thirty in 2002, and forty in 2008. Fully two-thirds of the AGs' multistate litigation during this period occurred since 2000.

In addition to becoming more common, multistate cases have involved a greater number of AGs over time. Figure 2.2 provides the size of the groups involved in multistate cases over each five-year period in the data set, broken down in small- (two to five and six to fifteen AGs), medium- (sixteen to thirty-nine AGs), and large-sized groups (forty to forty-nine and fifty AGs).

Although a substantial majority of early multistate cases involved AGs working together in smaller groups of fifteen or fewer states, larger suits

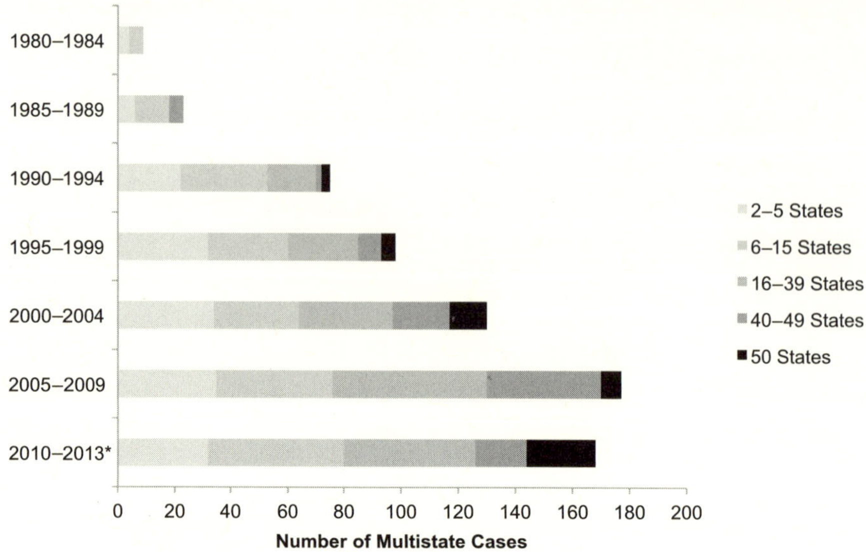

Figure 2.2. Number of AGs participating in individual multistate cases by five-year period. Source: Author's calculations. Note that the 2010–2013 bar represents only four years, in comparison to the five-year periods represented by the other bars.

and settlements have lately become more common. Litigation involving over half of the nation's AGs, once an unusual event, represents over 40 percent of all the multistate cases conducted since 2000.

Goals of Multistate Litigation

Coordinated state litigation has become significant not only because of its quantitative increase but also because of its rising qualitative importance. Although many of the earliest multistate litigation campaigns involved relatively minor issues—including multistate campaigns against telemarketers, sweepstakes firms, and manufacturers of food products—more recent cases have challenged broader practices of major multinational firms and significant policies of the federal government. This activity, as I suggested in chapter 1, increasingly constitutes a nationalization of state litigation through which coordinated groups of AGs have dictated the shape of national policy. Whether through settlements with national corporations or lawsuits directly against federal agencies, this coordinated, multistate litigation has served as an alternative venue for national policymaking. Below I describe three basic forms of coordinated state litigation, which I term policy-creating, policy-forcing, and policy-blocking litigation.

Policy-Creating Litigation

The first way in which AGs have attempted to influence national policy is through policy-creating litigation. This form of litigation, one of the more recent manifestations of regulation through litigation,[13] involves states bringing coordinated lawsuits against national corporations with the purpose of forcing them to the bargaining table. Most coordinated AG efforts are of this type, with 624 (91 percent) of the 686 resolved multistate cases targeting various aspects of corporate practice. The AGs base their policy-creating litigation on a variety of legal claims, including federal and state statutes as well as common law legal principles. Throughout these campaigns, however, courts play a relatively small role because the AGs' goal is not to win in court but rather to use the threat of active litigation to achieve comprehensive out-of-court settlements with their litigation targets.

As described in later chapters, this form of "bargaining in the shadow of the law"[14] is a powerful method of policymaking, in large part because it sidesteps the many veto points that are part of the American policymaking system. Increasingly, multistate settlements have included far-reaching provisions mandating that targeted industries comply with new requirements beyond anything contained in federal laws or regulations. Because these provisions are part of global settlements resolving the claims of many or even all of the fifty states, they effectively apply nationally. This is often a self-conscious result on the part of AGs, who have sought extensive regulatory provisions in the face of perceived failures of Congress or federal agencies to regulate corporate activities adequately.

A classic example is the AGs' tobacco litigation of the late 1990s, which came amid failed attempts of tobacco control advocates to achieve new national regulations in Congress. After years of investigations, forty-six AGs reached a Master Settlement Agreement (MSA) with America's leading tobacco firms that not only sent over $200 billion to the states but also established a new policy regime regulating the sale and marketing of tobacco products.[15] Among many other restrictions, the MSA prohibited tobacco firms from targeting youth with cartoons in cigarette advertising, banned the advertising of cigarettes in public transit facilities, and prohibited the use of cigarette brand names on merchandise. The MSA also created a complicated structure of payments from the tobacco industry to state treasuries that amounted to a new uniform national tax on tobacco products.[16] When AGs and the tobacco industry signed the MSA in 1998, it marked the first legal success against the tobacco industry after decades of failed private lawsuits. The MSA also created new national regulations covering the entire tobacco industry—all without involvement of the federal government.

The tobacco settlement received considerable scholarly and political attention, but AGs have since built on the tobacco experience to target the practices of many other industries. As Colin Provost has documented, state and federal consumer protection statutes serve as the basis for much AG litigation.[17] Such consumer protection litigation includes AGs' litigation against several national banks throughout the 2000s targeting alleged predatory lending practices.[18] It also includes the AGs' $26 billion settlement in 2012 with the six largest national banks to settle investigations into the banks' role in the mortgage crisis of the late 2000s.[19] Several AGs have also brought major antitrust litigation against national firms, which included a massive lawsuit against Microsoft accusing the software company of using its market power to thwart competition.[20] Former New York AG Eliot Spitzer made headlines throughout the 2000s for leading antitrust litigation against national insurance and brokerage firms based on the firms' use of contingent commissions and other allegedly illegal industry practices. These efforts resulted in new codes of conduct being applied across the national insurance industry.[21]

To determine which industries are the most common targets of multistate litigation, I identified the North American Industry Classification System (NAICS) code for the targeted defendants in each of the 624 cases in the data set involving settlements with private industry.[22] Table 2.1 contains the fifteen most common industry targets in AGs' coordinated litigation efforts against corporate firms.

Immediately apparent from table 2.1 is how often pharmaceutical companies are targets of coordinated AG efforts. Indeed, lawsuits and settlements with drug firms accounted for over one-fifth of all multistate litigation targeting private industry. Other frequent litigation targets have included large corporations with a strong national presence, such as tobacco firms, national banks, Internet firms, and telecommunications carriers. Although some multistate litigation involves firms that are strong at a regional level but not necessarily nationally, such as antitrust cases involving the merger of regional firms, most multistate litigation involves issues with salience beyond single regions. Approximately 85 percent of the multistate cases in

Table 2.1. Top Fifteen Industries Targeted in Multistate Litigation, 1980–2013

Sector Code	Industry Description	No. of Cases	% of Cases
3254	Pharmaceutical and medicine manufacturing	128	20.51
5221–5223	Commercial banking, consumer lending, and mortgage lending	39	6.25
5241–5242	Insurance carriers and insurance agencies/ brokerages	29	4.65
5418	Advertising, public relations, and related services	22	3.53
5171–5172	Wired and wireless telecommunications carriers	22	3.53
3112–3121	Food and beverage manufacturing	21	3.37
3241	Petroleum and coal products manufacturing	21	3.37
4461	Health and personal care stores	20	3.21
3122	Tobacco manufacturing	17	2.72
5191	Internet service providers, web search portals, and data processing	15	2.40
2211	Electric power generation, transmission, and distribution	15	2.40
3341–3349	Computer and electronic product manufacturing	12	1.92
5614–5617	Administrative and support services	11	1.76
3361	Motor vehicle manufacturing	10	1.60
5111	Newspaper, periodical, book, and directory publishers	10	1.60

Source: Author's calculations.

the data set involved AGs representing states from more than one region of the country.[23]

Although the strong national presence of the industries listed in table 2.1 partially explains why they are such frequent targets of multistate litigation, there is another dynamic at play as well. Several of the most frequent targets of multistate litigation are companies in industries featuring relatively high levels of market concentration. The tobacco industry is the clearest example, with only a few firms controlling nearly all of the tobacco market. Although not as concentrated as the tobacco industry, the frequently targeted pharmaceutical and banking industries consist of relatively few large firms whose products make up a significant portion of the market. Likewise, a relatively small number of leading firms dominate telecommunications, petroleum manufacturing, and health and personal care stores industries.[24] This level of market concentration is important because, as Michael Greve has suggested, regulatory provisions contained in settlements are considerably more effective when "the states and the targeted industry as a whole [are] able to reach an agreement."[25] New regulatory terms contained in settlements with the four largest tobacco or pharmaceutical firms will cover a larger percentage of the overall market, and involve easier compliance oversight, than settlement agreements with companies in more diffuse industries. For AGs seeking a nationwide impact on regulatory policy, the best use of resources is to target those industries in which settlement terms are most likely to have a broad impact across an entire industry.

Not all of the AGs are equally active in pursuing global settlements with national industries. When one or more AGs decide to engage an issue, the states initiating the action will often propose a multistate working group and offer to chair or co-chair the group. These lead states play a coordinating role, including organizing document reviews and performing similar litigation tasks.[26] Typically, the lead states will send out settlement information to the other states, including states not currently part of the investigation, to determine if they wish to join a proposed settlement.[27] In short, states taking the lead on settlement negotiations play the most important role in bringing a case to its conclusion, especially because AG participation in a case often involves little more than providing a signature on a draft settlement agreement that the lead states have already negotiated.

For nearly all (95 percent) of the 624 cases against private industry in the data set, I was able to determine every state that participated in the resolution of the case. For about two-thirds of the cases (69 percent), I was able to determine which AGs led the case. Table 2.2 lists the ten most active states participating and leading multistate lawsuits against private industry.

Only nine states participated in at least 50 percent of the cases, with Illinois's AG participating in the largest number of cases. Fourteen states, along with the six jurisdictions, were involved in less than a third of the cases. Several of the largest states are the most active in multistate litigation, though AGs from a few smaller states, such as Connecticut, Oregon, Iowa, and Vermont, have been relatively active as well.[28]

Many states participate in multistate litigation, but only a few states typically take a leading role in these efforts. Most striking is how frequently the New York attorney general's office has taken the lead in multistate cases against industry. The New York AG has taken a leading role in over a third of all multistate cases from 1980 to 2013, nearly doubling the percentage of the AG of the second-place state, California. This strong leadership role is consistent across all four of the major policy areas of multistate litigation,

Table 2.2. Most and Least Active States Involved in Multistate Litigation against Industry, 1980–2013

State	No. of Cases	% of Cases
	Top Ten Leading States	
New York	144	33.57
California	73	17.02
Massachusetts	66	15.38
Texas	63	14.69
Florida	59	13.75
Illinois	58	13.52
Ohio	57	13.29
Connecticut	44	10.26
Oregon	43	10.02
Washington	35	8.16
	Top Ten Participating States	
Illinois	374	63.39
California	341	57.80
New York	335	56.78
Texas	332	56.27
Massachusetts	323	54.75
Florida	322	54.58
Pennsylvania	319	54.07
Connecticut	310	52.54
Ohio	298	50.51
Washington	294	49.83
	Bottom Ten Leading States	
Wyoming	0	0.00
South Dakota	0	0.00
Alabama	1	0.23
Montana	1	0.23
Alaska	1	0.23
Oklahoma	1	0.23
Hawaii	1	0.23
West Virginia	1	0.23
Utah	2	0.47
North Dakota	2	0.47
	Bottom Ten Participating States	
Wyoming	145	24.58
Alaska	160	27.12
Utah	171	28.98
Georgia	176	29.83
South Dakota	177	30.00

continued on next page

Table 2.2. Continued

State	No. of Cases	% of Cases
North Dakota	182	30.85
Mississippi	184	31.19
South Carolina	186	31.53
New Hampshire	186	31.53
Indiana	187	31.69

Source: Author's calculations.

with New York leading the most cases in every area except health care litigation, where it places second behind Ohio. On the other end of the spectrum, twenty-six of the fifty-six jurisdictions have taken the lead role in five or fewer multistate cases from 1980 to 2013. The AGs from South Dakota and Wyoming (along with the five US territories) have never led a resolved multistate case, at least in the approximately two-thirds of the cases where the identities of the lead states are clear.

Previous research has indicated that coordinated litigation against private industries, at least coordinated consumer protection litigation, tends to attract largely bipartisan participation among AGs.[29] In one sense this is surprising, because one might expect Republican AGs to be more skeptical of litigation that effectively expands government oversight and regulation over the private sector. However, policy-creating litigation is largely a bipartisan endeavor because the settlements often require corporations to pay substantial fines, but only to the states signing the settlement. When a regulatory settlement will occur regardless of whether or not a particular AG participates, most AGs are likely to participate in order to get a share of the settlement proceeds even if they disagree with the underlying legal theories in the threatened lawsuit. This dynamic explains why, for example, Alabama AG William Pryor, a conservative Republican and consistent critic of his fellow AGs' use of litigation to regulate the tobacco industry, nevertheless signed the Master Settlement Agreement in 1998.[30]

Nonetheless, Democratic AGs are at least slightly more likely to participate in coordinated lawsuits against industry. Table 2.3 indicates the average percentage of AGs from each party participating in lawsuits or settlements across the four main policy areas of multistate litigation. On average, for example, multistate consumer protection cases garner the participation of 42.99 percent of all the Democratic AGs in office when the case is resolved while gaining participation from 37.72 percent of all Republican AGs in

Table 2.3. Democratic and Republican AG Participation and Lead Rates in Multistate Litigation against Industry, 1980–2013

Cases	Consumer		Antitrust		Environmental		Health Care	
	Democrat	Republican	Democrat	Republican	Democrat	Republican	Democrat	Republican
All Cases								
Participation	42.99%	37.72%	36.27%	34.90%	12.97%	9.58%	70.28%	69.76%
Lead	4.93%	2.39%	4.76%	4.14%	4.74%	0.96%	6.98%	5.96%
Cases since 2000								
Participation	49.66%	43.69%	36.00%	33.25%	12.08%	9.70%	72.76%	72.12%
Lead	5.19%	2.33%	4.85%	3.22%	5.36%	0.38%	7.11%	6.17%

Source: Author's calculations.

office at the time. Further, a look at which states lead, as opposed to merely participate in, coordinated litigation campaigns against corporations reveals a greater partisan split. Democratic AGs are more likely to serve as the lead states across all four areas, particularly in consumer protection and environmental litigation. In fact, Democratic AGs have led nearly all environmental litigation campaigns against corporations.

Policy-Forcing Litigation

Although AGs' multistate litigation most commonly targets corporations, several multistate litigation campaigns have featured the federal government as the defendant. By bringing policy-forcing litigation against federal agencies, states have attempted to force the federal government to take a more active regulatory approach. This approach has been particularly prominent in environmental litigation, especially concerning air pollution control. Policy-forcing litigation rose to prominence in the 1980s, when several AGs brought lawsuits to counter the Reagan administration's alleged failure to take steps to reduce sulfur dioxide emissions, the main precursor to acid rain. This strategy expanded over time, including successful efforts to challenge the EPA's decision not to regulate greenhouse gases during the George W. Bush administration.

The main legal mechanisms for these policy-forcing lawsuits are the citizen suit provisions that have been commonplace in federal environmental law since the 1970s. Several environmental statutes, including the Clean Air Act, Clean Water Act, and Safe Drinking Water Act, allowed "any person" to sue polluters as well as federal agencies tasked with regulatory enforcement.[31] These citizen suit provisions were built on earlier civil rights statutes creating private enforcement regimes that incentivize private litigants to sue alleged violators.[32] Unlike those earlier statutes, however, the environmental statutes specifically included states within the definitions of the "any persons" entitled to sue under the citizen suit provisions.

Policy-forcing litigation is unusual from the standard viewpoint of federalism. Rather than featuring states pushing back on an overzealous federal government, the states' lawsuits explicitly demand that the federal government expand regulation beyond what it has chosen to regulate. Several coordinated AG lawsuits during the George W. Bush administration, for example, demanded that the EPA expand its regulatory power to address acid rain and climate change. The particularly unusual aspect of these cases is that they sought greater federal control over the states in the form of strengthened federal mandates. The plaintiff AGs' concern was not that federal policy was interfering with state autonomy but that it was not doing enough to require states to reduce their own emissions. I return to this point in the context of the case studies contained in chapters 6 through 8.

Unlike the relatively bipartisan efforts against corporations, policy-forcing lawsuits feature wide partisan splits among the AGs that have grown over time. When AGs' policy-forcing strategies first became prominent in the acid rain litigation of the 1980s, the split between the AGs was largely regional. Nearly all of the AG plaintiffs represented Northeastern states claiming that they were especially affected by pollution that drifted into their states from Southern and Midwestern pollution sources. Over time, however, policy-forcing lawsuits have attracted wider AG involvement from across the country and have featured partisan rather than regional divisions. Since the George W. Bush administration, policy-forcing litigation has chiefly been an avenue for Democratic AGs to expand national regulation beyond the level preferred by Congress or federal agencies.

Further, policy-forcing litigation has attracted a broader network of advocacy groups that have worked closely with the AG plaintiffs in bringing these lawsuits. Environmental groups such as the Sierra Club and the Natural Resources Defense Council have viewed sympathetic AGs (nearly all Democrats) as partners in a battle to achieve stronger regulations through the courts. Meanwhile, groups fighting against stronger regulations, such as industry groups, have appeared alongside their AG allies (mostly Republicans) in opposition to the litigation brought by their fellow states.

Policy-Blocking Litigation

The third and final form of state litigation is policy-blocking litigation, which involves states' legal challenges to regulatory actions by federal policymakers. This form of multistate litigation has become particularly prominent during the Obama administration, with examples including the challenges to the Affordable Care Act and greenhouse gas regulations described in chapter 9 as well as a variety of challenges to federal financial policies and other environmental regulations. At first glance, this activity appears to be nothing new. After all, there is a long history of states bringing litigation against the federal government to prevent policy implementation, such as Southern states litigating against new civil rights statutes in the 1960s and other legal challenges to federal policies decades before that.[33] Additionally, policy-blocking litigation fits more comfortably with standard conceptions of the main conflicts inherent in the federal–state relationship. Rather than seeking an expansion of the national regulatory state, this activity typically seeks to push back on federal power in order to preserve alleged state prerogatives.

Yet recent policy-blocking litigation is different from past state litigation activity, and it shares much in common with the other types of modern state litigation. First, the same trends that have supported the AGs' collaborations on policy-creating and policy-forcing litigation have also supported policy-blocking litigation. As described in more detail later in this chapter, shifts in federal policy since the 1960s and 1970s have incorporated AGs into national policymaking, granting them both the interest and the capacity to engage in large-scale coordinated litigation with a national focus. Even the policy-blocking litigation based on constitutional claims, such as the Affordable Care Act litigation, is fundamentally tied into an underlying policy scheme in which states play a crucial role in federal policy implementation.

Further, the level of collaboration among the AGs and other actors is much closer than in previous state attempts to block implementation of federal policies. In the past, states typically challenged federal policies independent of one another, which reflected the AGs' assumption that their main duty was to represent the interests of their state alone. Multistate collaboration, when it did occur, came as amici curiae supporting another state's challenge to a federal policy.[34] Modern policy-blocking litigation, by contrast, has involved partisan collaboration among AGs as direct parties against federal policies and partnerships with a far broader network of like-minded advocacy groups. In the Affordable Care Act litigation, for example, the AG coalition that aligned against the legislation featured over half of the nation's AGs and involved close collaboration with the National Federation of Independent Business and key members of the conservative legal movement. Meanwhile, Democratic AGs and their liberal advocacy group allies countermobilized to square off with the plaintiff AGs in the case.

Similar to its policy-forcing counterpart, policy-blocking litigation has featured intensifying partisanship among the AGs, helping illustrate the way in which the institutional focus of the AG's office has shifted from a simple dualistic story of AG representing state prerogatives against the federal government. Instead, AGs have increasingly faced off against one another in court, as AG coalitions challenging federal law oppose other groups defending it. The Affordable Care Act litigation is one such example, as are AG efforts to challenge federal law in other politically salient areas such as gun control, voting rights, and same-sex marriage. A major reason this dynamic has appeared is a result of AGs becoming increasingly tied to a broader network of actors pursuing partisan and ideological political goals, which in turn focuses AG attention away from the institution's typical focus on defending state prerogatives. Policy-blocking litigation is in this sense similar to the other litigation examined in this book, as all three forms of litigation are part of broader efforts to coordinate partisan and interest coalitions to achieve policies not achievable in other political forums.

Multistate Litigation and Capacity Building in the Office of the AG

Two background conditions originating in the 1970s have been particularly important in helping to explain the significant rise in multistate litigation during the last couple of decades of the twentieth century. The first has been a substantial physical expansion of AG offices, which has included both significant budgetary increases across individual AG offices as well as the emergence of forums for collaborations among AGs and other interested actors. The second background condition, which is related to the first, has been the incorporation of AGs into the structure of the national social policy regime. Congress, federal agencies, and the courts have all contributed to creating new avenues for AGs to deploy their expanded resources to influence national policy through collaborative litigation. These federal actions, in addition to empowering the AGs, encouraged important shifts in the ways that AGs defined the interests they were tasked with representing.

AG Resources and Institutional Capacity

Helping fuel the rise of collaboration among AGs has been the substantial growth of their institutional capacity. As Eric N. Waltenburg and Bill Swinford documented, the mean number of attorneys in AG offices and median AG office budgets increased 300 percent and 500 percent, respectively, between 1970 and 1989.[35] The increase in AG budgets outpaced the growth of general government spending in every state throughout the 1970s and 1980s.[36]

Supplementing the growth of resources across individual AG offices was the emergence of new forums for multistate collaboration, the most important being the expanded role of the National Association of Attorneys General (NAAG). Founded in 1907, NAAG has served as an information exchange forum among the AGs, typically holding at least one annual national meeting attracting representatives of the various state offices. Beginning in the early 1980s, however, NAAG began to take a more active role in assisting its members' litigation efforts. Part of the impetus for NAAG's new role was the poor reputation AGs had as litigators, particularly in arguments in front of the Supreme Court, where "even state attorneys general had a perception that 'there was a gap in performance quality between what the federal government achieved and what the states did, both of them representing the public.'"[37] NAAG responded by establishing both the State and Local Legal Center and the Supreme Court Project in the early 1980s.[38] The Supreme Court Project provided several elements of litigation support to AGs, including organizing moot court sessions and coordinating state amicus curiae participation.[39]

Since that time, NAAG has set up groups within the organization that help not only with Supreme Court practice but also in facilitating investigations and litigation concerning particular industries. Such NAAG-sponsored task forces were key resources in both the Microsoft antitrust litigation and in the tobacco cases, for example.[40] Other more recently created groups have included, among others, a Craigslist Working Group, an Internet Safety Task Force, a Committee on Financial Practices, and a State–Federal Task Force on Mortgage Enforcement.[41] A number of the working groups are industry specific and more permanent, such as the Petroleum Products Working Group, while others are temporary and focus on specific investigations, including the Contact Lens Working Group, whose work led to a major antitrust settlement with three leading contact lens manufacturers.[42] The purpose of these task forces and working groups is to help facilitate the distribution of information relevant to ongoing multistate litigation.

Although AGs still work together on many issues, as they have on settlements with industry defendants, increased polarization among them has led to the creation of new forums reflecting divergent agendas. In 2000, former Alabama AG William Pryor expressed his frustration over what he viewed as activist liberal AGs driving the states' prosecutorial agenda. In the wake of the AGs' massive settlement with the tobacco industry, which Pryor charged was about "politics, not law" and that he had resisted for some time, he helped organize the Republican Attorneys General Association.[43] Democratic AGs followed shortly after in 2002 with the creation of the Democratic Attorneys General Association.[44] The primary missions of both organizations are to raise money and elect members of their respective parties, but both organizations also meet regularly to discuss various issues and strategies in ongoing litigation.[45]

AGs have not only worked closer together to help supplement their institutional capacity but have also increasingly reached out to external groups.

Most controversially, AGs have frequently hired private attorneys to assist their investigations. These private attorneys typically work on a contingency fee basis, receiving a substantial portion of any successful court judgments achieved or settlements reached at the conclusion of a lawsuit. Contingency fee attorneys were a large part of the tobacco litigation in the 1990s, helping investigate various elements of the litigation at the behest of the AGs who hired them, and eventually collecting billions of dollars in fees after the Master Settlement Agreement was signed in 1998.[46] More recently, AGs have hired contingency fee attorneys in litigation brought against the pharmaceutical industry. Several observers have criticized AGs' use of contingency fee attorneys, arguing that the use of private attorneys violates separation of powers and presents ethical conflicts of interest when AGs hire campaign contributors to work on particular cases.[47] AGs respond that the use of private attorneys saves taxpayer money and allows them to tap into different sources of litigation expertise.[48] Whatever the merits of this practice, the combination of contingency fee attorneys and settlements requiring payment of costs and fees has helped to increase AGs' capacity to conduct litigation.

As noted earlier in the chapter, AGs have also worked alongside advocacy groups sharing similar goals to those of AG plaintiffs. This collaboration sometimes involves AGs and interest groups working together on the same case, as groups such as the Sierra Club did with AGs in much of the states' environmental litigation against the George W. Bush administration. In other situations, it involves groups filing parallel lawsuits building on the AGs' efforts, as with lawsuits against the pharmaceutical industry and litigation against the Affordable Care Act. In both cases, the partnerships between advocacy groups and AGs have benefited both sets of actors through the building of larger coalitions seeking similar policy goals through litigation.

Multistate Litigation and the Modern American Policy Regime

The backdrop to the growth of AGs' institutional capacity has been provided by broader changes in the structure of national policy during the latter half of the twentieth century. As noted in chapter 1, the American response to calls for total justice in the 1960s and 1970s incorporated two distinctive aspects that differentiated it from the approach taken by other industrialized democracies: cooperative federalism and adversarial legalism. The widespread adoption of the cooperative federalism model, in which state and federal governments work together to achieve common objectives, integrated states into the operation of federal programs by requiring states to take on new responsibilities while affording flexibility about their implementation. The adoption of private enforcement regimes and citizen suit provisions in several policy areas differed markedly from the New Deal enforcement model that placed responsibility for federal regulation in centralized federal agencies.[49]

In part, Congress relied on cooperative federalism and litigation for the implementation of new social regulation because it allowed Congress to meet the demands for total justice while maintaining Americans' skepticism of centralized bureaucratic methods of implementation.[50] As part of the effort to ensure the effectiveness of this decentralized policy implementation regime, federal institutions provided critical resources to AGs that built up their capacity to influence national policymaking.

Especially important were congressional grants acting as seed money for state litigation. This facilitation of state action began with states' criminal enforcement capabilities. The Omnibus Crime Control and Safe Streets Act of 1968 provided millions of dollars in block grants to fund initiatives overseen by AGs, such as improving record keeping and data collection, training prosecutors, and facilitating new organized crime programs.[51] They also allowed states to move into new fields of enforcement, including the prosecution of economic crimes affecting consumers.[52] Congress soon after began bolstering AGs' civil enforcement capabilities, particularly in antitrust enforcement and efforts to fight health care fraud. The Crime Control Act of 1976 provided $25 million in grants for state antitrust enforcement, which enabled twenty-five states to create antitrust divisions in the AGs' offices for the first time.[53] The Medicare–Medicaid Anti-Fraud and Abuse Amendments of 1977 granted states resources to hire special prosecutors specifically tasked with tackling fraud within the government-funded Medicaid system.[54]

The grants provided by Congress in these enactments proved crucial in building capacity for state litigators. As an assistant AG in Virginia stated at the time, the federal money contained in the Crime Control Act of 1976 represented "the most important shot in the arm that state antitrust enforcement has ever received."[55] The grants provided as part of the Medicare–Medicaid Anti-Fraud and Abuse Amendments enabled states to create specialized prosecution teams that were able to conduct wide-ranging investigations of health care providers and pharmaceutical firms. Today, these federal grants for antifraud efforts total over $230 million, which has proven to be a major boost for AGs' litigation against prescription drug firms.[56]

In addition to Congress providing direct grants, federal agencies expanded resources available to state litigators by sharing resources and information with them to streamline enforcement efforts. Most importantly, federal agencies have aggressively promoted litigation working groups and task forces in numerous key policy areas, especially concerning antitrust matters, consumer protection, environmental protection, and health care fraud.[57] These groups have served as a vehicle for federal agencies to bolster state enforcement by providing specialists and additional attorneys to state litigators, as well as by sharing information and legal documents otherwise costly to the states.[58] The Federal Trade Commission, for example, set up databases of consumer complaints that they have made available to state litigators, offering them access to additional sources of information on which to rely for potential litigation.[59]

The provision of grants and information sharing has been a crucial boost to state enforcement capabilities, but Congress and the courts have also provided states with another important legal resource: the ability to directly enforce federal law. Federal courts have done so by interpreting ambiguities in existing law to expand the ability of states to sue under federal statutes. In several early citizen suit provisions, Congress did not explicitly include states among the "any persons" entitled to enforce the statutes. Nevertheless, federal courts have generally held that Congress implicitly intended for states to have enforcement powers under these statutes. With few exceptions, courts have allowed states to enforce federal statutes even when the statutes are silent about state enforcement.[60]

Courts have also been skeptical of federal efforts to preempt state enforcement. In *Cuomo v. Clearing House Association* (2009), for example, the Court held that federal law did not preempt the ability of AGs to enforce fair lending laws against national banks.[61] Federal courts have also overwhelmingly interpreted federal law that restricted private class actions as not applying to state litigation, thus allowing AGs a broader choice of venue than granted to private litigators.[62] Further, the Supreme Court announced in *Massachusetts v. EPA* (2007) that states should receive "special solicitude" when determining whether they have standing to sue because "states are not normal litigants for the purposes of invoking federal jurisdiction."[63]

Additionally, while courts have interpreted ambiguities in existing law to allow state lawsuits, Congress made explicit states' authority to enforce federal law in several new statutes since the 1970s. The first of these statutes, the Hart-Scott-Rodino Antitrust Improvements Act of 1976, specifically authorized AGs to sue in federal court based on alleged antitrust violations of the federal Clayton Act. Although used sparingly at first, provisions empowering state litigation became increasingly common by the early 1990s, particularly in the area of consumer protection. Congress enacted eleven new federal provisions specifically authorizing state litigators to enforce provisions of federal law in the 1990s and an additional sixteen in the 2000s. Table 2.4 displays several of the most important of these empowerment statutes.

Although earlier empowerment statutes involved specific and limited areas of jurisdictional expansion, such as enforcement of federal boxing regulations, more recent expansions are considerably broader. The Consumer Product Safety Improvement Act of 2008, for example, granted AGs the authority to enforce a wide array of federal product safety laws.[64] The Dodd-Frank Wall Street Reform and Consumer Protection Act in 2010 provided states with their broadest powers yet. This statute enabled AGs to enforce several existing and new federal consumer protection laws, including rules of the newly created Consumer Financial Protection Bureau, against national banks and other lenders.[65] At the same time, the enactment of broader enforcement statutes has proceeded parallel to a trend toward greater collaboration between state litigators and federal agencies. This has included the Financial Fraud Enforcement Task Force, which has involved collaborative efforts between state and federal prosecutors, as well as other major initiatives such as the DOJ's anti-Medicaid fraud HEAT Task Force.[66]

Federal Empowerment and the Shifting Institutional Purposes of AGs

For years, AGs were understood to represent the interests of a single client: the state itself. Starting with the initial empowerment of state litigators in the 1970s, however, federal institutions began encouraging AGs to understand themselves as representing not only the interest of their states but the people of the state as well. This shift was significant because by serving as the representatives of individuals and groups allegedly harmed by corporate conduct, AGs essentially became a form of class action litigator.

Central to this expansion of institutional purposes was the common law power of *parens patriae* (parent of the nation). *Parens patriae,* which traces its origins to England in the Middle Ages, has traditionally been the chief mechanism AGs have used to vindicate their state's sovereign interests.[67] In the early twentieth century, for example, AGs invoked this doctrine to bring lawsuits alleging that their state was harmed by spillover effects from neighboring states, such as pollution and infectious diseases.[68] By the mid-

Table 2.4. Selected Federal Statutes Empowering State Litigation

Year Enacted	Federal Law	Description
1976	Hart-Scott-Rodino Antitrust Improvements Act	Expands state enforcement of federal antitrust law
1976	Crime Control Act	Provides grants for state antitrust enforcement
1977	Medicare–Medicaid Anti-Fraud and Abuse Amendments	Provides grants for state health care fraud enforcement
1983	Housing and Urban–Rural Recovery Act of 1983	Authorizes state AG enforcement of provisions of the Real Estate Settlement Procedures Act of 1974
1990	Nutrition Labeling and Education Act	Provides for state enforcement of new food labeling laws
1990	Consumer Product Safety Improvement Act	Authorizes state AG enforcement of the Federal Hazardous Substances Act of 1960 and the Flammable Fabrics Act of 1953
1994	Freedom of Access to Clinic Entrances Act	Authorizes state *parens patriae* suits to enforce new abortion clinic access laws
1998	Children's Online Privacy Protection Act	Authorizes state *parens patriae* suits to enforce new Internet child safety laws
2003	Controlling the Assault of Non-Solicited Pornography and Marketing Act	Authorizes state *parens patriae* suits to enforce new e-mail communication regulations
2005	Deficit Reduction Act	Provides financial incentives for states adopting state-level antifraud statutes
2005	Class Action Fairness Act	Provides state AGs greater oversight of and information concerning private class action litigation
2005	Bankruptcy Abuse Protection Consumer Protection Act	Provides state enforcement of provisions of the bankruptcy code concerning debt relief agencies
2007	Energy Independence and Security Act	Provides state enforcement of new light bulb efficiency standards
2008	Consumer Product Safety Improvement Act	Authorizes state AG enforcement of federal product safety laws
2009	American Recovery and Reinvestment Act	Authorizes state *parens patriae* enforcement of the Health Insurance Portability and Accountability Act

continued on next page

Table 2.4. Continued

Year Enacted	Federal Law	Description
2009	Omnibus Appropriations Act	Authorizes state *parens patriae* enforcement of the Truth in Lending Act
2009	Credit Card Accountability, Responsibility, and Disclosure Act	Provides additional state *parens patriae* enforcement of federal mortgage laws
2010	Dodd-Frank Wall Street Reform and Consumer Protection Act	Authorizes state *parens patriae* enforcement of federal financial consumer protection law

twentieth century, however, several courts expressed concern that states were trying to stretch the doctrine by "merely litigating as a volunteer the personal claims of its citizens" rather than using *parens patriae* only when the states' own interests were directly implicated.[69] Courts consistently held that AGs could represent only the interests of their states as states, not classes of injured consumers.

This is when Congress began stepping in to expand state *parens patriae* authority beyond what federal courts were willing to do. The Hart-Scott-Rodino Amendments explicitly reversed judicial limitations of *parens patriae* by expanding how states could use this power in antitrust enforcement. As one of the House sponsors put it, AGs ought to bring *parens patriae* suits on behalf of not only state interests but "on behalf of their citizens or for injuries to their own general economies."[70] Under this approach of expanding *parens patriae,* therefore, AGs could sue in a representative capacity even without direct injury to the state they represented.

Legislators were cognizant of the fact that this altered the institutional purposes of state litigators. Defenses of *parens patriae* expansion during the hearings on the Hart-Scott-Rodino Amendments referred to these expansions as "providing the consumer an advocate in the enforcement process."[71] Several legislators argued that providing state litigators additional authority to represent the interests of consumers in their state could be a way to circumvent some of the problems with private class actions. Expressing concern that "restrictive judicial interpretations" of antitrust statutes made it difficult to ensure enforcement against smaller-scale violations of the antitrust laws, expanding state *parens patriae* claims sought to ensure more litigation to address these types of cases.[72]

Several groups, including the American Bar Association, echoed earlier courts' concerns that these expansions of *parens patriae* would allow AGs to pursue claims that were too remote from the direct interests of their states.[73] Congress proceeded despite these concerns, however, and especially beginning in the 1990s built on this innovation to expand the use of *parens patriae* in several areas of consumer protection, as indicated in table 2.4. The cumulative effect of these statutes was to enable AGs to serve as consumer class representatives in increasing areas of federal policy. Unlike the earliest statutes, few of these later state empowerment provisions generated much controversy.[74]

The federal courts, after initially rejecting this expanded view of *parens patriae,* have since been more sympathetic to the broader conception of this doctrine. Despite continuing concerns that AGs' expanded *parens patriae* standing allowed states to allege damage claims having only an attenuated connection to actual state interests, federal courts since the 1980s have interpreted this doctrine in a way allowing AGs to bring litigation even when state interests were only loosely related to the alleged harms.[75] AGs successfully relied on the expanded view of their new institutional role in early multistate antitrust lawsuits, with courts relying on Congress's intent to expand AGs' role "in protecting [their] citizens from violations" of antitrust law.[76] Several AGs relied on the *parens patriae* doctrine in tobacco litigation, for example, alleging that the tobacco industry committed violations of tort law that had a detrimental impact on the health and welfare of their states' residents. Since the tobacco litigation, states have continued to use broad uses of *parens patriae,* including litigation against lead paint and gun manufacturers as well as the pharmaceutical industry.[77]

Conclusion

Since the last couple of decades of the twentieth century, AGs have emerged as important players in the development of national policy. This influence stems from AGs' increased willingness to collaborate among themselves and other actors across state lines, particularly on large-scale litigation campaigns against corporations and federal agencies. The AGs' ability to conduct these campaigns has been bolstered through capacity building sparked by both the AGs and by federal grants and expansions of jurisdiction.

As the following chapters illustrate, considerable irony accompanies this federal support for AG litigation. The purpose of this capacity building was to bolster a regime of cooperative federalism in which states and the federal government would work together to achieve shared goals. Yet as AGs have been incorporated into the national policy regime, they have grown increasingly bold in using their capacity to challenge federal priorities. Policy-forcing and policy-blocking litigation feature the most direct challenges, with AGs suing federal agencies directly in attempts to reverse federal regulatory decisions. The AGs' policy-creating litigation has presented more subtle challenges to federal policy, using national settlements with private industries as an end run around the typical national regulatory process. The case studies in the next chapters detail several of the most prominent examples of this activity, illustrating how AGs have used their position in "the best job in politics" to have considerable influence in contemporary American politics.

CHAPTER THREE

LAWYERS, DRUGS, AND MONEY

Litigating Pharmaceutical Pricing

The goal is nothing less than changing the way the industry does business.

Mark Schlein, director of the Medicaid Fraud Control Unit within the Florida attorney general's office, referring to state litigation against the pharmaceutical industry

In late February 1994, President Bill Clinton listened as John Kiszkiel narrated his experiences as owner of the Greenville Drug Store in Norwich, Connecticut. "I've had people come in here and break down and cry," Kiszkiel said of many of his mostly elderly customers. "I've had people right here at the counter have to make the decision whether they were going to pay their rent that month or buy prescription drugs."[1] Kiszkiel's story was one of many told during Clinton's nationwide campaign to build support for his efforts to reduce the cost of pharmaceuticals. Throughout his presidency, Clinton claimed that the practices of the prescription drug industry resulted in higher drug costs for millions of Americans. To prevent people like John Kiszkiel's customers from having to make choices between their drugs and other essentials, Clinton argued that government needed to intervene to end drug industry practices that led to high drug costs. "This is a people issue," Clinton insisted.[2]

Contrast these concerns with those of "Flo," an arthritic Medicare beneficiary who near the end of the Clinton presidency starred in a national advertising campaign run by a coalition of drug manufacturers. Flo wanted Congress to "help more seniors get prescription drug coverage" but declared, "I don't want big government in my medicine cabinet!" Over the course of nearly a year, Flo questioned whether Clinton's proposals to expand government intervention in the prescription drug industry would really be beneficial to everyday Americans. Only the right sort of reforms, she argued, would continue to "guarantee research for tomorrow's cures."[3] These television appearances attempted to put a human face on industry arguments that government regulation would dampen research and development for the next wave of lifesaving drugs.[4]

Debates featuring these sorts of contrasting perspectives on the merits and demerits of expanded government regulation of the pharmaceutical industry have only intensified since the Clinton era, particularly as health care has become one of the most contested areas of American politics. Presidents, legislators, and numerous interest groups have clashed in a political battle pitting demands for lower drug prices against trepidations about big government. Even as policymakers in Washington, DC, debated these issues, however, some of the most important attempts to shape the national regulatory environment surrounding pharmaceuticals were occurring outside of the nation's capital and the typical policymaking process. Beginning in the late 1990s, AGs have used lawsuits and threats of litigation to achieve a significant expansion of government regulation of the multi-billion-dollar pharmaceutical industry. Chapter 4 examines how state litigation served to alter how drug companies market their products to doctors and consumers. This chapter describes how AGs, often working in conjunction with federal prosecutors and the private bar, used litigation as a way to achieve greater government oversight of pharmaceutical prices.

Both of these litigation campaigns, which target allegedly fraudulent pharmaceutical industry practices, have generated little political controversy. Indeed, federal lawmakers have actively encouraged state litigation against drug companies. This may seem unsurprising on the surface, as these prosecutorial lawsuits, fashioned as a simple matter of enforcing the law, involve complex and technical legal issues seemingly far removed from politics. After all, reducing fraud seems to be a goal with which everyone can agree.

Yet a closer examination reveals a sharper political side to this litigation. Although this activity appears to be straightforward law enforcement, these litigation campaigns have instead served as a form of law creation. This litigation has often followed in the wake of failures to achieve national policies through the typical avenues of congressional legislation or rule making by federal agencies. By using lawsuits and settlements, AGs sought to achieve what Bill Clinton and drug company critics in Congress could not: expanded government regulation of the pharmaceutical industry. As the quote at the beginning of this chapter suggests, this litigation aimed at nothing less than changing the way the pharmaceutical industry does business.

The Politics of Pharmaceutical Pricing

Starting in the late 1990s, AGs have initiated dozens of investigations and lawsuits against virtually the entire pharmaceutical industry concerning how the industry sets prices for prescription drugs. At the heart of this litigation campaign are claims that pharmaceutical firms conspired to defraud government health care programs. This litigation has resulted in verdicts and settlements that have collectively required the industry to pay billions for allegedly inflating drug prices at the expense of consumers and the government. Yet the very practices that the states have only recently labeled a fraudulent conspiracy had been well known and widely accepted by the pharmaceutical industry and government alike for decades. How did certain drug company practices go from acceptable and even encouraged to being the focus of one of the fastest-growing areas of state prosecution?

Answering this question requires attention to the broader politics of American pharmaceutical pricing. Prescription drug costs in the United States have for years been the highest in the world and have risen much faster than health care inflation generally.[5] The high cost of pharmaceuticals set off an escalating political battle over the role of industry practices in rising costs for prescription drugs. Throughout the late 1980s and into the 1990s, Congress convened numerous committees aimed at examining the high costs of pharmaceuticals. A number of legislators argued that the rise in drug prices was the result of the large profits garnered by pharmaceutical firms. "Now, how do they make these enormous profits?" Senator David Pryor (D-AR), one of the industry's biggest critics, asked on the Senate floor in 1992. "One, by outright price gouging of our American citizens who can least afford the medications—the elderly, the poor and the other vulnerable parts of the American population." Another critic of big pharma, Representative Henry Waxman (D-CA), suggested, "Unless the industry can provide an adequate explanation for these price hikes, one can only conclude that what is going on is greed on a massive scale."[6]

Industry critics in Congress spearheaded numerous efforts to counter pharmaceutical firms' perceived greed by proposing stricter price controls for prescription drugs. Several congressional proposals sought to eliminate tax subsidies for drug companies and provide a combination of carrots and sticks to ensure that increases in drug prices remained in line with overall inflation.[7] These legislative efforts to reshape drug industry pricing appeared to receive a major boost with the election of President Bill Clinton. Clinton made tackling drug costs a legislative priority, announcing a plan in 1993 that would expand drug coverage provided under government health care programs while also attempting to control inflation for pharmaceuticals. Among other ideas, Clinton proposed a new National Health Board tasked with investigating drug prices deemed unreasonable and armed with the power to require drug companies to turn over information to the government if the prices for any of their drugs in the United States exceeded those charged in other countries. Borrowing a popular idea from industry critics, Clinton also proposed allowing the secretary of Health and Human Services (HHS) to negotiate with pharmaceutical companies over drug prices paid by the government.[8]

Despite a two-year window in which Democrats enjoyed unified control of Congress and the presidency, these attempts to expand government regulation over the pharmaceutical industry failed in Congress. Clinton's proposals, like those percolating in Congress before his presidency, met fierce and successful resistance from the pharmaceutical industry. Representatives from drug companies denounced Clinton's pharmaceutical proposals as an attempt to achieve price controls on prescription drugs, an effort that would serve to "slow down or eliminate the volume of research" on new drug innovation.[9] They argued that greater competition in the drug industry, not government regulation, was the cure for high drug prices.

When the 1994 midterm elections gave Republicans control of both houses of Congress, the prospects for pharmaceutical pricing reform looked bleak. Clinton's major push for health care reform had failed even with a Democratic Congress, and it was unlikely that the new conservative legislative majority would look kindly on attempts to impose strict government regulation on drug companies. Advocates for lower drug prices continued pushing for new ways to control drug costs, such as allowing the reimportation of prescription drugs from Canada, where pharmaceutical prices are lower because of direct price controls imposed by the Canadian government.[10] The efforts, like those before them, foundered on concerns that they represented forms of price controls that would damage private sector innovation.

Legislative Efforts to Reform the Average Wholesale Price Payment System

After several legislative strategies failed, industry critics turned to an alternative route to control drug prices. These efforts involved changing how Medicare and Medicaid, which provide health coverage to elderly and lower-income Americans, respectively, pay for covered individuals' prescription drug coverage.[11] This strategy appeared promising because Medicare and Medicaid enrollees represent a crucial market for pharmaceutical firms. The government could use threats to close drug firms' access to this market to gain greater leverage over drug company practices.

The way in which Medicaid and Medicare pay for prescription drugs is complex. This complexity arises because the government does not pay pharmaceutical companies directly for drugs. Instead, firms make money by selling pharmaceuticals directly to health care providers who serve individuals covered by Medicare and Medicaid. These providers include pharmacies that dispense drugs to patients as well as doctors and hospitals that purchase physician-administered drugs directly from pharmaceutical companies for use at doctors' offices or in the hospital outpatient setting. The government then reimburses these providers according to a drug pricing benchmark known as the average wholesale price (AWP).

In theory, the AWP is meant to reflect the average price providers pay drug companies for prescription drugs. The AWP, however, has no statutory definition. Governments receive AWP information for drugs from private commercial publishers of drug pricing data, the most prominent being First DataBank. These commercial publishers in turn receive the AWP pricing information directly from manufacturers themselves.[12] Figure 3.1 illustrates the crucial role of AWP in government reimbursements for prescription drug coverage.

The problem is that the AWP, despite its name, is not an average price at all. The AWPs are often considerably higher than the actual amount providers pay for drugs, largely because they do not reflect the many discounts drug companies offer providers as an incentive to purchase their products. In this respect, the AWP is similar to the sticker price for vehicles in the automobile industry. The difference between this AWP sticker price and the actual price providers pay for the drugs is referred to as the spread. Because the government reimburses providers based on the AWPs—and not the actual amount drug companies charge providers for the drugs—providers can make extra money by prescribing drugs with high spreads. For example, a manufacturer might sell a physician-administered drug to a doctor for 30 cents a dose but set the AWP at $1 a dose. The government would then reimburse the doctor $1 a dose despite the doctor's actual cost being only 30 cents. The physician thus pockets a profit of 70 cents for each dose.[13] Drug companies, in turn, have an incentive to inflate their reported AWPs. The companies benefit because higher spreads serve as an incentive for providers to purchase their products over a competitor offering lower spreads.

The government has long been aware that these incentives could drive

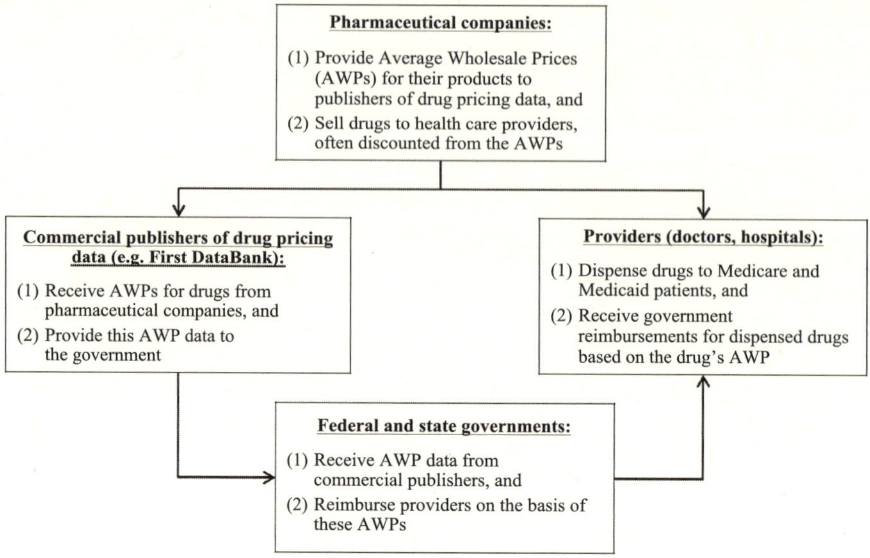

Figure 3.1. Pharmaceutical reimbursements under government health care programs.

up drug costs. As early as 1968, the Department of Health, Education, and Welfare noted that increasing the spread between actual drug costs and the reported AWP could be a way for drug companies to "maneuver against competing products."[14] In 1977, the Health Care Financing Administration actively tried to get state Medicaid programs to move away from AWP as a reflection of actual costs of drugs. As concern about rising health care costs increased in the 1990s, President Clinton noted the problems with what he characterized as a flawed, but legal, AWP system. In a 1997 address calling for additional efforts to reduce health care costs, Clinton explained the practices underlying the AWP system as examples of "waste and abuse" that "aren't even illegal [because] they're just embedded in the practices of the system."[15] For years, the difference between AWP and the actual market prices for drugs led pharmaceutical industry observers to refer to AWP as "ain't what's paid."[16]

This issue was important to many groups beyond government officials. Although AWP served as the main pricing benchmark for government reimbursements, it also was the price private insurers and health care plans were using to determine reimbursements for prescription drugs. This included Blue Cross/Blue Shield insurance associations, union health care plans, and self-insured employers across the country.[17] These groups, like the government, had for decades paid billions of dollars in prescription drug reimbursements based on the AWP benchmark for drugs.

Despite the many concerns raised about AWP, Congress continued the use of this manufacturer-reported benchmark. The reason had largely to do with lobbying efforts by physicians who argued that it would be impossible for them to stay in business and serve Medicare and Medicaid recipients without benefiting from the spread created by the AWP. According to these health care providers, the spread helped to make up for losses due to inadequate government payments for other professional services they provided under Medicare and Medicaid.[18] These arguments persisted in the face of the Clinton administration's significant push to change the system near the end of his presidency. In his 1998 budget proposal, Clinton proposed eliminating AWP and replacing it with a formula directly related to actual costs paid by providers. Congress rejected this proposal, instead making much less drastic changes to the drug reimbursement formula in the Balanced Budget Act of 1997.[19] The administration subsequently fought for larger tweaks to the AWP payment system in both 1999 and 2000, but neither of these proposals gained traction in Congress.

The Turn to Litigation in Pharmaceutical Pricing Regulation

Amid these numerous failed legislative attempts to control prescription drug costs, the locus of activity shifted from Congress to the courtroom. In 1997, at the same time that President Clinton began highlighting AWP as a potential driver of higher health care costs, several state and federal prosecutors began collecting information from leading pharmaceutical firms concerning their prescription drug pricing strategies.[20] After a lengthy investigation—and after further failures to change the pricing system in Congress—prosecutors explicitly began characterizing the way in which drug companies marketed the spread available to providers as fraudulent. One letter from New York attorney general Eliot Spitzer to Medicaid pharmacy directors across the country, for example, announced that the prosecutors' investigation "has revealed a pattern of misrepresentation by some drug manufacturers" resulting in Medicare and Medicaid "substantially" overpaying for certain drugs.[21] This marked the beginning of a lengthy litigation campaign aiming to force the elimination of AWP as a pricing benchmark, which was precisely the policy change President Clinton had pursued but Congress had rejected.

The first step was to pressure First DataBank, the largest commercial publisher of drug pricing data, to alter the way it reported prices for several prominent drugs. In the face of a growing joint federal and state investigation, the company agreed in April 2000 to list prices that the state prosecutors determined were closer to what providers actually paid for the drugs. After this informal agreement, Spitzer noted that this pricing change would likely result in "initial complaints or objections about lowered Medicaid payments" by providers.[22] This is precisely what occurred when the Health Care Financing Administration announced plans to use these new rates reported by First DataBank to compensate providers. After the predicted outrage from health care providers worried about lower reimbursement rates, Congress enacted the Medicare, Medicaid, and SCHIP Benefits Improvement and Protection Act of 2000. This statute, among other things, precluded the HHS secretary from "directly or indirectly decreas[ing] the rates or reimbursement . . . under the current reimbursement methodology."[23]

As Congress remained hesitant to proceed with any significant changes to the AWP system, state and federal prosecutors pressed ahead with their legal investigation. The government coalition reported that it had uncovered a variety of fraudulent behaviors involving drug reimbursements that had ultimately cost the federal and state governments billions of dollars. Some of the activity was the sort of garden-variety fraud that the states had been prosecuting for years, such as providers seeking reimbursements for drugs they never prescribed. Central to the investigation, however, was the notion that pharmaceutical companies' marketing the spread between a drug's listed AWP and the actual cost of that drug represented illegal fraud.[24]

The government coalition made clear that it was willing to turn to active litigation if necessary to recover government funds expended because of this alleged AWP fraud. The governments' legal hook relied on an innovative use of the False Claims Act (FCA), a Civil War–era statute that originally aimed to crack down on "rampant fraud" among defense contractors doing business with the Union army.[25] The purpose of the FCA is to recover money paid by the government to private contractors as the result of fraudulent claims. The FCA contains what are known as *qui tam* provisions, which allow private whistleblowers suing on the government's behalf to retain a substantial proportion of the proceeds of the suit.[26] After the filing of a *qui tam* complaint, government enforcers are granted a period in which to investigate the allegations and to intervene in the action. The *qui tam* whistleblowers thus serve as a sort of fraud alert system for government prosecutors.

For a variety of reasons, the FCA had fallen out of favor during and after

World War II, and government prosecutors rarely relied on it. However, Congress dusted off the FCA in the 1980s as part of an effort to cut down on fraud in defense contracting. As part of the False Claims Act Amendments of 1986, Congress increased the incentive of private whistleblowers to bring *qui tam* actions by increasing the cap on monetary recoveries from double to treble damages and increasing maximum mandatory penalties to $10,000 (up from $2,000). It also reduced the burden of proof necessary to prove a claim.[27]

Although fraud in defense contracting provided the impetus for the 1986 amendments, the FCA proved to be a strong ally in government prosecutors' threats of legal liability against the pharmaceutical industry as part of their AWP investigation. The prospect of FCA liability was particularly disturbing for pharmaceutical firms because every filled Medicare or Medicaid prescription might be considered a false claim subject to treble damages and the maximum penalty under the statute. These penalties could quickly add up to create potential exposure to these firms running into hundreds of millions of dollars. Additionally, if a company was found guilty of any criminal violations involved in a potential suit, the company could be excluded from Medicare and other federal health programs. Given the share of the overall pharmaceutical market that government programs represent, this penalty is akin to a "corporate death sentence."[28] Under these conditions, drug companies quickly realized that litigating government claims all the way to a jury verdict was risky and potentially fatal.

The Precedent for AWP as Fraud: The Bayer and TAP Pharmaceuticals Settlements

State and federal prosecutors understood the leverage they maintained over drug company defendants because of their FCA claims, and they sought to force a settlement with a major manufacturer in the hope that it would set a precedent for other companies to move toward a more accurate pricing system.[29] In January 2001, the government coalition achieved its first major victory. Since May of the previous year, the group had been in talks with Bayer Pharmaceuticals over the pricing of several of its drugs used to treat hemophilia and AIDS. The case originally arose when Ven-A-Care, an independent pharmacy in Florida, filed a *qui tam* complaint under the FCA alleging that Bayer inflated the AWP for these drugs. The federal and state governments intervened in the case, alleging that Bayer's marketing the spread to health care providers fraudulently inflated the cost of drugs under Medicaid in violation of the FCA.

Bayer, along with the rest of the industry, argued that setting prices for AWP was in no way fraudulent, given that the government had known for years that marketing the spread was an accepted industry practice and yet kept AWP as part of the government reimbursement system. Nevertheless, under pressure from threatened litigation, Bayer settled the prosecutors' allegations. Although the settlement required Bayer to pay $14 million, the injunctive relief was the most important remedy. The key provision of the settlement required Bayer to report a new pricing benchmark that prosecutors hoped would become an alternative to AWP. This new pricing benchmark, called the average sales price (ASP), sought to reflect actual prices providers paid for prescription drugs including all discounts, rebates, and other benefits tied to the purchase of the drug.[30] Because the ASP, unlike the AWP, was a defined term and set by actual market prices rather than by the manufacturer, this was intended to reduce the sort of price manipulation by the pharmaceutical industry involved in these cases. Because companies could not create a spread between the ASP and market prices, the aim was to reduce costs of drugs reimbursed under government health care programs. State Medicaid officials would be able to use the ASP data to set fair reimbursement rates for prescription drugs.[31]

The government prosecutors viewed the Bayer settlement as a watershed agreement that could be used to replace the existing AWP system with the theoretically more accurate ASP system. New York attorney general Eliot Spitzer characterized the settlement as "a significant victory . . . [that] sends a strong message to other pharmaceutical manufacturers and health care providers that we will not allow them to enrich themselves at the expense of taxpayers and those most in need."[32] This "strong message" resonated across the industry, as Bayer was but the first domino to fall in the government prosecutors' strategy to attack the AWP reimbursement system.

After the Bayer settlement was an even more significant agreement later in 2001 involving TAP Pharmaceuticals and its cancer drug, Lupron. In this case, the governments alleged that TAP engaged in a wide range of illegal conduct, some of which appeared to be clear fraud under existing federal statutes. However, as with the Bayer case, the allegations also included as evidence of fraud TAP's marketing the spread between its published AWPs for Lupron and the actual purchase price. This was despite the fact, as TAP argued, that marketing the spread and similar practices concerning AWP had been legal for years—and that Congress had even considered the spread an acceptable way to ensure that physicians and other providers remain in the Medicare and Medicaid programs. Despite the legally questionable nature of the AWP claims in the case, none of which had previously been tested in court, the accusations of illegal kickbacks and other violations of federal law were on firmer legal ground. Because these charges could lead to criminal as well as civil liability if proven in court, TAP faced the prospect of exclusion from Medicare and other federal health programs.

The threat of this corporate death sentence gave the state and federal prosecutors additional leverage to force a significant settlement related to not only the kickback claims but also to the alleged AWP fraud. In October 2001, the strategy came to fruition in the form of a massive $875 million settlement between TAP and the government prosecutors—the largest health care fraud settlement in history to that time.[33] As part of the settlement, TAP also entered into an agreement granting HHS strict oversight of TAP's marketing and sales practices for seven years, the first settlement to require this sort of strict scrutiny. Perhaps most importantly, the settlement required TAP to report the ASP for each of its drugs on a quarterly basis, similar to the provision the prosecutors had won in the Bayer settlement. This granted state Medicaid programs a new baseline with which to set revised, and likely lower, reimbursement rates for drugs provided under the program. The settlement also permitted the Center for Medicare and Medicaid Services (CMS), an agency within HHS, to rely on this ASP data to set reimbursement rates for TAP's products under Medicare.[34] This provision was remarkable given that it allowed CMS to go beyond its explicit authority established by Congress, which had specifically set Medicare reimbursement rates using AWP as the pricing formula.

The Expansion of AWP Litigation

The Bayer and TAP settlements were a watershed moment in the overhaul of the pharmaceutical pricing regime, serving as a wake-up call throughout the industry.[35] As one health care fraud attorney stated at the time, "The TAP settlement sent a huge chill through the pharmaceutical industry."[36] Not only did the size of the TAP settlement raise eyebrows throughout the pharmaceutical industry, but also the Bayer and TAP settlements introduced the notion that the AWP pricing mechanism, which had long been seen as standard company practice, was inherently fraudulent. These cases sparked an additional wave of state-by-state lawsuits by AGs and private class-action litigation. Ultimately, these efforts sought both to entrench perceptions that the AWP payment system was fraudulent and to force broad organizational changes in the pharmaceutical industry.

Kicking off the post-Bayer and TAP wave of state pharmaceutical litigation was Texas attorney general John Cornyn, who in the midst of the Bayer and TAP investigations filed the first individual state AWP lawsuit in fall 2000. The lawsuit arose after Ven-A-Care, the Florida pharmacy that also served as a *qui tam* whistleblower in the Bayer case, had alleged that Dey Laboratories had inflated the AWP for its asthma inhalants and marketed the spread to pharmacists.[37] After investigating the claims brought to light by Ven-A-Care, Cornyn filed suit against Dey and two other pharmaceutical firms, Schering-Plough (including its subsidiary, Warrick) and Roxane Laboratories.

Texas was in an unusual position to sue these firms relative to other states because it was one of the few states to have a state-level False Claims Act specifically targeting health care fraud. Enacted in 1995, this state FCA allowed Texas to recover double damages and costs from defendants found liable of Medicaid fraud.[38] Cornyn had also been one of the first AGs to create a civil Medicaid fraud section within his office in 1999. Additionally, Texas was the only state in the country requiring pharmaceutical manufacturers to certify the prices of their drugs, while other states relied on published pricing information from private publishers, including First DataBank.[39] This pricing data, provided directly by the manufacturers to the state as part of its Vendor Drug Program, was then used as the benchmark to calculate reimbursements under Medicaid.

These state laws provided Cornyn with the additional tools with which to bring his AWP case in September 2000. The allegations were similar to those in the Bayer and TAP cases, which had not yet reached settlement. The state accused the companies of falsely inflating the prices charged to the Vendor Drug Program, causing the state to pay more for the drugs than was appropriate. Cornyn claimed that the companies did so knowingly—the key standard to prove unlawful acts under the statute. He further alleged that each reimbursement constituted a separate violation under the state FCA, which could lead to penalties of up to $10,000 for each individual violation.[40]

The suit had a near-immediate effect on how Texas reimbursed drugs under its Vendor Drug Program. Shortly after Cornyn filed the case, the head of Texas's Medicaid program ordered an audit of its drug reimbursements and soon after cut the reimbursement rates for the drugs involved in the suit.[41] The reimbursement rate for Warrick's asthma inhalers was cut by more than half, for example, and the company's share of the state Medicaid market for asthma inhalers dropped from 71 percent to 42 percent in less than two years.[42] Eventually all three defendants named in Texas's AWP lawsuit reached settlements with the AG's office.[43] These settlements included combined monetary recoveries of over $55 million, representing nearly twice the damages allegedly caused by the defendants inflating their drug prices. The agreements also required the defendants to enter into pricing agreements with the state Medicaid division to ensure accurate pricing in the future.[44]

Texas's lawsuit was aided by the fact that manufacturers reported the pricing data upon which the state based its reimbursements directly to the state, rather than using an intermediary such as First DataBank. However, the lack of these advantages did not stop other AGs from bringing expansive AWP suits following Texas's example. In January 2002, Nevada AG Frankie Sue Del Papa filed a suit in Nevada state court accusing seventeen pharmaceutical companies of inflating the AWPs that they reported to First DataBank, which in turn were used to set the reimbursement rates for prescription drugs under Nevada's Medicaid program.[45]

Del Papa's lawsuit went well beyond that of Cornyn's in Texas. Not only did the state name a broader range of defendants, but the complaint also listed a variety of Medicaid fraud, antitrust, and consumer protection claims in the lawsuit.[46] In addition to allegedly using deceptive practices constituting consumer fraud that harmed Nevada residents and the state budget, Nevada alleged that the companies' behavior also constituted a racketeering enterprise aimed at deriving profits from states across the nation by inflating AWPs.[47] The complaint repeatedly referred to the pharmaceutical companies' behavior as part of an "AWP scheme"—a seeming attempt to coin a negative label for pricing behavior that had for decades been part of the government's reimbursement practice.[48] In addition to requesting damages of three times the amount unlawfully obtained and at least $5,000 for each allegedly false claim—monetary recoveries that could easily reach into the tens of millions—Nevada's complaint also asked for a redefinition of AWP. Rather than continuing with the long-settled notion that AWP represented the manufacturer-defined sticker price for prescription drugs, the complaint requested that "the Court enjoin defendants and order that any and all future disseminations of AWP . . . accurately reflect the average wholesale prices paid by physicians and pharmacies."[49]

Several AGs followed Del Papa's litigation strategy with expansive lawsuits of their own, most of which also targeted several industry defendants and included a variety of claims demanding significant monetary and injunctive relief. Most of these lawsuits ended in settlements, with only a handful proceeding all the way to a jury verdict. Table 3.1 indicates the progression of these state lawsuits over time.[50]

Table 3.1. AWP-Related State Medicaid Fraud Lawsuits through 2013

State	Date Filed	Defendants
Texas	September 2000	Dey Laboratories, Schering-Plough, and Roxane
West Virginia	October 2001	Schering-Plough and Abbott Labs
Nevada	January 2002	12 defendants
Montana	February 2002	18 defendants
Minnesota	June 2002	Pharmacia
New York	February 2003	Pharmacia and GlaxoSmithKline
Connecticut	March 2003	7 defendants
Florida	July 2003	3 defendants
Kentucky	September 2003	5 defendants
Massachusetts	September 2003	13 defendants
Arkansas	January 2004	4 defendants
Ohio	March 2004	5 defendants
Pennsylvania	March 2004	13 defendants
Wisconsin	June 2004	20 defendants
Alabama	January 2005	73 defendants
Illinois	February 2005	48 defendants
Missouri	May 2005	Dey and Warrick
California	August 2005	39 defendants
Mississippi	October 2005	86 defendants
Arizona	December 2005	42 defendants
Hawaii	April 2006	44 defendants
South Carolina	August 2006	5 defendants
Idaho	June 2007	10 defendants
Utah	September 2007	10 defendants
Iowa	October 2007	78 defendants
Kansas	November 2008	17 defendants
Louisiana	November 2010	18 defendants

Coordination and Collaboration in AWP Lawsuits

Although the lawsuits noted in table 3.1 involved individual AGs filing separately in state courts, AGs have collaborated closely on these cases. Two organizational mechanisms have been particularly important. The first is the Pharmaceutical Pricing Task Force established in 2002 under the auspices of the National Association of Attorneys General (NAAG). The task force's goal is to encourage communication and collaboration among the states, federal enforcement agencies, and the private bar. In addition to serving as an information clearinghouse for AGs bringing their own lawsuits, the task force has served as an umbrella under which several multistate lawsuits against the pharmaceutical industry have proceeded.[51] The second organizational mechanism helping to coordinate this litigation is the National Association of Medicaid Fraud Control Units (NAMFCU). This organization serves as a national coordination mechanism for specialized prosecution teams in each state, known as Medicaid Fraud Control Units, which investigate and prosecute alleged fraud in the Medicaid program. Through NAMFCU, the staffs of these Medicaid Fraud Control Units, which are under the direction of the AG in most states, work closely with NAAG in coordinating state pharmaceutical pricing litigation.

Also helping coordinate state legal strategies is close collaboration with private class-action litigators in the AWP cases. Most of the states bringing individual lawsuits against drug companies hired private outside counsel to handle many of the day-to-day litigation tasks, including developing initial complaints and drafting settlements with defendants. Working with private counsel is attractive to AGs because it allows them to leverage the expertise private counsel had built in previous pharmaceutical litigation for a relatively low cost. The private counsel work on a contingency fee basis, which means that they cost nothing to the state unless the state successfully achieves a settlement with or verdict against the corporate defendants. Additionally, working with a small number of plaintiffs' lawyers firms, the most prominent of which were Seattle-based Hagens Berman and Alabama's Beasley Allen, made it easier to achieve consistency across the states in this litigation. Nevada and Montana's initial AWP complaints, for example, were nearly identical, owing much to that fact that the same private law firm developed the complaints for both states.[52]

While coordinating closely across state lines and with private class-action attorneys, AGs have also worked alongside a coalition of advocacy groups targeting pharmaceutical industry practices in the courts. Many of these groups coordinate their litigation under the direction of the Boston-based Prescription Access Litigation project (PAL), a coalition of over a hundred organizations founded in April 2001 "working to end illegal pharmaceutical industry practices and fighting for more affordable drug prices."[53] The PAL alliance included unions and nonprofit health plans that claimed that AWP schemes cost them money. It also included several liberal interest groups, such as Health Care for All of Massachusetts, US Action, and various state public interest research groups (PIRGs), seeking a system change in how the pharmaceutical industry sold their products.[54]

In December 2001, the PAL coalition followed in the wake of the Bayer and TAP Pharmaceuticals settlements by filing a massive class-action lawsuit against twenty-eight drug companies in federal district court in Massachusetts.[55] This lawsuit adopted the characterizations of AWP as an industrywide scheme to defraud those paying for prescription drugs, similar to what the states were claiming in their ongoing litigation. Most of the defendants in this lawsuit were already under investigation by federal and state prosecutors, which the class-action complaint was quick to point out. For each of these defendants, which included TAP Pharmaceuticals and Bayer, the complaint prominently noted that the companies have "been the target of government investigations" and included information drawn from these investigations as part of the narrative of criminal complicity the complaint was attempting to build.[56]

By the mid-2000s, the sheer quantity of AWP litigation was staggering. Dozens of lawsuits by states, private parties, and advocacy groups targeted virtually the entire pharmaceutical industry. The public and private litigation shared the basic narrative that the way in which pharmaceutical companies priced their products represented a fraudulent scheme. The consistency of this narrative was aided by the fact that many of the same private class-action attorneys who collaborated with AGs on developing litigation strategies also did so for the PAL coalition. The similarities of the claims led to several of the pending AG lawsuits and private class actions to be consolidated with PAL's lawsuit in Massachusetts under the caption of *In Re Pharmaceutical Industry Average Wholesale Price Litigation*.[57] As discussed in more detail below, this consolidated litigation has been a major part of the law-based attack on AWP.

AWP Litigation as a Political Strategy

From the start of the AWP litigation campaign, AGs made it no secret that an important goal of their litigation was not only to recover millions of dollars from drug companies but also to alter practices in the pharmaceutical industry on a national scale. As Ohio attorney general Betty Montgomery, the first leader of NAAG's Pharmaceutical Task Force, put it, "Our major task is to change behavior. Money is incidental."[58] Indeed, the landscape of pharmaceutical pricing at the end of a decade of litigation looked much different than when the states first entered the field. At the start of the 2000s, Medicare and nearly all state Medicaid programs paid providers of prescription drugs on the basis of AWP, a practice that had been in place since shortly after the creation of both programs in 1965. Congress rejected attempts to alter the system, preferring to maintain this long-standing pricing benchmark as a way to entice providers to remain servicing patients covered by government programs. By the end of a decade in which it faced a barrage of litigation, AWP was dying. Few if any members of Congress now deny that the AWP system is fraudulent. Drug companies have paid out billions of dollars in AWP-related verdicts and settlements, and dozens of alternative pricing formulas emerged as candidates for permanently replacing AWP for the purposes of the Medicare and Medicaid programs.[59]

The story of AWP's decline and fall should not and cannot be dismissed as a mere lawyer's squabble over a highly technical and seemingly obscure area of the law. Instead, the fight over AWP was fundamentally political, set within the broader debate about the role of big pharma in American society. By transforming AWP from standard practice to actionable fraud, litigation produced a major shift in the locus of control for pharmaceutical pricing away from manufacturers and toward the government. Although formal price controls of the sort adopted in Canada and Europe continue to elude pharmaceutical industry critics in the United States, the decline of AWP marked at least a partial victory for advocates of greater government oversight of the pharmaceutical industry. State litigation played a crucial role in this fight by serving as both a direct method of policy creation and an indirect way to shape new legal understandings of long-standing industry behavior.

Policy-Creating Litigation against the Drug Industry

As noted in the previous chapter, policy-creating litigation has been a key way in which AGs have sought to expand regulation of national industries beyond anything required by federal policymakers. Out-of-court settlements with industry defendants have served as the central device for policy-creating litigation, which has been the case with AWP litigation as well. By reaching settlements, states and their litigation partners forced behavioral changes within the industry and built new structures of government oversight over drug industry defendants.

An important goal of early settlements with drug firms was to attain more information about the prices pharmaceutical companies actually charged providers for their drugs. Before the litigation, the only drug price information readily available to state Medicaid agencies were the AWPs listed by publishers of drug pricing data. Under existing law, drug companies were not obligated to provide any other pricing information because both federal and state governments had maintained AWPs as the preferred pricing mechanism. However, any successful attempt to replace the AWP system would need additional pricing information that could be used to establish an alternative benchmark.[60]

States used legal investigations and settlements to pry this information from drug companies. Subpoenas issued in the early stages of the investigation in the late 1990s granted states access to actual pricing information that they could use to highlight the extent of the spread between these prices and the listed AWPs. Subsequent lawsuits and settlements obtained additional information from industry defendants. The landmark Bayer and TAP Pharmaceuticals settlements required the companies to report drug price information to the government, which formed the basis for the newly developed alternative to AWP, the average sales price.[61] The settlements required that the ASPs be reported quarterly in order to make it easier for state Medicaid agencies to rely on this newly created price benchmark.[62] Individual state settlements enabled states to obtain similar information. The Texas AG's pioneering AWP lawsuits resulted in settlements requiring companies to enter into pricing agreements with the state Medicaid division that would ensure accurate pricing in the future. This in turn led to cuts in the amounts the state paid for drugs involved in the lawsuits.[63]

Even with these provisions in place, the question of enforcement remained. Because these new regulations were created through litigation and not through the typical policymaking process, which governmental entities ought to be tasked with oversight? Settlements with drug firms have addressed this issue by incorporating something similar to what Charles Epp has termed legalized accountability. In his study of law-based attempts to reform local government bureaucracies, Epp explains how activists used threats of legal liability as a lever to force localities to adopt new written rules, employee training programs, and new structures of managerial oversight.[64] The resulting framework sought to ensure compliance with emerging norms not otherwise required by specific laws or judicial decisions.[65] A process similar to this legalized accountability appears in settlements with pharmaceutical firms. The Bayer settlement, for example, required the company to appoint an internal compliance officer and create a compliance committee tasked with monitoring Bayer's day-to-day adherence to the settlement's regulatory terms. The compliance committee was required to create new written codes of conduct detailing the internal procedures Bayer would take to comply with the agreement, such as its new ASP reporting requirements.[66] In addition, the settlement required specific training and educational programs for employees to ensure compliance. Although the responsibility of implementing these provisions was placed on the company, all of its actions were subject to enhanced oversight by the federal government.[67] The TAP settlement reached the next year included similar provisions attempting to ensure the firm's compliance with new legal norms.[68]

Changing the Political Environment Concerning Pharmaceutical Pricing

At least as important as the provisions of the settlements themselves was the way in which litigation helped reshape legal norms surrounding AWP. Congress had been aware for years that when governments paid health care providers on the basis of AWPs, it meant that reimbursements to providers were often greater than what the providers actually paid to drug companies. Indeed, this is precisely why Congress maintained the system, as it operated as a way to compensate providers for losses incurred by their provision of other services under Medicare and Medicaid. Although this was a rather convoluted way of ensuring that health care providers were compensated highly enough to continue serving Medicare and Medicaid patients, the accepted system could hardly have been labeled fraud on the part of drug companies. Even when President Clinton pushed for an overhaul of AWP in 1997, he noted that the industry pricing practices were not illegal under current law.[69] Not surprisingly, the industry relied on and accepted AWPs as perfectly legitimate and even encouraged by Congress. "Three or four years ago, if you surveyed manufacturers and asked if AWPs were kickbacks," stated one industry attorney after the TAP settlement in 2001, "they'd have looked at you like you were from another planet."[70]

The AGs' litigation campaign altered this shared understanding by transforming the meaning of health care fraud to signify something much different from what Congress and the industry had understood it to mean for decades. Consistent throughout this litigation campaign was an attempt to replace the positive frame of AWP as a necessary part of the Medicare and Medicaid system with a negative frame of AWP as a fraudulent tool used by greedy pharmaceutical companies. It was no coincidence that prosecutors' legal complaints characterized the existing payment system as an AWP scheme and part of a racketeering enterprise. Prosecutors also used the media to advance these negative frames after settlements by issuing coordinated press releases containing frames of corporate malfeasance.[71]

As litigation alleging AWP schemes spread across the country, it empowered industry critics in Congress who had long advocated for action against alleged pharmaceutical greed and malfeasance. After years of refusing to substantially change the AWP formula for drug reimbursements, Congress began shifting its posture after the success of the Bayer and TAP settlements and the wave of state litigation that followed. Building on state and federal litigation, an increasing number of members of Congress decided to respond with their own investigations, incorporating information from these lawsuits as part of their investigations.[72] A few months after the Bayer settlement, and in the midst of the TAP investigation and increasing individual state litigation, Congress held its first hearing to discuss problems with the AWP system. The very title of the hearing was revealing, as it characterized the AWP "a broken system for patients and taxpayers" despite only months earlier requiring the Medicare system to continue using the AWP benchmark and prohibiting any alternatives.[73] Testimony during this hearing included the committee's chairman referring to a document obtained during the discovery process by state and federal prosecutors as an example of the "crazy AWP system at work."[74] After the first hearing in 2001, the number of congressional committees examining the issue proliferated.[75] AGs were invited to testify about their lawsuits and explain how drug companies committed fraud in their state Medicaid programs.[76]

By 2003, the terms of the debate had changed to such an extent that Congress reversed its decades-long support for AWP and began seeking alternatives for the system. For the first time, Congress, in the Medicare Prescription Drug, Improvement, and Modernization Act (MMA), provided a significant overhaul of the AWP system.[77] The MMA expanded drug coverage under Medicare through the new Medicare Part D prescription drug benefit and moved to end AWP as the baseline for reimbursement rates for prescription drugs already provided for under the program. In the place of AWP, now described as a flawed system, Congress adopted precisely the same pricing benchmark state and federal prosecutors had developed as part of the TAP and Bayer settlements—the average sales price. The MMA borrowed the definition of ASP directly from the settlements, defining it as an average of the actual final sales price of the drugs including all rebates and other discounts. Congress also required companies participating in the Medicare program to report the ASPs for their drugs to CMS on a quarterly basis, similar to the provisions previously achieved in the Bayer and TAP settlements. Congress, in short, nationalized the results of the Bayer and TAP Pharmaceuticals settlements, applying standards to the entire industry earlier agreed to by these two prominent firms.

The MMA's adoption of an alternative to AWP was only a first step in the decline of the pricing mechanism, because the provisions of the MMA pertained only to the pharmaceuticals provided under Medicare and not under Medicaid. Nevertheless, it was an important first step that demonstrated a new federal commitment to replacing AWP once and for all. Several subsequent proposals from Congress and President Bush sought to require state Medicaid programs to adopt ASP for drug reimbursements.[78] Two years later, Congress enacted another major statute targeting the supposed Medicare and Medicaid fraud prosecuted by state litigators. The Deficit Reduction Act of 2005 provided incentives for states to enact state-level False Claims Acts of the type that Texas's AG relied on in his groundbreaking lawsuits against pharmaceuticals firms.[79] The act also created new requirements for health care organizations associated with Medicaid programs to educate employees about the financial incentives and whistleblower protections available for anyone bringing fraudulent drug company behavior to the states' attention.[80] The purpose of these provisions was to make it easier for state litigation to police alleged pharmaceutical fraud.

In addition to shaping legislative responses to prescription drug pricing reform, state litigation also led to the courts accepting new legal norms about AWP in cases that actually did reach trial. After years of testimony from the AGs and class-action attorneys involved in the case, the judge overseeing the sprawling *In Re Pharmaceutical Industry* litigation adopted the AGs' characterization of AWP. In a crucial 2007 ruling, Judge Patti Saris characterized the actions of pharmaceutical industry defendants as "unscrupulously taking advantage of the flawed AWP system" in a way that was "outrageous" as well as "unethical and oppressive."[81] Additionally, the court adopted the characterization of the defendants' behavior as an AWP scheme benefiting the drug companies at the expense of old, sick, and needy patients. This language reflected just how effective the reframing of the AWP system through litigation was, given that just a few years earlier the AWP system was seen as so necessary to the government health care system that federal and state governments alike had continued to rely on it.

Both before and after Judge Saris's key ruling, the *In Re Pharmaceutical Industry* consolidated litigation proved an important vehicle for states to advance their AWP-as-fraud narrative.[82] GlaxoSmithKline (GSK) was the first defendant to resolve the claims it faced in the litigation, entering into settlements with five AGs and a number of private litigants concerning allegedly inflated AWPs for two of the company's cancer medications, Zofran and Kytril.[83] In addition to a $70 million monetary payment split between the various plaintiffs, the company was also required to report the ASPs for the two drugs to the states' Medicaid programs. Gaining this information was critical to the states because these prices, which were not previously available, could form a new baseline for Medicaid reimbursements in these states.[84] A member of the PAL coalition described this settlement as "without a doubt . . . the most important challenge to drug company greed going on in the United States today" and "a nail in the coffin of AWP and a move toward a more transparent system that will prevent drug companies from charging inflated prices that have no relation to the actual cost of a drug."[85] Eliot Spitzer, who led the multistate coalition settling with GSK, likewise described the settlement as a major effort to "stop a longstanding practice that inflated the cost of drugs for people suffering from cancer and cheated the Medicaid system."[86] Shortly after GSK settled, other defendants involved in the federal district court case did as well. This included AstraZeneca in May 2007 and eleven other companies in March 2008.[87]

Conclusion

Flo, the star of the drug industry's advertising campaign against President Clinton's prescription drug reform proposals, may not have wanted "big government in her medicine cabinet," but she got it—though in a much different way than she might have expected. As noted at the start of this chapter, several congressional proposals tried and failed to make much of a dent in the way the government paid for prescription drugs. After the failure of President Clinton's health care proposals and the Republican takeover of Congress, the prospects for national regulation imposing price controls on one of America's largest industries seemed unlikely.

Litigation provided an alternative avenue for expanding government regulation and oversight of long-standing pharmaceutical industry practices concerning how drug firms priced their products. Collaborating across state borders and alongside federal prosecutors, advocacy groups, and private class-action attorneys seeking similar goals, AGs were able to transform AWP from a necessary part of the government payment system to actionable fraud punishable by civil and criminal prosecution. Over time, the combined weight of these AWP litigation campaigns has led to the decline of AWP as the main pricing mechanism in government health care programs—precisely what industry critics had for years tried and failed to accomplish through Congress. This prompted a shift in pharmaceutical pricing from a system defined largely by manufacturers to one in which state and federal governments maintained greater control over drug prices and industry practices.

AWP lawsuits and settlements were only part of the broader litigation campaign waged by AGs against the pharmaceutical industry. As the following chapter explains, AGs aggressively used regulatory settlements to target the way in which drug companies market their products. These efforts also emerged out of failures to achieve stricter regulation in Congress and administrative agencies, and ultimately resulted in more government regulation and oversight of the prescription drug industry. In short, this litigation, as with the pharmaceutical pricing campaign described in this chapter, sought to fundamentally change the way the pharmaceutical industry does business.

CHAPTER FOUR

EXPANDING THE NEWEST WAR ON DRUGS

Litigating Pharmaceutical Marketing

One reason the states have been more and more active is that the federal government has been asleep at the switch.
Connecticut attorney general Richard Blumenthal, speaking of state litigation concerning prescription drug advertisements

Watch television in America and it will likely not be long before you're urged to speak with your doctor about whether the latest blockbuster drug is right for you. The high likelihood of encountering such an advertisement is unsurprising, given that the pharmaceutical industry spends billions in marketing its products to consumers each year.[1] What might surprise many Americans, however, is that television viewers nearly everywhere else in the world never see such ads. Only in two countries—the United States and New Zealand—is it legal for drug companies to market prescription drugs directly to consumers.[2]

The relative leniency of America's regulatory regime began taking shape in the late 1990s, when federal policymakers loosened restrictions on how drug firms could market their products. Congress and the US Food and Drug Administration (FDA) have since pursued a deregulatory approach to drug marketing, particularly during the George W. Bush administration. In addition to allowing manufacturers to run ads aimed at consumers, federal policymakers made it easier for the industry to persuade doctors to prescribe their products for purposes not specifically approved by the FDA. This so-called off-label marketing campaign is part of the drug industry's multi-billion-dollar advertising efforts aimed at health care providers.[3]

This state of affairs has generated criticism from many of the same critics who attacked the industry's drug pricing "fraud" described in the previous chapter. The proliferation of drug ads, according to industry critics, is another example of big pharma putting profits ahead of people and even, as the title of one book put it, "selling sickness."[4] By creating a regulatory regime that allows such business practices, federal policymakers have stood accused of aiding and abetting rising health care costs and jeopardizing patient safety. On the other side of the debate, the industry's defenders raise concerns about overintrusive government regulation. Supporters of deregulation argue that drug marketing restrictions not only prevent potentially lifesaving information from reaching patients but also raise serious concerns about free speech.[5]

This chapter explains how AGs, much as they did with drug pricing, have used litigation as a way to influence a broader debate about the pharmaceutical industry and to expand the reach of government regulation over prescription drug products. Building on their collaborations in the pricing litigation, AGs used lawsuits and settlements to attack allegedly fraudulent advertising practices. In the process, these actors have effectively created a patchwork national regulatory regime through settlements establishing stricter rules for pharmaceutical firms and increasing their own oversight authority over the industry. This form of policymaking has not only sidestepped Congress and federal agencies but also insulated the policies from constitutional concerns surrounding the regulation of drug marketing.

The Politics of Pharmaceutical Marketing

Political controversy over drug marketing has centered on two forms of industry practices. The first involves advertisements aimed at potential consumers, known as direct-to-consumer (DTC) advertisements. The second, promotion of prescription drugs for off-label treatments, concerns marketing efforts to persuade doctors and other health care providers to prescribe their medications for uses not specifically approved by federal regulators. The FDA has primary responsibility for regulating both forms of drug advertising in the United States, with its authority carved out of the Federal Trade Commission's regulatory jurisdiction over the marketing of most consumer products.[6] As a result of legislative shifts and constitutional concerns about free speech, the FDA began taking a more hands-off approach to both forms of drug marketing during the 1990s, particularly during the George W. Bush administration. This deregulatory approach became a point of contention within the broader debate about government regulation of the drug industry.

Direct-to-Consumer Advertising

DTC advertising of prescription drugs, unlike that for over-the-counter medicines such as Tylenol, is a relatively recent phenomenon. Since the Food, Drug, and Cosmetic Act of 1938 gave the FDA authority to require that pharmaceutical companies prove the safety of their products before advertising them, drug firms focused their marketing on doctors and other providers. This began to change in the 1980s, when several firms began aiming their advertisements directly to consumers. These advertisements initially appeared exclusively in print media, but the first television advertisement for a prescription drug medication appeared shortly after in 1983.[7]

Concerns about the possible adverse effects of DTC advertisements led the Reagan administration's FDA to impose a temporary moratorium on these ads the same year. The administration lifted this moratorium after a couple of years, however, in part because of concerns that restricting DTC advertisements would violate the First Amendment and because its belief that current federal law provided adequate consumer protections.[8] Even after the moratorium, however, most DTC advertisements remained in print as a result of a FDA requirement that the advertisements include all warnings, precautions, and adverse side effects for the advertised drug.[9] These requirements made short broadcast advertisements all but impossible.

In the mid-1990s, however, the FDA began reevaluating this policy. In 1997, the FDA released new draft guidelines pertaining to broadcast advertisement of prescription drugs. These guidelines, finalized in 1999, ended requirements that ads state every warning and side effect associated with the drug. Advertisements now needed only to notify consumers of "major risks" rather than all risks related to the drug, as long as they also granted consumers "reasonably convenient access to the advertised product's approved labeling" through a telephone number, website, or referral to a health care professional.[10] These FDA guidelines made it much easier for pharmaceutical firms to advertise their products in the broadcast media, contributing to a sharp increase in DTC ads. One study, for example, found that DTC advertising grew by 330 percent between 1996 and 2005.[11]

The sharp rise of DTC marketing generated significant debate about the merits of this form of advertising. On one hand, critics of loosening restrictions of prescription drug advertising focused on the potentially negative effects such advertisements had on consumers. Critics claimed that DTC advertisements were at best unnecessary and at worst completely misleading to consumers, prompting individuals to take drugs with little or even adverse effects on public health.[12] In addition, by heavily promoting the use of brand-name drugs rather than generic equivalents, DTC advertising could increase health care costs. One study in 2000, for example, found that the fifty drugs most frequently advertised to consumers were responsible for nearly half of the rise in retail spending on prescription drugs from 1999 to 2000.[13]

However, others have noted the public health benefits associated with DTC advertising. DTC advertising, for example, may help patients realize that their condition is treatable and may spur medically beneficial conversations with their doctors.[14] Pharmaceutical firms have also been quick to point out evidence that DTC ads may improve health care by increasing patient compliance with suggested therapies.[15] These arguments found a positive reception during the George W. Bush administration, which advocated a hands-off regulatory approach to DTC advertising. Officials at the FDA noted that there is "no evidence that DTC promotion is harming the public health," and the FDA's enforcement reflected these views.[16] One study noted that in 1997 the FDA had taken 142 actions concerning DTC advertisements it viewed as problematic, but only twenty-one in 2006.[17]

The agency's lenient regulatory posture made it a target of industry critics. In one congressional panel in 2001, for example, Sidney Wolfe, the director of Public Citizen's Health Research Group, told the panel of "an urgent need for more fine-tuned, better-staffed, and much tougher government regulation" of drug advertising. Wolfe cited the "sharp and steady decrease" in FDA enforcement, which included a 50 percent drop-off in overall FDA enforcement actions from 1997 to 2001.[18] Members of Congress also criticized the FDA's apparent lack of strong regulatory enforcement. Representative Henry Waxman (D-CA), a frequent critic of the pharmaceutical industry, issued a report in 2004 claiming that the FDA was guilty of "weak enforcement" of rules regarding "false and misleading" drug advertisements. Waxman's report demanded that FDA commissioner Mark McClellan explain why the agency was not taking more aggressive enforcement actions.[19] One theme running through these and similar criticisms was that the agency's alleged lack of oversight of DTC advertising had the effect of driving up the costs of health care by unnecessarily encouraging greater utilization of brand-name pharmaceuticals.[20]

Over the course of the 2000s, industry critics sought to reverse the deregulatory trend in pharmaceutical marketing by proposing new government controls on DTC advertising. While recognizing that outright bans on DTC advertising of the sort existing in other nations were not likely to pass scrutiny under the First Amendment, congressional proposals sought to grant the FDA greater power to review, or preclear, advertisements before they were aired.[21] Other congressional proposals sought to place a moratorium on all DTC advertisements within the first two or three years the drug is available for sale.[22] Several other bills proposed to make the cost of DTC advertisements more expensive by denying drug companies the ability to deduct the costs of such advertising as a business expense.[23] Few of these proposed restrictions on drug marketing gained traction in Congress, however, leaving the Bush administration's deregulatory stance as the operative approach.

Off-Label Marketing

The FDA has the responsibility to ensure that any drug marketed to consumers is "safe and effective for its intended use(s)" before a company can market it.[24] Each drug must have a label specifying its intended uses, which the FDA approves in what is an often lengthy process. Drug companies generally cannot market drugs for any purposes other than those listed on the label.[25] Although drug companies cannot promote off-label drug uses, doctors and other health care providers can nevertheless legally prescribe drugs for off-label purposes.[26] For a number of drugs, such off-label utilization is common. One study found that more than 20 percent of prescriptions written for the most commonly used prescription drugs in the United States were prescribed for off-label use.[27] For cancer drugs, off-label prescriptions reached as high as 75 percent.[28]

In the 1990s, drug companies more aggressively pursued efforts to educate providers about possible uses of their drugs beyond those approved by the FDA. Pharmaceutical companies sent sales representatives to speak with doctors about off-label uses for their products, which included disseminating information related to off-label use such as journal articles and the results of clinical studies. Firms also sought to maintain contact with health care providers through various educational programs, including sponsorship of continuing medical education programs and funding studies concerning off-label uses of prescription drugs.

To industry critics, allowing drug companies to suggest to health care professionals the benefits of off-label use of their drugs threatened to subvert the entire system of FDA regulation. By avoiding FDA evaluation, critics argued, off-label utilization may lead to the very sort of public health risks that necessitated stronger FDA regulation in the first place.[29] The Clinton administration's FDA, while loosening restrictions on DTC advertising in the late 1990s, took a stricter regulatory line with these drug company strategies. The agency issued guidelines suggesting that when drug companies distributed information to doctors about possible off-label uses for their drugs, even if done so without comment or endorsement, such activity would constitute illegal marketing.[30]

Soon after, however, Congress moved in the opposite regulatory direction by enacting the FDA Modernization Act of 1997. This law, which after a string of compromises won bipartisan support in Congress as well as Clinton's signature, abolished the long-standing prohibition on drug manufacturers disseminating information related to off-label uses of their products.[31] Although this statute maintained the general prohibition on off-label promotion, it provided a safe harbor from this general prohibition by allowing firms to provide doctors with neutral information about the off-label uses for their drugs. For example, the statute specifically allowed firms to disseminate peer-reviewed scientific journal articles regarding off-label uses for their products.[32] Doctors, as they were previously, remained free to prescribe drugs for off-label uses. These legislative changes reflected attention to a different set of concerns than those raised by critics of off-label promotion, as supporters of these changes emphasized the benefits to public health of off-label prescriptions. Given that the FDA approval process can take years, off-label utilization potentially saves lives by making treatments available to patients sooner. Fostering greater dissemination of information regarding such off-label use opens new options for doctors and patients in their health care treatments.[33]

The FDA Modernization Act was a step toward deregulating off-label promotion, though it also placed several regulatory requirements on firms wishing to take advantage of the statute's safe harbor. Before disseminating information about off-label uses to doctors, firms first had to submit various materials to the FDA, including the materials the companies planned to disseminate as well as an application to approve the drug for off-label use. However, these regulations soon became enmeshed in constitutional controversy. A libertarian interest group, the Washington Legal Foundation (WLF), sued the government claiming that the regulatory provisions of the FDA Modernization Act were an unconstitutional restriction of free speech. The federal district court hearing the case agreed, holding that the drug ads, because they contained truthful information, were a form of protected commercial speech that the government could not regulate.[34]

This holding prompted the FDA to announce that it would not prosecute companies for disseminating information about off-label uses for drugs.[35] In 2006, Congress allowed the regulations of off-label promotion in the

FDA Modernization Act to expire, thereby formally ending the policies the WLF had challenged as unconstitutional. A week before Barack Obama took office in January 2009, the Bush administration's FDA finalized new guidelines making it easier for drug firms to provide doctors with possible off-label applications of their products.[36]

Much as it did with DTC advertising, the FDA's deregulatory approach to off-label marketing spurred several congressional proposals seeking to place stricter regulations on drug companies' advertising strategies to doctors. Some proposals aimed to place a flat ban on drug firms' dissemination of the results of research studies to health care providers, closing what many critics (but not the FDA) viewed as a loophole in the general prohibition of off-label marketing. Other proposals sought to force drug firms to disclose more of the information they used to target doctors. One such proposal was the Enhancing Drug Safety and Innovation Act of 2006, which would have required the establishment of a publically available clinical trials database containing information about clinical trial results.[37] However, advocates' attempts to win congressional approval of stricter limits on off-label promotion, as with curbs on DTC advertising, proved largely unsuccessful.

State Policy-Creating Litigation and the Regulation of Pharmaceutical Marketing

As with the pharmaceutical pricing regulation discussed in chapter 3, state litigation emerged as a response to failed efforts to expand government regulation through legislation. By the time that the drug marketing debate began heating up in Congress, AGs had already aggressively investigated the pharmaceutical industry in the context of drug pricing. This experience of coordination and collaboration in the area of pharmaceuticals served as a springboard for the expansion of the states' efforts to reform industry marketing through litigation. Out-of-court settlements served as the main regulatory mechanism, serving to regulate DTC advertising, limit how drug firms disseminate information about off-label uses to doctors, and mandate new disclosure requirements on drug firms. These settlements used the broad prohibitions against fraudulent and deceptive business practices in state law as a hook to achieve requirements that, settlement by settlement, extended throughout the pharmaceutical industry. By doing so, AGs essentially adopted the arguments of drug advertising's congressional critics and transformed them into a form of national regulation—all while bypassing the typical avenues and constraints of national policy development.

Regulating DTC Advertising through Litigation

The first rumblings of the states' now expansive role in drug marketing litigation occurred shortly after George W. Bush's inauguration in 2001, when several AGs began investigating Pfizer's advertising of its blockbuster antibiotic, Zithromax. Zithromax was (and is) approved by the FDA as a safe and effective treatment for childhood ear infections, and Pfizer marketed the drug for this purpose. However, the AGs claimed that although Pfizer's advertisements contained all of the information necessary to pass muster under federal law, they also contained false and deceptive claims under state consumer protection statutes. In particular, the AGs claimed, Pfizer failed to disclose information about possible antibiotic resistance and misrepresented the efficacy of Zithromax in treating ear infections in comparison to other antibiotics on the market.[38]

Pfizer, however, noted that it was marketing Zithromax consistently with all applicable federal laws and the FDA-approved labeling for the product. In fact, Pfizer had voluntarily submitted these exact DTC advertisements to the FDA for review before running them, and the FDA had approved them.[39] Nevertheless, the AGs' legal theories rested on state consumer protection law, not federal labeling laws. The states claimed that under the laws of the nineteen states involved in the investigation, Pfizer's failure to disclose certain information and claims about the efficacy of the drug represented fraudulent misrepresentation and deceptive trade practices.[40]

Pfizer publicly denied the states' claims. However, faced with the prospect of a protracted and public litigation battle with nearly half of the nation's AGs, Pfizer agreed to a national settlement of the claims in December 2002. The settlement required Pfizer to pay $6 million, two-thirds of which went directly to the AGs to cover their investigatory costs and attorneys' fees, and placed various restrictions on Pfizer's DTC advertising of Zithromax in the future. In addition to requiring Pfizer to cease the DTC ads that were the subjects of the investigation, the settlement required the company to make a series of highly specific statements about Zithromax in all of its future advertisements for the product. Pfizer was also required to disclose any company connections with scientific studies cited in consumer ads and make such studies available to consumers on its Internet site.[41] Federal law or the FDA required none of these various disclosures and advertising changes. By requiring them in this settlement, however, the AGs wanted to send a "strong message" not only to Pfizer but also to the pharmaceutical industry generally that "advertisements that mislead or fail to provide complete information about pharmaceutical products will meet with tough enforcement actions."[42] These enforcement actions, the AGs made clear, would occur regardless of the FDA's position.

The Zithromax settlement was the first in a line of increasingly aggressive attempts to expand government oversight of DTC advertisements, especially when it became clear that legislative attempts to expand industry regulation would be unsuccessful. A key example involved the AGs' investigation of Merck's marketing of its blockbuster arthritis drug, Vioxx. In 2001, the FDA delivered a warning letter to Merck expressing concerns about the potentially harmful side effects of the drug. The agency did not take any additional action after its issuance of the letter, however, deeming the matter "satisfactorily resolved."[43] Vioxx thus remained on the market until September 2004, when Merck voluntarily recalled the drug after a company-sponsored study found that the drug nearly doubled the risk of heart attack and stroke.[44]

Shortly after the Vioxx recall, several AGs began investigating Merck's marketing of the drug, claiming that the company had waged an aggressive DTC advertising campaign misrepresenting the safety of Vioxx and concealing increased risks associated with the product's use.[45] The investigation led to a $58 million settlement that, among other new regulatory requirements, increased the authority of the FDA to oversee Merck's advertising. The settlement required Merck to submit its television commercials to the FDA for approval before broadcasting any DTC advertisements, a process known as preclearance. It also required the company to comply with any FDA recommendation to delay advertising for new pain medications.[46] In a subsequent settlement with Merck over another of its drugs, Vytorin, AGs extended the requirement for FDA preclearance to all of Merck's products, not just the drugs involved in the investigations.[47]

These preclearance settlement provisions, which served as a model for subsequent settlements with other drug firms, came amid increasing calls for Congress to adopt preclearance requirements across the entire industry. Initial versions of the Food and Drug Administration Amendments of 2007 contained language imposing stricter curbs on DTC advertising long sought by industry critics, including requirements for FDA preclearance of drug advertising. However, after heavy lobbying efforts by drug and advertising firms, these regulatory provisions were removed from the final version of the bill. The AGs' Vioxx settlement, signed a few months after this legislative failure, contained preclearance provisions similar to those that had failed in Congress.

In addition to increasing FDA oversight of Merck's DTC advertising, the

Vioxx settlement also granted AGs power to enforce federal law governing drug regulation—a power nowhere in the statute itself but rather one delegated specifically to the FDA. In the settlement, Merck agreed to refrain from making false, misleading, or deceptive promotional claims under state law as well as under the federal Food, Drug, and Cosmetic Act and FDA regulations. Merck was already under an affirmative obligation to adhere to federal law and regulations or face potential penalties from federal enforcers. However, this provision allowed the AGs themselves to oversee Merck's compliance with federal law, providing them with additional leverage to forge ahead with the enforcement of federal law even where the FDA had allegedly failed to do so.

One problem with the Vioxx settlement from the AGs' perspective was that despite granting themselves additional ability to enforce existing federal law, the AGs still relied on the FDA to actually review the DTC advertising that the agency received from the company. If the agency failed to review the advertising, the preclearance provisions would have little effect. The AGs addressed this problem in a subsequent settlement with Pfizer in October 2008, which supplemented their own capacity to preclear DTC advertisements. This settlement resolved thirty-three AGs' investigation of Pfizer's alleged off-label marketing of a pair of the company's drugs, Celebrex and Bextra.[48] The $60 million settlement included many similar requirements that several previous settlements had, becoming the second AG settlement to include a requirement that a company receive preclearance for all of its DTC advertisements before broadcasting them.[49] Unlike the Merck settlement, however, the Pfizer settlement required the company to report to a newly established Multistate Executive Committee of AGs if the FDA did not act within a certain amount of time. Pfizer was required to provide this multistate committee with all of the DTC advertising information that the company gave to the FDA. In short, this provision created a two-layered enforcement regime that simultaneously expanded the FDA's authority while also granting the AGs additional information with which to enforce their new preclearance regulation if the FDA did not act to enforce it.

Limiting Off-Label Drug Promotion through Settlements

The fastest growing area of state drug marketing litigation involves the pharmaceutical industry's promotion of the off-label use of prescription drugs. In some of these cases, AGs have collaborated with federal enforcers to achieve significant regulatory settlements tying together Medicaid fraud and consumer claims. In other cases, the states operated independently of federal enforcers to reach settlements based on state law. Through this litigation, AGs have sought to require stricter limits on off-label marketing in a way effectively rolling back earlier efforts to deregulate off-label promotion.

Much as collaboration between federal and state prosecutors served as the spark for an expansion of drug pricing litigation, a major federal–state settlement with an industry leader did the same in the context of off-label marketing. The settlement involved Warner-Lambert's marketing of Neurontin, which the FDA had approved to treat epilepsy but which also proved highly effective in treating general pain, attention-deficit disorder, and bipolar disease.[50] Prosecutors had alleged that Warner-Lambert had promoted these off-label uses of Neurontin by offering illegal kickbacks to prescribers, in the form of trips and falsely labeled consulting fees.[51] The governments also claimed that Warner-Lambert disseminated information to doctors about the off-label uses of the drug in such a way that it constituted illegal off-label marketing. These off-label marketing violations, prosecutors claimed, led to the increased utilization of Neurontin under the Medicaid program, helping to drive up costs for the federal and state governments.

The federal Department of Justice concentrated on the criminal allegations in the case and collaborated with states on the civil Medicaid fraud aspects of the case, while the AGs activated not only their fraud enforcement personnel for this case but also their consumer protection divisions. The AGs' consumer protection investigation focused on alleged violations of state consumer protection laws occurring when Warner-Lambert promoted the drug for off-label uses. Both of these Medicaid fraud and consumer protection claims rested on innovative interpretations of existing law, raising constitutional concerns as well as questions about the theories of causation used in the case. For one, the government enforcers suggested that pharmaceutical companies could and should be held liable for false claims providers made to health care programs. This was despite the fact that the company was likely unaware that any of these claims were made by the physicians.[52] Further, because the alleged communications by Warner-Lambert about off-label uses were actually truthful, the claims sought to penalize speech potentially protected by the First Amendment.

Warner-Lambert initially fought these claims in federal district court, but after losing a pair of key rulings at the motion to dismiss and summary judgment stages, the company opted to settle.[53] The government prosecutors announced a $430 million settlement in May 2004, representing the largest health care settlement since the 2001 TAP Pharmaceuticals case discussed in chapter 3. The bulk of the monetary recovery consisted of criminal fines paid to the federal government, although the settlement directed Warner-Lambert to pay federal and state Medicaid programs $190 million for losses allegedly incurred by the company's off-label marketing of Neurontin. The size of the settlement, much as in the TAP Pharmaceuticals case, was meant to send a message to the industry that prosecutors would enforce broad and innovative interpretations of antifraud provisions in existing law regardless of the regulatory posture of Congress or federal agencies.

On the same day as the Warner-Lambert settlement, forty-six AGs also entered into a separate but closely related settlement resolving their state consumer protection claims. In addition to injunctive provisions aimed at barring Warner-Lambert from continuing its alleged off-label marketing, the AGs' settlement established a new Neurontin Multistate Executive Committee headed by the AGs of California and North Carolina.[54] This new committee would administer the new Attorney General Consumer and Prescriber Education Grant Program, funded by a $21 million payment by Warner-Lambert, the purpose of which would be to fund programs around the country designed to educate physicians and patients about prescription drug marketing and other related issues.[55] Governmental entities, academic institutions, and not-for-profit groups would be eligible to apply for grants from this program, which the AG members of this committee would administer.[56] These funds led to the creation of organizations such as PharmedOut, an activist project at Georgetown University that subsequently grew to be a major critic of the pharmaceutical industry, as well as funding the launch of an educational website by another activist group that seeks to combat off-label marketing.[57] An additional $6 million of the states' settlement was allocated to a "corrective advertisement campaign" regarding Neurontin to be run by Warner-Lambert, and $10 million went directly to the AGs' offices to compensate them for investigation and litigation expenses.[58]

The landmark federal–state settlement with Warner-Lambert served as a spark for extensive prosecutorial investigations of dozens of other pharmaceutical companies in relation to alleged off-label marketing. This has often come in the context of alleged FDA failures to protect consumers, as with the AGs' investigation involving Purdue Pharma's powerful pain reliever OxyContin. For several years, AGs and various consumer interest groups criticized the FDA for ignoring how Purdue Pharma was persuading providers to prescribe more frequent doses of the drug than that approved by the FDA. Connecticut AG Richard Blumenthal took the lead in criticizing the agency, filing a petition in 2004 to require stronger labeling of OxyContin "expressly warning prescribers of the increased occurrence of side effects or potentially serious adverse reactions resulting from off-label prescribing at more frequent dosing intervals."[59] Blumenthal claimed that the FDA had "turned its back on its serious responsibility with regard to OxyContin," citing the alleged off-label marketing of OxyContin as only "the latest grim example of corporate greed and arrogance causing death and serious injury."[60]

After the perceived unwillingness by the FDA to address the issue, AGs took matters into their own hands. West Virginia AG Darrell McGraw was the first to sue Purdue Pharma over its alleged marketing violations, reaching a $10 million single-state settlement with Purdue in which the company agreed to fund various "education programs for doctors, law enforcement drug-prevention programs, and community drug-rehabilitation programs."[61] A group of twenty-six AGs followed up McGraw's settlement with an investigation of their own. This ultimately resulted in a 2007 settlement with Purdue in which the company agreed to pay $19.5 million to the states as well as significantly reform its practices. In addition to requiring the company to cease engaging in off-label promotion and "other improper marketing of OxyContin," the settlement contained a number of additional restrictions on the marketing of the drug.[62] Purdue was required to maintain an "abuse and diversion-detection program" to detect problematic prescribing and to ensure that all of their sales representatives undergo training in the program before promoting OxyContin.[63] The agreement also contained various provisions regulating Purdue Pharma's internal operations, prohibiting the company from sponsoring any events in which it knew that a speaker would recommend the off-label use of OxyContin, and restricting it from basing bonuses of its sales representatives solely on the volume of OxyContin prescribed.[64]

The OxyContin settlements, along with other agreements, served as a way for AGs to force pharmaceutical firms to disclose various aspects of their operations, including many that policy advocates in Congress had tried and failed to achieve through legislation. An AG settlement with Bayer in January 2007, for example, was the first to require a company to disclose the results of internal clinical studies of drugs. To that point, neither Congress nor the FDA placed requirements on companies to disclose the results of both positive and negative clinical drug studies—an issue that was the subject of contemporaneous debate in Congress.[65] This changed with the AGs' settlement with Bayer over its cholesterol reduction drug Baycol, which required Bayer to disclose all results from its internal clinical trials, not just those with positive outcomes.[66] These clinical trial provisions, as with other regulations, have become a common part of subsequent state settlements.[67]

Settlements also achieved other restrictions on off-label promotion that industry critics had been pressing in Congress. In 2007, thirty-two AGs reached a settlement with Eli Lilly over claims that its "Viva Zyprexa!" marketing campaign illegally promoted its schizophrenia medication for purposes beyond those approved by the FDA.[68] The $62 million settlement placed a variety of regulatory restrictions on the company. Among other requirements, the settlement barred Eli Lilly from giving product samples of Zyprexa to health care providers whose specialties are not consistent with Zyprexa's label or from using any grant funds to promote the drug.[69] The settlement also required Eli Lilly's medical staff, rather than its marketing staff, to have the ultimate responsibility for the medical content of references regarding Zyprexa.[70] In addition to these regulatory provisions governing internal company operations, the agreement also required a significant amount of new disclosures, including information about grants received, lists of "promotional speakers and consultants who were paid more than $100 for promotional speaking and/or consulting," and the results of the company's clinical trials.[71] Echoing a number of his colleagues, Florida attorney general Bill McCollum described the agreement as a "landmark settlement [that] sends the message that pharmaceutical companies will be held responsible for their actions, including any inappropriate marketing practices which may promote off-label uses that have not been approved."[72]

States also used multistate settlements to address emerging controversies over ghostwriting in the industry, in which companies would pay authors to put their names on independent research that was instead actually conducted by the pharmaceutical company. The Vioxx settlement discussed earlier required anyone named on a Merck-sponsored study to adhere to a variety of authorship conditions before their names could appear on the study.[73] Certain guidelines regarding these practices had been suggested by the International Committee of Medical Journal Editors but had not been required by any law or regulation in the United States before this settlement.[74] The Vioxx settlement provision, subsequently extended in other settlements, essentially adopted the guidelines promulgated by this international committee and turned them into an affirmative requirement not otherwise required by national law.

AGs initiated several investigations related to drug firms' off-label advertising during the George W. Bush administration, but they have become even more aggressive as the Obama administration has initiated a stricter regulatory approach to off-label pharmaceutical advertising practices. A $181 million settlement with Johnson & Johnson's pharmaceutical unit in

August 2012, the largest multistate consumer protection settlement with a drug company in history, barred any sales staff from disseminating reprints of scientific journal articles to health care providers.[75] Other settlements expanded restrictions reached in previous settlements to other industry leaders including Abbott Labs, Pfizer, and AstraZeneca. In addition to their own multistate lawsuits, AGs collaborated with federal prosecutors to press claims about allegedly illegal off-label advertising and reach massive settlements with drug firms. This included a $2.3 billion settlement with Pfizer in 2009, a $3 billion settlement with GlaxoSmithKline in 2012, and a $2.2 billion settlement with Johnson & Johnson in 2013.[76]

Pharmaceutical Marketing Litigation as a Political Strategy

Since the early 2000s, pharmaceutical advertising settlements have increased in terms of the number and extensiveness of their regulatory provisions. Table 4.1 summarizes several of the AGs' major multistate drug marketing cases against pharmaceutical firms in recent years.

By achieving successive settlements with some of the nation's largest pharmaceutical firms, the AGs established stricter marketing restrictions on industry than anything required by federal statutes or regulations. The policies created through multistate settlements have included several that industry critics had proposed in Congress but never successfully navigated the legislative process. This included full drug company disclosures of internal clinical drug studies, preclearance provisions concerning DTC advertising, and limits on the dissemination of information pertaining to off-label uses.[77] The settlement provisions were also a direct response to the FDA's deregulatory posture toward drug marketing. Beginning during the George W. Bush administration, when the FDA minimized enforcement and issued new guidelines signaling a less stringent approach toward drug marketing, AG settlement provisions served to counter this deregulatory approach.

Just as importantly, these efforts have provided a new regulatory baseline that the entire industry must follow to be certain that they will not be subject to potentially expensive multistate investigations. This is why the AGs' frequent talk about these settlements sending a message to the entire pharmaceutical industry is not mere bluster. Indeed, the impact of the settlements beyond the significant consequences for the individual companies involved in the agreements was apparent when the pharmaceutical industry's peak association adopted new voluntary guidelines, mirrored after recent AGs

Table 4.1. **Selected Multistate Settlements Pertaining to Pharmaceutical Marketing through 2013**

Defendant	Product	Year Settled	Significant Settlement Terms
Pfizer	Zithromax	2003	$6 million; specific alterations to advertisements
Warner-Lambert	Neurontin	2004	$430 million; corrective advertisements
Bayer	Baycol	2007	$8 million; disclosure of clinical trial results
Medicis	Loprox	2007	$10 million; limits on off-label marketing
Purdue Pharma	OxyContin	2007	$19.5 million; various marketing restrictions and disclosure requirements
Merck	Vioxx	2008	$58 million; preclearance provisions, bans on "ghostwriting"
Cephalon	Provigil; Gabitril; Actiq	2008	$425 million; limits on off-label marketing; oversight of marketing practices
Eli Lily	Zyprexa	2008	$62 million; various disclosures and marketing requirements
Pfizer	Celebrex; Bextra	2008	$60 million; preclearance provisions, clinical trial disclosures
Bayer	Yaz	2009	$20 million; preclearance provision, corrective advertisement campaign
Merck	Vytorin	2009	$5.4 million; preclearance provisions, disclosure of clinical trial results, various conflict-of-interest regulations
Pfizer	Geocon	2009	$33 million; various disclosures and limits on off-label marketing
AstraZeneca	Seroquel	2011	$68.5 million; various disclosures and restrictions on off-label marketing
Abbott Labs	Depakote	2012	$100 million; various disclosures and restrictions on off-label marketing
Janssen Pharma	Risperdal; Invega	2012	$181 million; various marketing and clinical trial disclosures and restrictions
GlaxoSmithKline	Avandia	2012	$90 million; clinical trial disclosures; marketing restrictions
Pfizer	Zyvox and Lyrica	2012	$43 million; various off-label restrictions
Victory Pharma	Naprelan, Xodol, Fexmid and Dolgic	2013	$12 million; various off-label restrictions

settlements, aiming to help avoid liability for its members.[78] After settlements with other firms, several individual companies have announced reforms to their advertising practices to help them avoid future liability.[79]

Sidestepping Constitutional Concerns through Regulatory Settlements

A crucial advantage of using settlements as a form of policymaking is that they have proven capable of not only bypassing Congress and the FDA but also of sidestepping important constitutional concerns. One of the main barriers to drug marketing regulation in the United States is that such restrictions face free speech concerns that do not exist in other nations. Since the US Supreme Court's 1976 decision of *Virginia State Pharmacy Board v. Virginia Citizens Consumer Council,* which held that the government could not limit pharmacists' ability to advertise prescription drug prices, courts have provided First Amendment protection for purely commercial speech.[80] The Washington Legal Foundation's successful lawsuit against the government's regulation of companies' distribution of truthful information was one example of this in the pharmaceutical marketing context. Although the constitutional issues in that case were not litigated beyond federal district court, the Supreme Court has more recently indicated the continuing vitality of commercial free speech protections in connection to drug advertising. In *Thompson v. Western States Medical Center,* decided in 2002, the Court held that provisions of the FDA Modernization Act of 1997 restricting DTC advertising of compounded drugs violated the First Amendment.[81] In a 2011 decision, *Sorrell v. IMS Health,* the Court struck down a state law limiting pharmaceutical marketing practices. The case, which pitted Vermont's AG against a drug company, involved a state law restricting how drug firms could use data about doctors' prescribing practices in their marketing efforts. The Court held that this state statute represented an unconstitutional content-based restriction on speech that discriminated specifically against pharmaceutical firms.[82]

From the perspective of pharmaceutical industry critics, the constitutional vulnerability of state statutes like Vermont's and congressional legislation like the FDA Modernization Act of 1997 has been a major roadblock to reform. Even industry critics have been forced to acknowledge the limits the First Amendment places on potential restrictions on drug marketing.[83] Restrictions on off-label dissemination of information may unconstitutionally restrict commercial speech, particularly when the information distributed by companies is entirely truthful. Granting the FDA the ability to preclear drug advertisements before airing likewise raises concerns about unconstitutional restraints on speech. Neither Congress nor the FDA enacted any such preclearance requirements, largely because of these constitutional concerns.

The AGs' method of policymaking has served as a way to at once leverage judicial power to force settlements while simultaneously shielding the regulations they contain from constitutional challenge. Settlements have limited the ability of drug firms to disseminate truthful information about off-label uses to doctors, and AGs achieved the same preclearance provisions that even industry critics in Congress realized were constitutionally problematic. Because the AGs' regulations have been the result of agreements between the AGs and the involved companies, these requirements are insulated from the same sort of constitutional challenges to which a congressional enactment or agency regulation would be exposed. Further, the characterization of the drug companies' actions as fraud—despite being legal under federal law—helped blunt First Amendment concerns. As Eliot Spitzer put it while dismissing constitutional concerns about his litigation, "You cannot invoke free-speech arguments as a defense to fraud."[84]

Yet if these constitutional concerns were actually tested in court, there is reason to believe that they would not pass judicial scrutiny. The Supreme Court's decisions in *Western States Medical Center* and *IMS Health* provide strong arguments that FDA preclearance and restrictions on distributing truthful information about off-label drug uses violate free speech protections. Indeed, in one of the few cases actually testing these sorts of provisions, the Second Circuit held in 2012 that the truthful distribution of information concerning off-label uses of drugs is speech protected by the First Amendment. In overturning the criminal conviction of a pharmaceutical sales representative who had promoted a drug for off-label uses, the court held squarely that the government "cannot prosecute pharmaceutical manufacturers and their representatives . . . for speech promoting the lawful, off-label use of an FDA-approved drug."[85]

If it is unlikely that the settlement provisions sought by AGs would pass constitutional muster, then one might wonder why companies would not simply fight the charges the states are levying against them and refuse to agree to such settlement provisions. The problem from the companies' perspective, however, is that protracted litigation presents serious risks. A long litigation struggle ending in a jury verdict may end up costing far more money than the cost of a settlement. One telling example involved Arkansas AG Dustin McDaniel's lawsuit against Ortho-McNeil-Janssen Pharmaceuticals involving the company's alleged violations of state law when it sent letters to thousands of Arkansas doctors promoting a drug for off-label use. The company decided to fight the lawsuit to a jury trial, a decision that subsequently backfired. In April 2012, a jury found Ortho-McNeil-Janssen liable under state consumer protection law, and the judge assessed an astonishing $1.2 billion fine for the company's issuance of these letters.[86] Although the company succeeded in having this judgment overturned after an appeal to the state supreme court, the case nevertheless indicates the high risk present for companies choosing to fight AG claims in court rather than settle.

Multistate settlements also serve as a way to resolve several AG investigations at once, helping avoid a situation in which one protracted litigation campaign in New York, for example, is simply the prelude to another in California. This dynamic helps explain why so many companies initially raise constitutional objections to settlement provisions before ultimately acceding to them in order to resolve all of the government litigation involving the drug. A settlement in 2010 illustrated that firms will even agree to provisions requiring them to drop pending free speech lawsuits against the FDA in order to end investigations of off-label promotions.[87]

The Role of State Consumer Protection Law

America's federal system has enabled this new form of policymaking through litigation, and not simply because AGs would not exist without the states as an entrepreneurial platform. Although AGs' pharmaceutical settlements are national in scope and feature close coordination among AGs, the threatened lawsuits are largely based on generous interpretations of state statutes, particularly state consumer protection law.

Although similar to federal consumer laws in many ways, these state consumer protection statutes often provide different—and stricter—regulatory standards than those found in federal statutes. Although both sets of laws target unfair and deceptive business practices in various industries, federal laws tend to tightly define unfair and deceptive practices to target specific practices that Congress chooses to address. By contrast, state laws often fail to define what unfair and deceptive practices are, and often there are few court decisions available to help with the interpretation.

The many differences in state and federal consumer protection laws were the focus of an empirical study in 2009 by Northwestern University's Searle Center on Law, Regulation, and Economic Growth. The researchers found that state consumer statutes allow enforcers to pursue different types of claims, including many that do not involve conduct that would be illegal under federal standards for consumer protection. As part of the study, the researchers surveyed a group of five individuals with substantial expertise in consumer protection issues, derived from experience working with the Federal Trade Commission (FTC), the federal agency with chief jurisdiction over enforcing federal consumer protection statutes. This Shadow Commission examined summaries of actual state consumer protection case decisions and determined whether the underlying practices would prompt FTC action. The Shadow Commission found that most cases did not meet FTC illegality standards and that the FTC would likely enforce even fewer cases. Business practices that may have constituted deceptive advertising under strict state laws, for example, rose merely to the level of exaggeration and puffery not warranting enforcement action under more tightly defined federal laws.[88]

The ability to pursue different types of claims under state law was crucial in the states' reaching settlements with national drug firms because it granted AGs stronger legal weapons than federal enforcers possessed on the federal level. AGs were able to use the broad prohibitions in state consumer protection law to regulate the sorts of drug marketing practices Congress and federal agencies explicitly chose to allow under federal law. Although it is not unusual in the history of American federalism for individual state statutes to prohibit activity otherwise legal in other states, what is new is the AGs' effort to use the strict standards of state law for a form of national regulation—something that has become increasingly common in the area of marketing by the nation's largest pharmaceutical firms.

The FDA as a Resource and a Foil

A recurring dynamic in the AGs' attempt to regulate prescription drug advertisements through litigation is the way in which the AGs have simultaneously relied on the FDA for information while criticizing the agency for its regulatory approach. The AGs' rhetoric concerning the FDA's allegedly abysmal policing of drug advertisements is rarely in short supply, as former Connecticut attorney general (now US senator) Richard Blumenthal's quotation at the start of the chapter illustrates. Nevertheless, the FDA also serves not only as a focus of criticism but also as a resource for entrepreneurial AGs seeking to place further regulatory restrictions on DTC and off-label pharmaceutical advertising.

One of the main enforcement mechanisms the FDA retains under federal law is the ability to send warning letters to companies notifying them of promotional pieces or practices that the FDA considers to be in violation of the law.[89] These warning letters give companies the ability to take corrective actions without being subject to formal enforcement actions. AGs, however, have relied on these FDA warning letters to help notify them of new opportunities for litigation. The Vioxx investigation, for example, was spurred at least in part by a 2001 FDA warning letter expressing concern about the drug's advertisements.[90] As a West Virginia deputy AG noted after securing a $4.5 million consumer protection settlement against Johnson & Johnson in 2004 that relied heavily on a FDA warning letter, "It's the best evidence I think you can get. That was the crux of our entire case."[91]

In another settlement with Bayer concerning Yaz, a birth control pill, AGs relied on a FDA warning letter to Bayer stating that two of the company's advertisements were misleading because they overstated the efficacy of Yaz and minimized serious risks associated with its use. In its letter, which the agency posted publically on its website, the FDA asked Bayer to stop using the ads immediately and to submit a written response describing Bayer's intent to comply with the agency's request. Bayer responded to the warning letter and pledged to work with the FDA in regards to the full range of its Yaz promotional materials.[92] Several AGs were not content with this regulatory approach, and soon after, they began investigating the company's advertising of Yaz. The FDA's warning letter was a key part of the state's case. According to one Florida assistant attorney general, the warning letter was the "canary in the coal mine" in the Yaz litigation, adding that warning letters "have served as the impetus or trigger for many attorney general investigations."[93] The AGs used the allegations made by the FDA in its warning letter to threaten litigation based on state consumer law, subsequently achieving a significant regulatory settlement in 2009.[94]

By using the FDA as both a foil and a source of information for their own lawsuits, AGs have built themselves up as powerful pharmaceutical regulators on the state level. Not only have they used state law to create nationally applicable regulations not required by Congress or federal agencies but they have also used these settlements to extend government regulatory oversight over drug company advertisements into the future. The new requirements that the FDA preclear DTC advertisements, for example, granted the agency powers that it did not even seek for itself. At the same time that they helped to build the FDA's regulatory power, AGs also built up their own by providing themselves greater regulatory oversight across the prescription drug industry.

Conclusion

The states' litigation campaign targeting drug advertising, like the drug pricing litigation, served as a way to reregulate an industry at a time when federal policymakers were moving in a different regulatory direction. By relying on a variety of innovative and legally untested claims broadening the meaning of corporate fraud, many of which were based on state law, AGs built a stricter regulatory regime on top of the looser regime maintained by federal policymakers. These state litigation campaigns, which had the explicit aim of reshaping the entire pharmaceutical industry, raise a number of broader issues about the nature of contemporary American politics. In the next chapter, I discuss the elements of American politics helping sustain this activity as well as several of the broader implications of this new form of national policymaking.

CHAPTER FIVE

STATE LITIGATION AND NATIONAL PHARMACEUTICAL POLICY

Once the attorneys general have entered a field, they don't go out.
Former Maine attorney general James Tierney

In both litigation campaigns described in the previous two chapters, states served to expand the reach of the national regulatory state across one of the largest and most important industries in America. Despite the intense polarization in contemporary American politics over issues of health care and government intervention in the private sector, this regulatory expansion has occurred gradually and generated little controversy. What helps to explain how this activity came to be and why it persists?

This chapter examines several broader issues pertaining to the AGs' pharmaceutical policymaking through litigation. Both the pricing and marketing litigation used a powerful tool, policy-creating litigation, to pursue new industry regulations that federal policymakers had declined to create through typical policymaking processes. Yet despite this litigation effectively challenging the national policy status quo, federal policymakers have contributed to the existence of these challenges. By building the structure of the American health care regime in a peculiar way—particularly by combining elements of cooperative federalism and adversarial legalism—federal policymakers have served to invite and empower AGs to take on a greater national role in health care. AGs have taken advantage of their expanded entrepreneurial space to create regulations on the pharmaceutical industry stricter than those pursued by federal authorities, in turn altering the balance of concerns at the heart of the national regulatory regime.

Expanding the National Regulatory State through Policy-Creating Litigation

The states' pharmaceutical litigation has occurred amid a broader debate about how to best balance various competing concerns about government regulation of prescription drugs. At the heart of this debate are concerns about the effects of corporate conduct on drug prices and consumer safety on the one hand, and trepidations about the negative effects government regulation could have on private sector innovation and efficiency on the other. In the pharmaceutical pricing context, federal policymakers were also attentive to the possibility that altering the long-standing average wholesale price system might lead doctors to stop servicing Medicaid and Medicare patients. With drug advertising, policymakers sought to balance consumer protection with consumer education. Although direct-to-consumer (DTC) advertising and restrictions of off-label marketing might drive up drug costs, they also educate consumers about existing drugs that could help their medical condition. The First Amendment also forced lawmakers to consider how efforts to limit drug advertising in the name of consumer protection might clash with commercial free speech rights.

Through policy-creating litigation with the drug industry, AGs pursued their own vision of the best balance of these various concerns, achieving policy goals that pharmaceutical industry critics had attempted but failed to achieve through legislation. By doing so, AGs operated quite differently from typical portrayals of how federalism operates. Rather than pushing back against a federal government intent on expanding national power at the expense of the states, the AGs' pharmaceutical litigation sought instead to expand the reach of the national American regulatory state. The key mechanism for doing so was settlements with industry members that combined significant financial penalties, new industry regulations, and enhanced government oversight of corporate practices.

The first important aspect of these settlements has been the monetary provisions, which are often substantial. Settlements with drug companies routinely involve tens of millions of dollars each—even into the billions when the federal Department of Justice brings criminal prosecutions parallel to the AGs' efforts. In the three and a half years between 2009 and the summer of 2012, pharmaceutical companies collectively paid over $18 billion in financial penalties to federal and state coffers because of government antifraud litigation.[1] In 2012, New York alone received $335 million from its AG's participation in multistate settlements.[2] As states and the federal government struggle to contain health care costs, this litigation has been used to recoup money and lower the costs of drugs in a way that has effectively served as a de facto tax on the pharmaceutical industry. This aspect of the litigation is particularly valuable to the government prosecutors at a time in which both federal and state governments are running substantial deficits and the political will to raise taxes is lacking. In this context, legal settlements targeting ever-expanding definitions of fraud and deceptive trade practices are an attractive way to raise additional government revenue—especially when this revenue is derived from an unpopular industry already under fire for its alleged corporate greed and malfeasance.

While important, these monetary provisions are only part of the story. Former Ohio AG Betty Montgomery, who served as the chair of the National Association of Attorneys General's Pharmaceutical Task Force, described the money involved in settlements as merely "incidental" because "our major task is to change behavior."[3] Settlement provisions have served as the vehicle for AGs to do so. Such provisions have required the disclosure of the results of internal clinical tests and pricing information that governments could use to set more accurate reimbursement rates under Medicaid. They have also required changes to various drug advertisements and marketing practices.

AGs sought to enforce these new regulatory norms, none of which was required by federal law, by creating a three-tiered oversight structure in which companies, states, and the federal government shared enhanced responsibility for enforcing new regulations not otherwise required by federal law. Settlement provisions first sought to legalize accountability by forcing companies to police themselves, such as by creating new compliance committees and new codes of conduct. The AGs supplemented these internal compliance mechanisms by bolstering their own regulatory power in various ways, including creating new Multistate Executive Committees armed with the power to review planned drug advertisements, collect information gleaned from newly required drug company disclosures, and distribute settlement proceeds to groups of the AGs' choosing. AGs also used settlements as a way to grant themselves the ability to enforce federal laws that Congress already placed explicitly under the jurisdiction of federal agencies.

In addition to internal compliance mechanisms and supplementing the AGs' own power, settlement provisions also enhanced the federal government's regulatory power. As part of their settlements, state and federal prosecutors negotiated expansive Corporate Integrity Agreements, in which companies submit to enhanced oversight by the Department of Health and Human Services (HHS) in exchange for continued participation in government health care programs. The TAP Pharmaceuticals settlement, the first to require this sort of strict scrutiny, allowed agencies within HHS to contravene an explicit congressional mandate limiting how it could alter reimbursement rates for prescription drugs. In the marketing litigation, multistate settlements granted not only the AGs but also the Food and Drug Administration (FDA) additional powers not otherwise granted by law, including the ability to preclear drug advertisements before airing.

Regulation during the New Deal, Stephen Gardbaum has argued, "unshackled the states" because the goal was not simply to increase federal power over the states but to expand government regulation over the private sector, regardless of the source.[4] Contemporary policy-creating litigation exhibits a similar regulatory dynamic. Multistate settlements, rather than being simply a manifestation of state–federal conflict, have sought to unshackle the regulatory power of government at all levels—even when existing federal policy served to cabin the national regulatory state.

The Power of Policy-Creating Litigation

Gerald Rosenberg famously dubbed the Supreme Court a "hollow hope" for policy reformers because of the many constraints the judiciary faces, echoing Alexander Hamilton's argument in *Federalist* No. 78 that the judiciary's lack of power over the purse or the sword made it the "least dangerous branch."[5] However, scholars have also noted the importance of "bargaining in the shadow of the law," in which disputants negotiate resolutions to avoid official judicial actors and the substantial costs of litigation. Even when official legal actors are not present, the law lurks in the background, structuring the negotiations on the basis of how each side believes active litigation would play out.[6]

The states have used this bargaining in the shadow of the law as a way of leveraging the law to achieve policy objectives in a way that sidesteps the normal constraints on the ability of courts to implement decisions. Unlike most court opinions in constitutional cases, settlements specify a number of highly detailed responsibilities on the part of the defendant entities. They resemble administrative regulations both in terms of this detail and because they serve to regulate corporate entities directly. Because settlements are fashioned as agreements between parties, they do not require the actions of other political actors to enforce compliance. Instead, regulatory provisions in settlements are largely self-implementing. They depend not on constrained courts to implement them but rather on mechanisms of legalized accountability and threats of future litigation if the defendants fail to comply with their agreed-on requirements.

In addition to sidestepping the constraints on courts, policy-creating litigation's power resides in its ability to sidestep the lengthy process associated with typical lawmaking and rule making. The policy process in the United States, as numerous scholars of American politics have noted, contains a host of veto points making policy development difficult. The fragmentation of power among several institutions spurs a greater number of veto players who seek maintenance of the policy status quo.[7] These veto players are advantaged by the existence of several roadblocks in the policy process, such as the congressional committee structure, the senatorial filibuster, and the presidential veto. Even when proposals successfully navigate this arduous legislative process, the policy implementation stage allows veto players additional opportunities to shape policy. Under the Administrative Procedure Act (APA), which has served as the basic framework for agency decision making since the New Deal, new agency regulations must typically provide a notice-and-comment period allowing for public comment before the publication of any final rule.[8] For controversial proposed regulations, this process can be lengthy and contentious. Further, the APA allows for judicial oversight of agency rule making—a power that has been invoked frequently, especially since the 1970s.[9]

Policy-creating litigation avoids these many veto points on the path to policy development by effectively reducing the number of veto players involved. The only veto players present in the AGs' regulatory process are those whom the AGs themselves invite to the negotiating table. By bypassing several typical legislative hurdles, regulatory provisions in settlements require only the assent of the AG plaintiffs and their corporate targets. The prospects of both sides "getting to yes" is made even more likely given the significant leverage government prosecutors maintain in the context of negotiating pharmaceutical settlements. When the alternative consists of total exclusion from participation in government health care programs—the so-called corporate death sentence—abiding by new regulatory requirements in return for ending an investigation is a preferable outcome for drug firms.

Further, because they are the product of negotiated settlements rather than the typical rule-making process, settlement provisions are not subject to the APA. This also reduces the number of actors who have a hand in creating new regulations and overseeing their implementation. Unlike typical regulations, members of the interested public affected by regulatory settlement provisions—including, for example, the doctors whose income would be directly affected by changes in the drug reimbursement system—do not have the opportunity for formal comment. Instead, the process of regulation through settlement occurs largely behind the closed doors of the settlement negotiating room, and the only parties having a say in the development of settlement provisions are those directly involved in the negotiations.

Unlike typical regulations subject to the APA, settlement provisions are also subject to little or no judicial oversight. At most, multistate settlements must gain the assent of a single judge in a fairness hearing before going into effect, though even then judges rarely void settlements reached by prosecutors and industry defendants. Once approved, settlement provisions are essentially immune from further judicial review. This is particularly important because settlements have so frequently been based on legal arguments that, if tested in court, would likely have a difficult time passing scrutiny. The contention that AWP was fraudulent faced a number of legal problems, including the fact that doctors, not pharmaceutical firms, directly benefited from the AWP spread, as well as the fact that governments knew for years that AWP really meant "ain't what's paid" and did not accurately reflect the true cost of drugs. Attempts to regulate drug advertising, either by requiring preclearance of DTC advertising or by restricting companies' ability to distribute truthful information about their drugs to physicians, raised important free speech issues arising under the First Amendment.

If these policies were part of a statute or agency regulation, they would almost certainly face legal challenge from industry members or advocacy groups. When Maine became the first state in the nation to enact a price control law for prescription drugs in 2000, for example, the industry's trade group sued to block implementation of the statute because of its allegedly unconstitutional encroachment on federal law.[10] The industry also sued to block implementation of a Washington, DC, law that made selling patented medications for an "excessive price" illegal.[11] As noted in chapter 4, the FDA's attempts to restrict drug advertisements faced legal challenges from the libertarian Washington Legal Foundation claiming that the restrictions unconstitutionally limited free speech.[12] By contrast, settlement provisions attempting to achieve similar policy goals, including variants of price controls and advertising restrictions, are not vulnerable to similar constitutional challenges because the regulations are voluntarily entered into by the defendant companies. The ironic result is that AGs have leveraged judicial power to force new regulations through settlements while simultaneously insulating these regulations from future court review.

Unlike the tobacco Master Settlement Agreement, which was resolved in one massive agreement with virtually the entire tobacco industry, settlements with pharmaceutical firms have proceeded on a more piecemeal basis. Although this approach limits the reach of any one settlement to those defendants actually signing the agreement, it also presents benefits for AGs seeking to regulate the industry. Agreements that include entire industries, such as the tobacco Master Settlement Agreement, limit the prospects for future regulatory innovation because a settlement, once signed, becomes locked in place to provide certainty for the parties involved. By contrast, a settlement-by-settlement approach allows AGs flexibility to experiment with new legal arguments and regulatory requirements that were not part of previous settlements. The piecemeal settlement approach also makes it more difficult for the industry to defend itself as a whole. Each company makes a decision to settle on the basis of its own self-interest, even if it involves agreeing to new regulatory provisions that set negative precedents for the future of the industry at large.

Further, the piecemeal settlement approach can have radiating effects beyond the specific companies signing on to a settlement agreement. State prosecutors frequently remark that litigation against industry leaders is meant to send a message to the broader industry. The intended message is that companies wishing to avoid future liability ought to alter their conduct to reflect practices followed by companies covered by other settlements. Industry members have frequently reacted to this message, as several companies not involved directly in settlements have nevertheless voluntarily changed their behavior in order to avoid future prosecution.[13] Litigation also prompted PhRMA, the industry's peak association, to adopt new codes of conduct to help their members ward off litigation, further radiating the effects of landmark settlements across the entire industry.[14]

Even when individual companies do proceed to trial, the existence of new legal norms created through previous litigation may mean a reduced chance of success for industry defendants. The notion that the AWP pricing system constituted fraud was difficult to fathom in the late 1990s, but the underlying legal norms had shifted so far by the mid-2000s that the judge overseeing the most important consolidated AWP case adopted the prosecutors' characterization of AWP as a fraudulent scheme perpetuated by greedy drug companies.[15] Although some individual companies have achieved success litigating state claims all the way to trial,[16] the broader AWP-as-fraud narrative advanced by litigation has already radiated throughout the entire political system. As noted below, Congress ratified the results of much AG litigation, essentially adopting provisions in individual settlements and applying them nationwide via federal statutes. Likewise, state Medicaid agencies have announced their intention to modify their state's prescription drug pricing system following AG lawsuits, regardless of how those cases were ultimately resolved.[17]

Federal Support for the AGs' National Policymaking

AGs' pharmaceutical ligation is essentially an effort to sidestep Congress, place a thumb on one side of the balance of interests considered by the legislature, and otherwise encroach on the regulatory ground thought to reside with the federal government. One might expect Congress to react with strong concern about the states' efforts to intrude on their regulatory turf and seek to preempt their efforts to create their own national policy. Yet something closer to the opposite has happened. Rather than discouraging further attacks on federal policy by these state actors, Congress has instead encouraged them to be policy entrepreneurs and often ratified the results of the AGs' policy-creating litigation.

The American Health Care Regime and Cooperative Federalism

This support begins with the peculiar structure of the federal health care regime itself, which has provided new opportunity points for AGs to shape federal policy through litigation. Health care provision in the United States is highly fragmented, relying not only on the private sector to a greater degree than in other industrialized democracies but also on the separation of program responsibilities and oversight between levels of government and among its branches.[18] Several federal programs, including the Medicaid program that has been at the heart of state pharmaceutical litigation, adopted a framework of cooperative federalism. As Daniel Elazar put it, cooperative federalism consists of a "partnership" between "several [power] centers that must negotiate cooperative arrangements with one another in order to achieve common goals."[19] This structure has embedded state actors, including AGs, into the processes of national policymaking.

Congress enacted Medicaid contemporaneously with Medicare as part of the Social Security Amendments of 1965, but both programs adopted a much different structure. The federal government controlled program operations for Medicare, which policymakers viewed as a broad-based program to benefit deserving elderly Americans. Medicaid, by contrast, was from its inception more closely associated with the sort of welfare programs that had traditionally been under state jurisdiction. The program aimed to supplement earlier state-based programs that had provided more limited health benefits to lower-income Americans.[20]

For that reason, the Medicaid system adopted a framework of cooperative federalism that maintained a crucial role for states. Under the program, every state joining Medicaid must create an agency to implement the program. Although they must conform to broad federal baselines, these state agencies also maintain wide control over the details of program administration. This includes enrollment of eligible individuals in the program, determining the benefits to be covered, and accounting to the federal government for its share of Medicaid funds.[21] State participation in Medicaid is voluntary, though every state has been part of the program since the early 1980s. A major reason for this full participation is the significant federal funding available for states that join the program. As of the 2014 fiscal year, the federal government covers between 50 and 73 percent of each state's total program costs, depending on the state.[22] In 2012, the total program costs for Medicaid were $421.2 billion, representing a significant portion of state budgets.[23]

Although not a sufficient condition on its own, Medicaid's status as a system of cooperative federalism was a necessary factor in the emergence of the states' pharmaceutical litigation. The cooperative federalist structure of Medicaid provided AGs, armed with the sole claim to represent their states' interests in litigation, with the basis for their claims that drug companies were cheating state treasuries and taxpayers. Ironically, the Medicaid program was fragmented to maintain the traditional American commitment of keeping welfare provision at the state and local level. AGs took advantage of this commitment to states' rights in the Medicaid program, though for the considerably different purpose of expanding rather than constraining the reach of the national regulatory state.

The American Health Care Regime and Adversarial Legalism

Cooperative federalism gave states an interest in the operation of Medicaid, but subsequent federal encouragement of adversarial legalism in the program has served to build the AGs' capacity for expansive litigation campaigns targeting Medicaid fraud. The origins of this support trace back to the late 1970s, when growing concern about widespread fraud in the system, such as doctors double billing Medicaid for services covered under the program, served as an impetus for state and federal governments to create new state-level special prosecution teams tasked with uncovering

Medicaid fraud.[24] After New York's pioneering effort that introduced anti-Medicaid fraud special prosecutors, Congress enacted the Medicare–Medicaid Anti-Fraud and Abuse Amendments of 1977. This enactment granted additional resources to the states for establishing special prosecutors to investigate health care fraud, similar to New York's program.[25] These prosecutors became part of specialized Medicaid Fraud Control Units (MFCUs) placed under the AGs' control in nearly all states.[26] The MFCUs were granted wide discretion to initiate antifraud litigation independently of any other state actors. In fact, federal requirements prohibited state Medicaid agencies from reviewing or overruling any activities of the MFCU, a requirement instituted to prevent conflicts of interests that could occur if the same agencies tasked with administrating the program were also tasked with investigating waste, fraud, and abuse within the same programs.[27]

In addition to providing prosecutorial independence for MFCUs, the federal government has provided considerable funding to encourage them to bring antifraud litigation. After an initial three-year trial period in which the federal government covered 90 percent of the costs of the MFCUs, Congress decided to make the federal funding of these units permanent. The federal government continues to fund the majority (typically 75 percent) of each state's MFCU. The grant amounts to the states under the MFCU program totaled over $217 million as of 2012, enabling these units to employ over 1,900 staff members collectively.[28] Thanks to the considerable federal and state funding of these units, most MFCUs retain a number of experienced attorneys and investigators on staff. For example, New York's MFCU, the largest in the nation, retained 317 attorneys and other staff as of 2012.[29]

In addition to increasing funding for state-level prosecutors, Congress has continued to encourage fraud prosecutions through other enactments as a way to cut costs. As part of the Deficit Reduction Act of 2005 (DRA), Congress offered a variety of grants for states to strengthen their state antifraud efforts.[30] Specifically, the DRA provided financial incentives to states that enacted strong False Claims Acts by allowing these states to keep larger portions of the settlement proceeds from any antifraud prosecutions. As of 2014, thirty states had enacted state-level FCAs, granting AGs greater incentive to bring Medicaid fraud litigation.[31] The Patient Protection and Affordable Care Act of 2010 (ACA) further strengthened the federal FCA, making it an even more attractive weapon for both federal and state prosecutors to bring litigation against drug firms.[32] Other proposals and enactments have likewise sought to make it easier for prosecutors to bring antifraud litigation against the health care sector.[33]

The growth of collaborative anti-Medicaid fraud networks has also served to encourage pharmaceutical litigation. The MFCUs have cooperated closely with one another as well as with federal agencies, especially through the National Association of Medicaid Fraud Control Units (NAMFCU), which was established in 1978. The NAMFCU provides a forum to discuss multistate investigations and helps to coordinate state actions with the many federal agencies involved in combating Medicaid fraud, including chiefly the Office of the Inspector General within HHS, but also including the Department of Justice, the FBI, the IRS, the Post Office, and others.[34] NAMFCU also works closely with the National Association of Attorneys General (NAAG) in coordinating state actions, facilitated by the fact that both organizations are located on the same floor of the same building in Washington, DC.[35] Especially since the start of the Obama administration, federal prosecutors have significantly ramped up their collaborations with AGs and the NAMFCU. In May 2009, the Obama administration announced the creation of the cabinet-level Health Care Fraud Prevention and Enforcement Action Team (HEAT) Task Force, which aimed to strengthen the existing federal–state collaboration in health care litigation. This has contributed to a significant increase in pharmaceutical pricing and marketing litigation. Since HEAT's creation in 2009, federal and state prosecutors concluded nearly as many fraud settlements with the pharmaceutical industry in four years as they had in the previous eighteen years combined.[36]

When MFCUs first entered into operation, the focus was on what one might characterize as run-of-the-mill fraudulent behavior by health care providers concentrated within individual states. Prosecutors targeted activities such as health care providers billing Medicaid for blood tests or x-rays that they never performed.[37] These law enforcement activities generated little controversy because they usually involve fairly clear and obvious schemes to defraud the Medicaid system. As illustrated in chapters 3 and 4, however, the type of so-called fraud investigated by AGs has expanded well beyond these sorts of clearly illegal schemes. Law enforcement against fraud now encompasses attempts to change nationwide pricing practices of the pharmaceutical industry in ways often indistinguishable from changes in public policy. Yet Congress and federal agencies have continued to empower adversarial legalism as a method of regulating the pharmaceutical industry, even as the federal policy regime has become the target of these prosecutions as much as any single corporate defendant.

Ratifying the Results of Policy-Creating Litigation

As AGs took advantage of the institutional fragmentation in America's health care regime to develop national policies, federal policymakers have frequently ratified the results of these challenges. After the success of the Bayer and TAP Pharmaceuticals settlements and the wave of state drug pricing litigation that followed, for example, members of Congress began with their own investigations of industry pricing practices. Ultimately, Congress increasingly accepted the view of AWP as fraud. The Medicare Prescription Drug, Improvement, and Modernization Act of 2003 even codified the new average sales price benchmark created by and defined in the legal settlements and complaints against the drug industry. Congress likewise adopted several policy changes following successful landmark drug marketing settlements with drug firms. The Food and Drug Administration Amendments Act of 2007 mandated various additional disclosure requirements on drug firms, including the expansion of required clinical trial disclosures similar to those AGs were achieving in their settlements.[38] The ACA contained a host of new sunshine provisions requiring drug firms to report certain payments to doctors—requirements that several companies were already obligated to provide under settlements negotiated by state prosecutors.[39]

In his studies of environmental and welfare policy, R. Shep Melnick noted the ways in which Congress frequently ratified federal courts' interpretations of a variety of statutes even though the decisions appeared to go beyond Congress's original intent.[40] Similarly, Congress ratified new regulatory baselines adopted by AGs' out-of-court settlements, despite these settlements encroaching on their policy jurisdiction and contravening the choices of previous Congresses. The underlying dynamic resembles a regulatory ratchet, with state litigation and federal legislation building off one another to expand the reach of the regulatory state. Federal policies create entrepreneurial space for AGs to bring litigation; AGs accept the invitation and use litigation as both a regulatory tool and a method of refocusing congressional attention on new frauds and deceptive practices of drug companies; and subsequent federal policies then ratify and extend the results of this litigation.

AG Litigation and the Expansion of Coordination

In 1960, E. E. Schattschneider suggested that the "central political fact in a free society is the tremendous contagiousness of conflict." How a particular conflict is resolved, he argued, will depend largely on the breadth of its scope. Political fights that draw in additional participants and adequately socialize conflict are more likely to have an impact on the existing political status quo.[41] Critical to the government litigators' efforts to change pharmaceutical firms' organizational culture and policy on a national scale was their ability to draw in additional participants to the conflict over pharmaceutical practices. These additional participants included private class-action attorneys as well as advocacy groups that had long sought stricter regulation of the pharmaceutical industry through legislation. As Ron Pollack of Families USA, a health care advocacy group, described it, "Consumer groups, government agencies, hospitals, insurance companies and others are now saying enough is enough. They've decided that if they can't succeed through the legislative process, then they will challenge the companies through the legal process."[42]

Among the most important collaborations were those between state-level public prosecutors and private plaintiffs' lawyers. Stung by criticism of the AGs' relationships with private contingency-fee attorneys in the tobacco litigation, the AGs initially signaled that their litigation against pharmaceutical companies would be different. "This is not going to be another windfall for plaintiffs lawyers around the country," stated the spokesman for the first chair of NAAG's Pharmaceutical Pricing Task Force, Ohio AG Betty Montgomery.[43] A number of AGs had a "lingering ill will" toward the lawyers in the tobacco cases over the size of their legal fees, and other AGs were concerned that the private lawyers' focus on large monetary settlements would interfere with the AGs' goal of obtaining regulatory changes throughout the industry by means of this litigation.[44]

Despite these early concerns, the private bar has played a major role in the pharmaceutical litigation. This was especially true in the AWP litigation, which created the greatest prospects of large monetary recoveries. The AGs bringing AWP litigation, with the exception of Texas's AG, hired contingency attorneys to handle these cases in the name of the state. The reason for this, as the AGs themselves stated, was to supplement their limited resources with the expertise of these plaintiffs' lawyers. This was particularly useful in the AWP litigation, which involved a number of highly complex issues with which the AGs had little previous experience. For the private contingency fee attorneys, on the other hand, "this fell hand-in-hand with a lot of consumer work [they did]."[45] One plaintiff's firm in particular, Hagens Berman, handled much of the day-to-day litigation for several of the states joining the campaign against drug companies.[46]

This coordination with a small pool of plaintiffs' lawyers had the effect both of harmonizing the AWP-as-fraud narrative—the legal complaints written by Hagens Berman in separate state AWP cases bear a great deal of similarity with each other—and providing private attorneys with additional resources to be used in later private class-action litigation. Coordination with states has proven to be an effective way for the private class-action bar to join the conflict over AWP, because AGs have a key resource that private attorneys do not: the ability to sue on behalf of the public interest by framing the AWP system as defrauding taxpayers and state treasuries.

After the AGs' initial successes, several advocacy groups also joined the growing litigation campaign against drug companies. The Prescription Access Litigation (PAL) coalition, consisting of various unions and progressive advocacy groups, formed shortly after the initial Bayer and TAP Pharmaceuticals investigations. Operating as a project of Community Catalyst, a national advocacy organization for consumer rights in the health care system, PAL formed to use class-action litigation to "advance important legal and public policy goals." The coalition is not hesitant to explain the policy-oriented purpose of its lawsuits:

> The longer-term goal [of PAL's class action lawsuits] is to put a halt to drug company practices that keep the cost of drugs high. The lawsuits will move the issue of access to prescription drugs to the forefront of the public eye. Historically, class action lawsuits have been a vehicle to encourage legislative leaders to take action on a particular policy issue. It is our hope that the actions of the PAL initiative will persuade state and Congressional legislative leaders to address the high price of prescription drugs and the problems many people experience in obtaining needed medications.[47]

The litigation goals articulated by the PAL coalition shared much in common with those of the AGs. Much as PAL sought a "system change" in their litigation, the prosecutors sought "nothing less than changing the way the industry does business."[48] Given this shared focus on similar public policy goals, it is not surprising that the lawsuits filed by the PAL coalition have built directly on the AWP-as-fraud frame developed by the government prosecutions. Assisting the convergence in goals was the fact that the same private class-action firms that had worked with the states applied their experience to the PAL coalition, further coordinating tactics among the different parts of the anti-AWP coalition.[49]

AGs' position as advocates for the public interest offered them advantages that helped them serve as a vanguard for a broader litigation campaign. For one, by framing their litigation strategies as merely enforcing the law against rogue drug companies, AGs were able to create what Eugene Lewis termed an "apolitical shield" around activities that are actually very much political.[50] Unlike interest groups whose purposes are tied explicitly to ideological goals, AGs have the advantage of claiming that they were working for the public interest at large by neutrally prosecuting illegal activity. This apolitical shield made it considerably more difficult for pharmaceutical industry defendants to claim that the legal attack they faced was motivated by groups with an ideological axe to grind. Similarly, by serving as the face of the litigation campaign, AGs could more easily avoid charges that the campaign was motivated simply by money rather than the public interest. This is in contrast to private class-action coalitions more easily painted as consisting of greedy trial lawyers.

One important aspect of the expansion of AGs' antifraud litigation campaign is that it has remained largely bipartisan. This is despite the fact that this litigation seeks regulatory expansion in health care policy, one of the most polarized areas of American politics. Liberals long concerned with the actions of big pharma have supported prosecutions of drug firms as a way to fight corporate greed, but this litigation has also appealed to conservatives who have viewed state prosecutions as a way to fight waste, fraud, and abuse in burgeoning federal social programs. Republicans praised legislative efforts to encourage state AWP lawsuits against drug companies, for example, as a way to help US taxpayers "recover the billions of dollars stolen through fraud every year."[51] As Senator John McCain (R-AZ) put it, pharmaceutical pricing fraud was another example of "wasteful and unnecessary" government spending.[52]

Helping advance this antigovernment waste argument was the fact that the coalition of prosecutors litigating against drug companies throughout the 2000s included a bipartisan group of Republican and Democratic AGs as well as members of George W. Bush's Department of Justice. Indeed, few differences exist in the propensity of Democratic or Republican AGs to participate in antifraud litigation against pharmaceutical firms.[53] In a polarized era in which few political compromises seem possible—particularly when dealing with government regulation in health care—this bipartisan approach to regulatory expansion in the drug industry is all the more remarkable.

AG Litigation and the National Pharmaceutical Policy Regime

The pharmaceutical industry practices at the center of the AGs' litigation were problematic in several respects. The AWP benchmark almost certainly resulted in higher prices for prescription drugs under Medicaid and Medicare. Drug companies have tiptoed close to the line between the dissemination of neutral drug information to physicians and the explicitly illegal marketing of off-label uses of their products. In these cases, however, Congress and other federal regulators were aware of these industry practices but chose to maintain the existing system for years before the AGs' litigation campaigns. Critics may point to pharmaceutical company lobbying and agency capture as the main factors behind this federal inaction, but the explanation is more complex. These areas involved a delicate balance of competing concerns that made alteration of the system difficult and even undesirable. The AWP system, flawed as it may be, helped to compensate providers for losses they incurred when providing other services under government health care programs. DTC advertising and dissemination of information related to off-label uses of pharmaceutical products, while potentially driving up costs, also provide consumers and physicians with useful information about drugs that can ultimately promote public health.

By using their position as legal representatives of their states to expand the federal regulatory regime, the AGs' litigation sought to privilege one set of concerns at the expense of the others. This in turn has threatened to unleash certain unintended results throughout the national pharmaceutical policy regime. When the AGs' litigation precipitated an alteration in government reimbursement rates for prescription drugs, many AGs viewed this as a victory for consumers and state budgets. Yet at the same time, these changes threatened to eliminate a significant source of revenue for health care providers without replacing it with an alternative. This reduced compensation meant less incentive for health care providers to offer services to Medicare and Medicaid recipients. Particularly because the shortage of primary care physicians is already a major problem in the United States, this seemingly obscure regulatory change threatened to have a major impact on the quality of care for Medicare and Medicaid patients.

Similarly, the AGs' drug advertising litigation aimed to protect consumers and slow the growth of drug costs. Yet the stricter regulations they achieved in settlements could come at the expense of public health by making it more difficult for physicians to consider off-label uses of drugs and for consumers to learn about potentially helpful treatments for their conditions. New regulations pertaining to DTC advertising, such as preclearance provisions, might lead to companies becoming more conservative about DTC advertising and result in fewer opportunities for consumers to learn about beneficial medications.[54] While the off-label use of pharmaceuticals raises legitimate questions about drug safety, restricting information about potentially beneficial off-label uses may actually have net negative effects on patient health. Prosecution of off-label promotion by drug companies also threatens to result in a reduction in funding for educational and clinical research in this area. Other regulatory changes achieved through litigation present similar drawbacks. The regulations in the Zyprexa and Vioxx settlements relating to conflicts of interest may, for example, deter significant numbers of well-qualified physicians from engaging in promotional relationships with pharmaceutical companies or from participating in continuing medical education activities altogether.

Evaluating whether the changes prompted by the AGs' litigation have had a net positive or negative effect for patient health is beyond the scope of this book. The purpose of raising these issues is instead to note a fundamental difficulty with the AGs' policy-creating litigation. By seeking to reshape the existing national regulatory regime, AGs recalibrated the balance of concerns that propelled the creation of the original federal regulatory regime without consideration of how to deal with unintended consequences. The litigation left it up to Congress to decide how to compensate doctors adequately after recharacterizing the long-standing AWP system as fraudulent. Prosecutions created new uncertainty in the industry about how companies might be penalized for distributing truthful information about potentially life-saving treatments to consumers and doctors.

AGs did not undertake a consideration of potential unintended consequences of their preferred regulatory approach because they did not need to. Federal agencies, including the FDA, are staffed by experts in their respective areas and are tasked with making determinations about inevitable regulatory trade-offs. The lengthy process of regulatory rule making, while imperfect, aims to uncover as many of the competing concerns involved in any regulatory decision as possible. By contrast, AGs have neither the technical expertise of those in the FDA nor the incentive to worry about how pulling on one thread of the national regulatory scheme may affect the larger tapestry. Instead, their focus remains on resolving individual cases brought to address only one set of concerns, such as drug costs, without consideration of the bigger picture.

In the next three chapters, I turn to a different policy area that nevertheless shares much in common with the AGs' pharmaceutical litigation. As with their pharmaceutical litigation, AGs have used litigation to expand regulatory controls on the energy industry. In doing so, they sought to alter national air pollution policy in a way that focused greater attention on the problems of acid rain and climate change. As with their prescription drug lawsuits, however, the AGs' efforts to spur greater air pollution controls through litigation altered the national environmental policy regime in ways that created new regulatory problems.

CHAPTER SIX

FIGHTING A GUERRILLA WAR IN THE COURTS

Litigating Acid Rain

What is necessary is a full-scale, all-out war, which can only, in my opinion, be carried out by Congress. . . . In the meantime, we are fighting a guerrilla war to use whatever weapons we have.
Connecticut attorney general Joseph Lieberman, referencing multistate acid rain litigation against the Reagan administration

Ever since the rise of environmental consciousness in the 1960s and the celebration of the first Earth Day in 1970, environmental issues have maintained a high-profile role in American society. Hollywood blockbusters frequently dramatize the negative effects of pollution, and books from Rachel Carson's *Silent Spring* to Al Gore's *Earth in the Balance* have topped the New York Times best-seller lists.[1] Even as environmental issues have played a strong cultural role in American society over the past several decades, they have played an even larger role in American regulatory politics. Few sectors of the economy remain untouched by regulatory programs seeking to address problems such as acid rain, smog, and climate change.

The expansiveness of America's contemporary environmental policy regime has helped make it a battleground for political contestation, frequently pitting arguments for more government regulation to protect human health with concerns about the impact of such regulation on economic growth. These debates have transpired across several venues, including not only Congress and federal agencies but also the courts. The Clean Air Act of 1970 was the first to contain a citizen suit provision granting court access for lawsuits against polluters or the Environmental Protection Agency (EPA). This proved invaluable for environmental advocacy groups, including the Sierra Club and the Natural Resources Defense Council, which developed litigation teams challenging perceived inaction on the part of federal regulators.

These advocacy groups would soon have a powerful ally in state attorneys general. Since the 1980s, AGs have challenged the federal government's performance on air pollution control in several multistate litigation campaigns, focusing first on acid rain and later on climate change. For the last several decades, they have continued experimenting with a variety of legal strategies to address these environmental issues. In addition to policy-forcing litigation based on the citizen suit provisions of the Clean Air Act, AGs built on their successful policy-forcing litigation strategy developed in the 1990s—most prominently in the area of tobacco—to bring lawsuits against polluters directly as a method of policy creation.

This chapter and the following chapter 7 examine the development of the AGs' litigation campaigns pertaining to acid rain and climate change, respectively. Much as it did in the context of pharmaceutical policy, state litigation served as a method of challenging deregulation and expanding the regulatory state to impose stricter controls on American industry. Rather than following the familiar narrative of states' rights in which states fight a federal government determined to violate state prerogatives through new and costly federal mandates, the litigation discussed in these chapters involves state efforts to force the federal government to promulgate stronger and more expansive environmental regulations. As coordinated state litigation has unfolded over several presidential administrations, it has become a major new front in escalating battles over environmental policy.

The Politics of Acid Rain

The broader politics of acid rain during the Reagan administration served as the backdrop for the emergence of AGs as national environmental policymakers. During this time, the issue of acid rain became increasingly politically salient yet typical avenues for policymaking appeared unlikely to address it. Acid rain refers generally to precipitation with an unusually high acidity caused when certain pollutants, chiefly nitrogen oxide and nitrogen dioxide (collectively referred to as NO_x) and sulfur dioxide (SO_2), enter the atmosphere and become chemically altered by atmospheric processes. The term *acid rain* itself dates to 1872, but interest in the issue as a potentially serious environmental problem did not grow until the 1970s. New studies at that time indicated an increase in acid rainfall in the northeastern United States brought on by NO_x and SO_2 emissions from the Midwestern industrial region.[2] This acid rain allegedly caused a variety of environmental ills in these states, resulting in reduced fish populations, polluted drinking water, and damaged historic buildings and monuments.[3]

These concerns led to calls for stricter government controls of SO_2 and NO_x emissions. Proponents of tighter regulations faced two main problems in the late 1970s, however. First, the scientific evidence remained mixed concerning the harms of acid rain and the contribution of SO_2 and NO_x emissions to alleged environmental problems.[4] Further, it was not clear that existing federal statutes could properly deal with the problem of acid rain. Congress enacted the central federal air pollution statute, the Clean Air Act of 1970 (CAA), well before acid rain emerged as an issue. This created a problem because acid rain was a different type of pollution than the type anticipated by the CAA's drafters. The CAA targeted air pollutants that, once emitted, tended to diminish ambient air quality in the surrounding area. Coal burning, for example, releases pollutants leading to the smoky haze, or smog, that became infamous in American cities after World War II. Congress designed the CAA to reduce this sort of pollution in part by adopting national ambient air quality standards (NAAQS) requiring that the level of specified pollutants remain under a certain threshold in the ambient air. The EPA establishes NAAQS for these pollutants, after which every state must submit state implementation plans to the EPA detailing how it will achieve the levels required by the federal government.[5]

By basing the regulatory system on the quality of the ambient air in each state, the NAAQS regulatory system assumed that air pollutants affected only the areas surrounding the sources of pollution. Acid rain raised a different problem. Unlike smog, which nearby energy plants generate, acid rain results from the mixture of pollutants at higher levels in the atmosphere. This not only makes it difficult to pinpoint the pollution sources responsible for acid rain but also means that pollution generated in one location could affect a much broader area compared to the types of pollution anticipated by the drafters of the CAA. This was particularly a problem for states, like those in the Northeast, that were expected to detail to the EPA how they would improve air quality in their states even as the sources of pollution causing declining air quality were outside of their regulatory control.

This dynamic led to increasing interstate and even international conflicts, as Canada joined Northeastern US states in their complaints that upwind (primarily Midwestern) pollution sources were interfering with their pollution control regime. Congress amended the CAA in 1977 to address certain types of interstate pollution, but acid rain was not among them. Rather than instituting new regulations, Congress and the EPA pursued a more limited approach toward facilitating additional acid rain research. The EPA earmarked $4 million to study the problem in 1979, and a year later, Congress enacted the Acid Precipitation Act of 1980, creating a ten-year study of the causes and effects of acid rain.[6] Meanwhile, environmental interest groups increasingly identified acid rain as their biggest policy priority, and they sought major changes in the CAA that would go beyond funding new studies.[7] Several EPA officials argued that the mismatch between the existing structure of the CAA and the problem of acid rain required further amendments to the statute.[8] Given that Congress had enacted significant changes to the CAA only three years before, legislative efforts to combat acid rain seemed within the realm of possibility.

Acid Rain and the Reagan Administration

The prospect of legislative solutions to acid rain, however, faced a major challenge with the election of Ronald Reagan in November 1980. Throughout his presidential campaign, Reagan emphasized the need for a smaller federal government and reduced regulation. His victory, which brought along with it a Republican Senate majority for the first time in nearly thirty years, led some environmental advocates to declare that the "environmental decade is indeed over."[9] Early in his administration, Reagan proposed cutting EPA funding by nearly 75 percent, and his appointment of the business-oriented Anne Gorsuch as EPA administrator signaled a different regulatory approach to environmental policy.[10] The Reagan administration joined a growing chorus that was critical of burgeoning federal air pollution regulation, which critics viewed as harming economic growth and contributing to the growth of the federal government. The Reagan administration proved to have little appetite for expanding the CAA's style of command-and-control regulation, instead signifying support for market-based regulation and a smaller role for the federal government in air pollution control.[11]

The Reagan administration proposed new CAA amendments that cut back on federal regulation and mentioned little about acid rain. Representative Henry Waxman (D-CA), then chair of a key environmental subcommittee, labeled the administration's proposal as "nothing less than a blueprint for the destruction of our clean air laws."[12] Legislators, especially from Northeastern states most affected by acid rain, introduced several proposals to require stricter reductions in emissions leading to acid rain.[13] However, these bills met with strong opposition from Midwesterners concerned with the burdens new regulations would place on industries in their states.[14]

Given this political context—with the administration seeking to scale back the CAA and substantial regional conflict in Congress—the prospects for federal action on acid rain appeared slim. Members of both the House and the Senate stated that acid rain legislation was unlikely to reach the floor because the issue was "tremendously polarizing."[15] Many members, particularly from the Midwest, wanted the costs of any acid rain program to be spread around the country (through a nationwide tax, for example) to avoid electricity price shocks in their regions.[16] Nevertheless, a number of proposals attempting to do this, such as one introduced by Representative Waxman, met defeat in subcommittee.[17] Every time that acid rain legislation would move forward in committee—as when the Senate Environment and Public Works Committee nearly unanimously passed a compromise proposal to require reductions in SO_2—it died before reaching a full floor vote.[18] The various attempts at compromise received increasingly less support from environmentalists, labor, and industry groups in the early 1980s.[19]

State Litigation and the Guerrilla War over Acid Rain

Amid increasingly polarized congressional debates about acid rain, a new approach to acid rain regulation was developing in the states. Two years before President Reagan's election, Democratic Bronx borough president Robert Abrams succeeded his long-time Republican predecessor as New York's AG. Abrams, who had frequently criticized state Republicans as being too "cozy" with big business, pledged to make his office "the people's law firm" by taking stronger enforcement actions to protect consumers and the environment.[20] Reagan's election in 1980 and the deregulatory approach it ushered in gave Abrams and like-minded AGs a new target.

In December 1980, only a month after President-Elect Reagan's victory, Abrams declared that he would sue the federal government if the EPA continued to allow coal-burning plants in several Midwestern states to emit the same levels of SO_2. This threat was possible because of the citizen suit provision in the CAA, which allowed "any person"—including states—to sue the EPA alleging that the agency failed to carry out a nondiscretionary duty under the statute.[21] In a letter to outgoing EPA administrator Douglas Costle, Abrams charged that SO_2 emissions had increased since 1978 and that he was particularly concerned that the EPA would relax emission standards in the future—a clear reference to the incoming Reagan administration. According to Abrams, the EPA had "a legal obligation under the Clean Air Act to consider the effect on downwind areas of relaxed emission standards at any power plant," and if necessary, he would use the his power as AG in an unprecedented state effort to force the EPA to fulfill this obligation in court.[22] Over the next few years, Abrams and other AG allies backed up this threat by leading a policy-forcing litigation campaign against the Reagan administration's EPA. The litigation campaign resembled a guerrilla war in the courts, as Connecticut AG Joseph Lieberman put it, in which the states used a jumble of legal strategies to try to force strict federal regulations concerning acid rain.

Litigation under the Interstate Abatement Provisions of the Clean Air Act

In January 1981, Abrams filed a petition with the EPA asking the administrator for a finding that emissions of SO_2 and NO_x from Midwestern sources were polluting New York's air. Abrams acted under §126 of the CAA, which Congress had added as part of the 1977 amendments. This section allows a state to ask the EPA for a finding that pollution generated in other states interfered with the state's ability to achieve its NAAQS requirements. A few months after Abrams's petition, Maine AG James Tierney filed a similar §126 petition alleging that the same Midwestern sources prevented his state from meeting its NAAQS requirements. Tierney noted that he acted because "in large part we have to rely on the federal government to protect us from long-range air pollution" that harmed Maine's forestry, fishing, and tourism industries.[23] Three additional states subsequently filed §126 petitions.[24]

The EPA held hearings on the petitions during the summer of 1981 but did not act on any of them. Throughout the process, the EPA maintained that action on acid rain was premature and not cost-effective, given the lack of scientific consensus on the issue.[25] Other Reagan administration officials echoed this position, emphasizing the uncertainty in the scientific data on acid rain and that "no clear link has yet been established between man-made emissions and acid precipitation."[26]

The petitions remained pending for nearly three years. With the EPA declining to take action on acid rain and legislation addressing the issue stalled in Congress, AGs adopted a more aggressive strategy. In January 1984, five AGs, now joined by three environmental interest groups, sued the EPA in the US District Court for the District of Columbia. The AGs pointed to the provisions in the CAA requiring the agency to respond to their §126 petitions within sixty days, a period that had long since expired. This was despite allegedly "exhaustive evidence before it showing that Midwestern states' sulfur dioxide emissions are interfering with Northeastern states' ability to meet national air pollution standards." The AGs' lawsuit demanded that the EPA issue a prompt and final decision in the §126 proceedings, order several Midwestern states to revise their implementation plans to bring about compliance with the interstate air pollution requirements of the CAA, and take "all other actions necessary" to eliminate the "offending" interstate pollution.[27]

The EPA, for their part, did not deny that the statutory limit had expired, but it asked the court for more time to respond to the petitions. Because of the technical complexity and public significance of the issues presented in the petitions, as well as the myriad other demands on the agency's resources, the agency argued that it was impossible for it to comply with the short time limit specified in the statute. The district court rejected this argument, ordering the EPA to respond to the states' petitions. If the EPA "desires a certain degree of flexibility in its evaluation of section 126 petitions," the court noted, "the defendant must look to Congress, not the courts."[28] Abrams praised the court for "finally flush[ing] the EPA out into the open," but he warned that he would sue again if the EPA failed to impose acid rain controls.[29]

That was precisely what the EPA chose to do in its response to the court's order. Rather than appeal the District Court ruling, the agency denied the AGs' petitions, claiming that the states failed to show that out-of-state emissions had contributed to their NAAQS nonattainment. Most critically, the states did not identify specific sources of harmful emissions but instead wanted the EPA to reject other states' implementation plans for not dealing with acid rain and interstate pollution—something that the CAA did not explicitly require.[30]

Abrams declared that the EPA's action represented "an additional blow to human health, enormous financial loss due to property damage, and irreversible destruction to our environment," and he pledged to challenge the EPA's actions.[31] As soon as the EPA finalized its determinations, Abrams, along with five other AGs, brought another lawsuit in the DC Circuit Court of Appeals. As they had in their original petitions to the EPA, the AGs argued that the CAA placed a duty on the EPA to determine whether other states were adequately preventing pollution that had adverse impacts on theirs.

In a decision written by Judge David Sentelle and joined by future Supreme Court justice Ruth Bader Ginsburg, the DC Circuit rejected the states' arguments in the summer of 1988. The court held that the language of §126 was quite specific, allowing states only to petition the EPA "for a finding that any major source" is polluting in violation of the CAA but not allowing states to challenge the validity of other states' implementation plans. If Congress had wanted the EPA to review the adequacy of existing state plans, the court continued, it could have explicitly required it. In a short concurring opinion, Judge Ginsburg noted that Congress is "fully capable of instructing the EPA to address particular matters promptly" but that it "did not supply such direction in this instance; instead, it allowed and has left unchecked the EPA's current approach to interstate air pollution. The judiciary, therefore, is not the proper place in which to urge alteration of the Agency's course."[32]

The AGs petitioned for certiorari to the Supreme Court, which declined review and thus ended the AGs' ultimately unsuccessful attempt to use §126 to force the EPA to reduce pollution in the Midwestern states.[33] The AGs acknowledged that the DC Circuit Court's opinion meant that the states' attempts to use these provisions to address acid rain were "pretty much dead" but noted that they would continue their efforts to make acid rain a priority for the next presidential administration.[34]

Litigation under the International Abatement Provisions of the Clean Air Act

As the states' §126 litigation progressed, they pursued a parallel policy-forcing strategy under another new provision added by the 1977 CAA Amendments. Before these amendments, Canada had joined Northeastern states to complain that upwind pollution sources were interfering with its pollution control regime. To partially address this concern, Congress added §115 to the CAA. This section required the EPA to abate the offending emissions whenever the administrator made findings regarding the international impact of US pollution. Triggering abatement action under this provision required only the rather liberal basis that the administrator has reason to believe that upwind pollution had international impacts on public health and welfare.[35]

This provision became directly relevant in January 1981, only days before the Reagan administration took office. In response to an international report on acid rain deposition, outgoing EPA administrator Douglas Costle sent a letter to Senate majority leader George Mitchell and Secretary of State Edmund Muskie expressing his belief that the report "confirms that acid deposition is endangering public welfare in the US and Canada." Costle expressed similar themes in an EPA press release issued shortly after.[36] However, the EPA solicited no comments on the letters and did not publish them in the *Federal Register*. Costle's immediate successor, Anne Gorsuch, concluded that these letters and press release were of "no legal significance" and declined to take any actions under §115.[37]

Nevertheless, several AGs viewed Costle's actions as a possible legal hook to force the EPA to take action on acid rain. Following Gorsuch's determination that the letters were without legal significance, a coalition of seven AGs and several environmental groups demanded that the EPA implement the §115 international abatement procedures on the basis of Costle's alleged findings in his letters. When it declined to do so, the coalition again turned to the courts under the CAA's citizen suit provisions, seeking an order compelling the EPA to act. In an unusual twist, the Canadian government did not appear as a party in this lawsuit filed in the DC federal district court but instead authored the legal brief presented to the court by the AGs.[38]

The brief claimed that Administrator Costle's letters legally obligated his successors in the EPA to identify the states in which pollution responsible for acid rain originates and to order those states to abate their emissions. According to the suit, Costle's letters represented a formal determination that American SO_2 emissions were endangering public health in Canada, a determination known as an endangerment finding. Because §115 requires EPA action after an endangerment finding, the EPA's failure to do so constituted a statutory violation. The suit sought a court order requiring the EPA to publish emission limitations and compliance schedules for eight states allegedly generating high levels of transboundary emissions.[39]

Shortly after the initiation of the AGs' suit, Administrator William Ruckelshaus, who had recently replaced Gorsuch at the EPA, made clear his opposition to the use of §115 to deal with acid rain. He noted that §115 was "a very cumbersome way" to regulate SO_2 emissions because using this provision would require the agency to force states to revise their implementation plans on the basis of their proportionate share of emissions and establish plan revisions for any states that refused to do so. This regulatory route, Ruckelshaus noted, would not only be time-consuming, costly, and perhaps ultimately impossible, but would also be "a prescription for a decade's worth of court suits" over the new state implementation plans. Rather than "stretching" sections of the CAA to serve purposes for which they were not intended, it would be more sensible "if the country wants to do something about acid rain . . . [to] deal with it frontally" through legislative revisions to the CAA.[40]

Despite the agency's protestations, the AGs achieved initial success in federal district court. The court held that the AGs had standing to sue, despite the EPA's argument that the AGs and environmental groups were merely attempting to act as surrogates for the Canadian government. The district court also agreed with the AGs that Costle's letters and press release constituted "official agency actions" triggering the requirements of §115. This in turn compelled the agency to require states to revise their implementation plans to prevent further harm to Canada.[41]

The AGs hailed this "dramatic victory" in the district court and expressed hope "that the decision will spur some action in Congress" on the acid rain issue.[42] As one assistant AG from New York commented, this case "represents the first time a court has ordered the executive branch of the US government to abate acid rain and is perhaps the first time in history that a court has ordered air pollution emission reductions in its own country for the protection of another nation."[43] This celebration was short-lived, however, because the EPA appealed the decision after its determination that it had neither the time nor the resources available to comply with the court order.[44] The EPA also reiterated Administrator Ruckelshaus's earlier criticism that §115 was not intended to deal with acid rain.[45] Four AGs representing Midwestern states intervened in the case in favor of the EPA's position and against their colleagues, as did dozens of utilities from the upwind states. The groups noted that because the EPA never formally published the Costle letters, they never had a chance to comment on these alleged findings.

The DC Circuit, as with the §126 litigation, reversed the district court. In a short opinion released only a day after the Senate confirmed him to the Supreme Court, Judge Antonin Scalia wrote for a three-judge panel holding that Costle's letters and press release was not an official agency finding triggering the state implementation plan review procedures of §115. Scalia noted that any agency determination allegedly binding all future EPA administrators to review state implementation plans constituted a rule. As a rule, Scalia continued, the findings in Costle's letters required notice-and-comment rule making to constitute official agency judgments. It was unnecessary to consider any of the plaintiffs' additional §115 arguments: "Because the findings were issued without notice and comment, they cannot be the basis for the judicial relief appellees seek."[46]

Despite the decision, Abrams vowed to continue, and the AGs made another push to use the §115 provisions to force the EPA to deal with acid rain. In 1988, the AG-led coalition, now totaling nine states in addition to official involvement by the Canadian government, petitioned the EPA to publish the now eight-year-old Costle letters for official notice-and-comment rule making.[47] After the EPA responded that the petition was "premature" and that the agency was "working vigorously" to "devise an appropriate program to deal with the acid deposition problem" in both the United States and Canada,[48] Abrams announced yet another §115 lawsuit together with fellow AGs and the Canadian government. In this case, *Her Majesty the Queen v. EPA*, the AGs again met defeat in the DC Circuit when the court deferred to the EPA's conclusion that it did not have sufficient evidence to identify the specific sources of pollutants in the United States that allegedly caused harm to Canada. The court also noted that the National Acid Precipitation Assessment Program, which Congress set up in 1980 to identify the sources and causes of acid rain, was to be completed by the end of 1990. The court accepted the EPA's argument that the conclusions of this program would help the EPA determine whether a §115 process was appropriate.[49]

The Clean Air Act Amendments of 1990

As the 1980s ended, the states' guerrilla war against the deregulatory-minded EPA did not appear to be going well. After initial successes in the federal district court, the AGs' lawsuits met greater skepticism in DC Circuit Court. Even as the AGs' litigation campaign faltered, however, legislative proponents of acid rain controls were finally achieving success. Before 1990, there were many proposals but little action in Congress on the issue. The third and final EPA administrator under Reagan, Lee Thomas, maintained that the acid rain legislation percolating in Congress would be extremely expensive and did not rise to the level of "ecological emergency" requiring immediate controls.[50]

The tenor on the issue changed under President George H. W. Bush, who pledged to bring the acid rain problem under control.[51] While promising action on acid rain, Bush remained critical of the command-and-control approach taken by the CAA and sought to institute market-based solutions to air pollution control. Most importantly, Bush proposed a cap-and-trade program in which the government would specify maximum allowable emissions but create economic incentives for private industry to meet those targets.[52] Bush's proposal formed the framework of what would eventually become the CAA Amendments of 1990, enacted overwhelmingly by Congress and signed into law by the president in November 1990.[53]

These amendments represented a major overhaul of the CAA, ambitiously addressing several major air pollution issues including urban air pollution, toxic air emissions, automobile emissions, and acid rain. Title IV of the amendments dealt with acid rain, aiming to reduce SO_2 emissions substantially by the year 2000 by creating emissions trading markets. This emissions trading market first established an 8.9 million ton annual cap of total SO_2 emissions by the year 2000. The EPA would then issue SO_2

emission allowances to existing sources, which could then bank their allowances or sell them, depending on how much SO_2 they emitted. Congress also directed the EPA to develop emission standards for NO_x, which would apply to the plants also subject to SO_2 controls.[54]

Expanding the Battleground: The Second Wave of Acid Rain Litigation

Federal legislative and executive action on acid rain created a temporary lull in the sort of policy-forcing litigation that had been so prominent during the Reagan years, but the AGs' guerrilla war was far from over. The EPA may have won the early skirmishes in the AGs' attempts to force the Reagan administration to address acid rain, but they nonetheless proved to be key moments in the development of modern state litigation. As conflicts among states continued to smolder over interstate air pollution, these early coordinated litigation efforts foreshadowed expanded and more successful collaborations among AGs. During both the more pro-regulatory Clinton administration and the return of a deregulatory approach during the George W. Bush era, AGs created new avenues for pursuing stricter air pollution requirements on American industry. This included new policy-creating strategies building on the approach that had proved so successful in the tobacco litigation of the late 1990s.

State Litigation and the Clinton Administration

Apart from a handful of skirmishes with the George H. W. Bush administration after passage of the CAA of 1990, the coordinated state litigation against the EPA that had been prominent during the Reagan administration largely dissipated.[55] Carol Browner, President Bill Clinton's EPA administrator, was a "self-proclaimed environmentalist" with close ties to Vice President Al Gore and his "ardent environmentalism."[56] Browner's EPA gradually implemented the acid rain emissions trading program throughout the Clinton presidency, which proved quite successful in reducing SO_2 emissions.[57]

With a self-proclaimed environmentalist leading the EPA, pro-regulatory AGs that had for so long been a thorn in the EPA's side proved to be valuable allies for the agency. When an EPA rule imposing stricter air pollution controls on Eastern states faced a legal challenge from the Virginia AG and a handful of business associations, the AGs of several of the Northeastern states facing stricter regulation under the EPA's program intervened to defend the agency's position.[58] The EPA even encouraged state litigation against itself as a way to expand air pollution controls. In 1997, a coalition of AGs petitioned the EPA under §126 of the CAA alleging that the EPA had failed to regulate certain NO_x emission sources in the Midwest and Southeast.[59] Shortly after the states threatened litigation, AGs and the EPA reached a settlement agreement requiring the EPA to promulgate stricter regulations on the Midwestern emission sources based on an accelerated schedule.[60] Less than three months after the settlement, the EPA issued a preliminary assessment of the §126 petitions agreeing with the states' findings that upwind sources were contributing to their failure to meet federal requirements, marking the first time ever that the EPA sided with the states in a §126 petition.[61] Documents obtained by industry groups opposed to the settlement suggested that the EPA had welcomed the AGs' suit to help provide it with political cover to obtain further NO_x reductions from Midwestern sources.[62]

A New Approach to New Source Review

Coordination among AGs not only served to help along a pro-regulatory EPA by placing it under legally binding demands that the agency itself wanted, but also helped devise a new strategy to expand controls on pollution emissions allegedly contributing to acid rain. Until the late 1990s, AGs had sought stricter regulations exclusively through policy-forcing litigation brought against the EPA. Beginning at the end of the Clinton administration, AGs looked to their massive settlement with the tobacco industry in 1997 as a blueprint for another approach. The tobacco settlement required the tobacco industry to pay over $200 billion and adhere to a variety of regulations not required under federal law. The settlement served as a prime example of how coordinated state litigation could create new policies governing major American industries that federal institutions could not or would not adopt. Following the tobacco example, AGs sought to use settlements to achieve strict air pollution regulations on the energy-generating industry.

The AGs' main legal hooks were ambiguities in the New Source Review (NSR) program, which is a crucial part of how government regulates pollution from large stationary sources such as factories and power plants. The NSR program, which began in the mid-1970s, requires that utilities and other industrial pollution sources planning new construction first obtain permits that "specify what construction is allowed, what emission limits must be met, and often how the source must be operated." The purpose of this program is to ensure that new construction will be as clean as possible and that new emissions do not significantly worsen air quality.[63]

The NSR permitting process applies not only to brand-new stationary sources but also to major modifications of existing sources. Congress defined a major modification as "any physical change in, or change in the method of operation, of a stationary source" that resulted in significant increases in existing emissions or the emission of a new pollutant.[64] Early in the program's existence, the EPA specified that "routine maintenance, repair, and replacement" would not constitute major modifications triggering NSR.[65] The distinction between major modifications and routine maintenance makes millions' of dollars worth of difference to the affected facilities because a facility subject to NSR must lower emissions by installing expensive pollution-reduction equipment. The problem, however, was that from NSR's inception in 1974, neither Congress nor the EPA made clear what constituted routine maintenance. Despite countless pages of rules attempting to define the exclusion, the ambiguity of the term led to considerable confusion regarding the applicability of the NSR process.[66]

AGs took advantage of this ambiguity to pursue a narrow reading of routine maintenance, bringing their acid rain campaign directly to the doorsteps of American industry. During his first few months as New York's attorney general, Eliot Spitzer had grown increasingly frustrated with what he viewed as a lack of progress in reducing pollution from Midwestern stationary sources that contributed to acid rain in the Northeast. Two weeks after the apparent collapse of negotiations between the EPA and several states concerning how best to achieve these reductions, Spitzer sent letters to seventeen electric power plants in the Midwest and Southeast announcing his intent to sue them under the citizen suit provision of the CAA in September 1999. Spitzer alleged that the plants violated the NSR provisions of the CAA because they did not obtain the necessary preconstruction permits before making major modifications to their facilities. The pollution generated from these newly modified sources in turn emitted SO_2 and NO_x, allegedly contributing to the formation of acid rain in New York and other Northeastern states.[67] In rhetoric reminiscent of his predecessor, Robert Abrams, Spitzer explained that the lawsuit was necessary because "while we in New York are striving to protect our residents and our natural resources with tough environmental standards, we are under siege by airborne pollution originating far beyond our borders."[68] He described the lawsuit as a landmark because it marked the first time that any state had directly sued a polluter in a different state for alleged violations of the CAA.[69]

Spitzer's suit, however, came as a surprise to the EPA, which was already in the process of preparing its own enforcement actions against many of the same utilities. EPA administrator Carol Browner noted that "we were working on [the issue of SO_2 and NO_x], trying to do things strategically. Eliot became impatient."[70] The EPA, in fact, had for the past two years instructed several investigators to examine utility permits in an effort to determine whether specific plants had made plant modifications resulting in higher SO_2 and NO_x emissions. Spitzer, on the other hand, asserted that his office acted "to pull the EPA along a little bit," claiming that the "EPA had been a little hesitant on these cases."[71] In part Spitzer defended his actions as necessary to enforce the law that the EPA, which he suspected of being afflicted with "regulatory capture," had failed to implement.[72]

Only six weeks later—while Spitzer was still waiting for the expiration of the CAA's required sixty-day waiting period between his intent to sue and the actual filing of his lawsuit—the federal Department of Justice (DOJ) sued many of the same utilities in its own action. As with Spitzer's suit, the DOJ alleged that the targeted utilities triggered NSR coverage by making major modifications at some of their plants that did not qualify as acceptable routine maintenance or repair under the Clean Air Act.[73] After the initial lawsuits, the DOJ soon amended its complaint to include several additional plants in the Midwest, bringing the total number of plants targeted in the suit to twenty-four.[74] The EPA, after its initial hesitation, also took several additional administrative enforcement actions against a broad range of emission sources over a large geographic area.[75]

Once Spitzer and the federal DOJ became involved, other AGs began to hitch their offices to this new litigation campaign. Two weeks after the DOJ's announcement, Connecticut AG Richard Blumenthal announced his intent to sue sixteen of the seventeen plants named in Spitzer's lawsuit.[76] With the DOJ now already litigating in US District Court in Ohio, Blumenthal and Spitzer opted to join the DOJ's suit as proposed plaintiff intervenors, filing their actions in late November 1999.[77] By the middle of December, six other Northeastern AGs joined the action, along with several environmental interest groups, creating a similar litigation coalition as in the earlier acid rain lawsuits in the 1980s.

The defendant companies claimed that regulators had long considered the type of work done at their plants as routine maintenance under the CAA and thus not subject to the act's NSR provisions.[78] None of the projects were designed to increase the plants' electricity-generating capacity, which the defendants argued was the crux of what triggers the NSR permit process.[79] Several other industry groups viewed the lawsuits as "rulemaking in disguise," alleging that the states, along with the EPA, were attempting to set a new NSR standard by using a broad interpretation of routine maintenance in the lawsuits.[80] This was in marked contrast with the case-by-case approach the EPA had previously been using to determine actions triggering NSR.[81] Others noted how prosecutors were using the enforcement process to accomplish interpretations of the CAA not explicitly authorized in the legislation or existing regulations. Former EPA general counsel E. Donald Elliot noted that while changes to the NSR provisions could be done through legislation or a series of rule changes, the states and the Clinton administration had instead sought to "change the law through aggressive enforcement" and getting courts to defer to these actions, thereby changing the law.[82] By doing so, the lawsuits sought not only to impose the new rules without normal rule-making procedures but to do so retroactively.[83]

In the last few months of the Clinton administration, the plaintiff states and the DOJ reached agreements in principle with several of the utility defendants. Despite industry qualms about the lawsuits, the settlements largely reflected the EPA's new NSR interpretation. A December 2000 agreement with Cinergy Corporation, for example, called for Cinergy to install state-of-the-art pollution control equipment in several of its plants. Cinergy agreed to either shut down or repower with natural gas nine small coal-fired boilers at three of its power plants by 2004. In addition, the company agreed to build four additional SO_2 scrubbers starting in 2008, upgrade its existing pollution control systems, and phase in NO_x reduction technology year round starting in 2004.[84] The parties estimated that the costs to Cinergy would amount to at least $1.4 billion, making it the largest Clean Air Act settlement in history, surpassing a $1.2 billion agreement the DOJ and states reached with the Virginia Electric Power Company a month earlier.[85] Cinergy also agreed to pay $8.5 million in fines and $21.5 million in "supplemental environmental projects" in the plaintiff states. The parties stated that the agreement would lead to 400,000 tons of annual reductions in SO_2 emissions and annual cuts of NO_x totaling 100,000 tons.[86]

Following the agreements in principle, Eliot Spitzer stated that he "couldn't be happier" with the results.[87] This was hardly surprising because the settlements accomplished nearly everything the AGs sought in their lawsuits. Rather than "spending years in time-consuming and wasteful litigation," and to "gain certainty regarding any future operations," two of the nation's largest energy firms agreed to install the types of new state-of-the-art pollution reduction equipment demanded by the government litigators.[88] This was despite the fact that the companies maintained that no such action was required under federal law. During the George W. Bush administration, states would continue this regulation-through-settlement approach to win similar pollution reductions by other industry leaders, including a major settlement with American Electric Power in which the company agreed to spend approximately $4.6 billion to install new pollution-reduction technology in several of its plants.[89]

Clear Skies, Messy Litigation: Challenging the Bush Administration on NSR

Despite Spitzer's blindsiding Carol Browner and the EPA with the announcement of his lawsuits against energy firms, AGs maintained a generally cooperative posture with the EPA and DOJ during the early stages of this NSR litigation. Carol Browner remarked that she was "constantly looking for ways [to make sure] that the things I cared about would continue even if there was a Republican administration. Having Eliot Spitzer in the mix was one way to do that."[90] This view of Spitzer as an insurance policy against future regulatory reversals became relevant during the George W. Bush administration. The Bush administration took a much different administrative and legislative approach to NSR, even as several NSR lawsuits remained on the docket. This transition led to increased tensions between the federal enforcers, the EPA, and AGs.

The first signs of conflict appeared early in Bush's presidency. As President Bush debated adopting a new national energy policy throughout the spring and summer of 2001, the administration signaled that it was considering withdrawal from all NSR lawsuits.[91] As part of Vice President Dick Cheney's Energy Task Force recommendations, the White House called on the DOJ to review the existing NSR actions for consistency with the CAA.[92] The state and environmental interest group plaintiffs decried this "outrageous" action, charging that this review meant that the targeted companies had no incentive to settle the suits as long as the review was pending.[93] Richard Blumenthal bluntly suggested that industry groups were driving this review. "Make no mistake," he told an EPA panel convened to discuss the new strategy. "Energy industry political pressure is the reason for this review. False pleas by energy special interests are the engine driving these proceedings."[94] The states also accused the Bush administration of shutting them out of the NSR litigation review process.[95]

About a year after taking office, President Bush announced his plans to address the ambiguity of the NSR process by proposing a Clear Skies initiative aimed at "encourag[ing economic] growth that will provide a better life for citizens, while protecting the land, the water, and the air that sustain life."[96] As an alternative to the "confusing, ineffective maze of regulation . . . that has created an endless cycle of litigation" typifying the NSR approach, Clear Skies would replace key aspects of NSR with a cap-and-trade system modeled after the successful approach taken in the 1990 CAA Amendments. This approach would be part of a "multi-pollutant strategy" targeting SO_2, NO_x, and mercury.[97] The EPA also initiated an administrative strategy to revamp the NSR program by developing regulations greatly expanding the number of modifications that would fall under the definition of routine maintenance.[98]

Amid the Bush administration's legislative and administrative attempt to revamp and replace the NSR process, the states received a pleasant surprise when the federal DOJ completed its review of the NSR cases by concluding that the "EPA reasonably may conclude that the enforcement actions are consistent with the Clean Air Act and its regulations."[99] Thus, the existing NSR suits could move forward as a matter of law, leaving it to the EPA to decide whether this was good policy.[100] Eliot Spitzer, not surprisingly, took this as a stamp of approval for his lawsuits, though he suggested that the EPA's parallel administrative actions on NSR might turn the DOJ's report into mere "disingenuous camouflage of another capitulation to the President's industry supporters."[101]

From the AGs' perspective, this was precisely what occurred. After the DOJ's report, the DOJ and EPA's respective approaches to NSR enforcement took on an incongruous quality. The DOJ forged ahead with the NSR suits it inherited from the Clinton administration, setting trial dates and in some cases settling some of the lawsuits.[102] The EPA, meanwhile, simultaneously moved forward with an attempt to administratively eliminate the central basis of both the DOJ's and the AGs' NSR lawsuits.[103] Reports also emerged that the EPA would drop any new NSR enforcement cases against major sources as part of any effort it viewed as changing the NSR requirements through litigation or regulatory enforcement.[104]

It was in this context that the AGs' relationship with federal enforcers continued to deteriorate. This was especially true after both Cinergy and Virginia Electric Power refused to sign finalized consent decrees and backed out of their respective agreements in principle signed back in 2000. The departing head of the EPA's Office of Regulatory Enforcement, who had previously served under the Clinton administration, charged the Bush administration with sabotaging settlement negotiations in these cases. As he put it, "Companies with whom we were close to settlement have walked away from the table. . . . We were getting settlements, and getting it done. The companies that settled must be feeling pretty stupid now."[105] Members of Congress later repeated this criticism, particularly after a General Accounting Office report suggested that other EPA staff members believed the agency's NSR approach negatively affected the existing litigation.[106] The Office of Inspector General simultaneously concluded that the new EPA rules "seriously hampered" existing enforcement efforts.[107]

In response, EPA administrator Christine Todd Whitman claimed that the Bush administration maintained a "firm commitment to fully enforcing our environmental laws," pointing to its participation in finally bringing the Virginia Electric Power negotiations to a final settlement in 2003 along with the state plaintiffs.[108] Nevertheless, the AGs asserted that in contrast to the "enthusiastic collaboration" between the Clinton administration EPA and the states in these suits, the collaboration between them and "the highest levels" of the Bush administration was at best grudging. They noted, for example, that the Virginia Electric Power settlement was identical to the agreement in principle reached two and a half years earlier. The only reason the deal was delayed, the AGs argued, was because the company was holding out for a better deal. The Bush administration would be perfectly willing to give them this deal, the AGs claimed, if it had not been for the states' involvement in the negotiations. Indeed, without their continued involvement in the lawsuits, no settlements would have been possible at all. "The administration would really prefer the aggressive states to go away," a top attorney in the New York AG's office charged.[109]

The states continued their uncomfortable relationship with the Bush administration concerning the NSR suits throughout the administration's tenure. The posture was complicated because of the diverging enforcement approaches of the DOJ and the EPA. In 2003, for example, the DOJ and the AGs together achieved a major victory at trial against Ohio Edison, persuading the federal district court judge that the utility's plant modifications were not routine maintenance and thus were performed without Ohio Edison receiving the required NSR permits.[110] The prosecutors viewed this as a strong victory because of the potential cascade effect it would have on the other NSR cases.[111] Before the subsequent remedy portion of the trial, however, Ohio Edison argued that in considering remedies, the court should consider that under the EPA's new NSR rules, Ohio Edison's supposed violations of the CAA would not be violations at all. The EPA's actions thus supplied industry defendants with legal ammunition in the government prosecutors' case against them.[112]

This continued tension between active enforcement by state and federal prosecutors and the EPA's undermining the suits through rule making convinced AGs to renew their vow to press on with all of their NSR lawsuits, regardless of the federal government's enforcement posture. In reaction to the reports that the EPA would drop all new enforcement actions, Eliot Spitzer called on the EPA to turn over its enforcement files to the states so they could take the lead on these lawsuits independently.[113] In 2004, a trio of AGs, led by Spitzer, filed a NSR lawsuit against a utility without any federal DOJ intervention for the first time.[114] Although the federal government was not involved in this suit, the AGs used EPA compliance data and DOJ briefs filed in other NSR cases as part of their own lawsuits.[115] One industry attorney involved in the Ohio Edison case noted that this and other state NSR investigations and lawsuits were important in the politics of NSR because "it keeps the NSR issue alive, at least periodically," even as the Bush EPA attempted to replace NSR altogether with a different regulatory strategy.[116]

As the AGs pressed ahead with their Clinton-era interpretation of routine maintenance in their NSR lawsuits, they coupled their innovative regulation-through-settlement strategy with lawsuits aimed at frustrating the EPA's attempt to alter NSR through administrative rule making. These rules became more prominent when the Bush administration's Clear Skies legislation, which would have replaced key elements of the NSR program with a cap-and-trade system for SO_2, NO_x, and mercury, stalled in Congress when the bill failed to move out of the Senate Environment Committee.[117] With Clear Skies facing little prospect of passage in Congress, the EPA pursued parallel plans to achieve the essential contours of Clear Skies via administrative rule making.

The EPA finalized its first set of rules pertaining to NSR in November 2002, basing them on proposed rules first announced by the EPA during the Clinton administration in 1996. The new rules would establish plantwide emission caps allowing facilities to make changes within a plant as long as the emissions did not exceed the plantwide cap. This marked an important change from the current rules, which subjected all individual emissions units within a plant to NSR such that an increase in emissions from any one of them would trigger the permitting process. The rules would also establish a ten-year grace period allowing so-called clean units recently receiving NSR permits to continue making modifications without triggering NSR. Other changes also proposed to make triggering the NSR process less likely for most plants.[118] The EPA claimed that these rules would be better for the environment than the current program because the current system created disincentives for utilities to invest in clean technologies by subjecting too broad a range of modifications to expensive NSR procedures. By allowing more flexibility for industry, the EPA claimed, the rules would result in cleaner and more efficient factories.[119] These rules generated considerable controversy and received more public comments than had any previous EPA rule.[120]

A number of AGs immediately entered the fray, accusing the Bush administration of "endangering air quality by gutting a key component" of NSR, with Connecticut attorney general Richard Blumenthal accusing the administration of "appeas[ing] the energy industry by sacrificing the lives of people in the Northeast."[121] The AGs filed a lawsuit against the EPA in late December 2002 challenging the new package of rules (*New York v. EPA*). Led by Eliot Spitzer and initially joined by eight (eventually growing to thirteen) additional AGs, the AGs' key argument was that modifications under NSR were required whenever a change "increases the amount of any air pollutant." By contrast, they argued, the EPA's new rules resulted in an impermissible interpretation of the meaning of "increases" in that provision (though the CAA did not define the term).[122]

A bevy of amici eventually joined the AGs, such as a group of several Democratic senators that included Democratic presidential nominee John Kerry.[123] Meanwhile, the National Association of Manufacturers mobilized against the AG suits, asking its member companies to contribute between $500 and $5,000 to defend the regulations.[124] The state coalition lost on its initial attempt to achieve a stay of the rules in 2003,[125] but the DC Circuit's decision in 2005 handed the states a victory on several of their challenges. Although the court upheld some of the EPA's rules, it vacated both the clean-unit grace period and other NSR exemptions that the EPA had allowed. The EPA's interpretation of pollution increases, the court held, contravened the "plain language" of the CAA and therefore was not entitled to deference. The court also rejected all of the industry contentions that the existing NSR regulations resulted in stricter regulations than permitted under the statute.[126] The AGs viewed the decision as "a victory for clean air and for accountability," with Eliot Spitzer noting, "Today's court decision fully upholds the basis of all of our enforcement cases against coal-fired power plants."[127]

At the same time that the AGs' challenges to these NSR rules worked their way toward resolution, the AGs continued their approach of suing the federal government directly by challenging another new EPA rule, the Equipment Replacement Provision (ERP). This EPA rule, issued in October 2003, sought to expand the NSR exemption concerning routine maintenance.[128] The purpose was to substantially reduce the number of smaller equipment changes subject to NSR. These efforts, like the previous NSR rules finalized by the EPA, aimed to eliminate another disincentive for electric utilities to replace inefficient equipment.[129]

An AG coalition similar to the previous iteration in NSR cases brought a policy-forcing lawsuit against the ERP (*New York v. EPA*, known as *New York II*), claiming that their states would be harmed by the increased SO_2 and NO_x emissions allegedly resulting from the rule.[130] The plaintiff AGs argued that the ERP was contrary to the plain text of the CAA because the definition of modification in that section, which applies to NSR, applies to "any physical change" resulting in increased emissions.[131] The EPA claimed that the terms "any" and "physical change" were both ambiguous, and interpretation of these provisions should be left to the agency. In this case, several AGs intervened on the side of the EPA, arguing that vacating the ERP would have a negative effect on them "by increasing the costs of enforcement, constricting their enforcement options, and frustrating the achievement of the Act's pollution control goals in a more efficient and cost-effective manner."[132]

The plaintiff AGs obtained a stay of the ERP in December 2003, a decision Spitzer described as "one of the most important environmental victories in many years."[133] In 2006, the plaintiff AGs ultimately achieved an even larger victory in the case when the DC Circuit vacated the entire ERP. According to the court, "The petitioners' approach, by adopting an expansive reading of the phrase 'any physical change,' gives natural effect to all the words used by Congress and reflects both their common meanings and Congress's purpose in enacting the 1970 and 1977 amendments."[134] This successful policy forcing litigation, along with other state challenges to the EPA's attempts to modify NSR requirements not discussed here, marked a significant setback to the Bush administration's administrative approach to reform NSR.[135] This litigation continued throughout the Bush administration, frustrating the EPA's efforts to cabin its own regulatory authority all the way to the start of the Obama administration.

Conclusion

Unfolding over several presidential administrations, state acid rain litigation has opened up a major new front in the broader battles over environmental policy since the 1970s. Initial efforts targeting Reagan's deregulatory approach met defeat in the courts but signaled new forms of collaboration among the states that expanded over time. These expanded strategies, including both policy-forcing and policy-creating litigation, served as a major challenge to the George W. Bush administration's approach to air pollution control, particularly as the DC Circuit Court of Appeals proved more receptive to the AGs' increasingly prevalent arguments.

In the following chapter, I examine how states continued their guerrilla war concerning air pollution control by expanding their efforts to include the emerging issue of climate change. As calls for federal action to address the impact of greenhouse gas emissions grew, state litigation on the issue became increasingly aggressive. These efforts helped define the shape of the federal government's approach to climate change, even as environmental advocates found themselves stymied by congressional gridlock.

CHAPTER SEVEN

FROM SO_2 TO CO_2 Litigating Climate Change

Some may say that the states have no role in this kind of fight or that there's no chance of success. To them I would say: think tobacco.

Connecticut attorney general Richard Blumenthal, discussing the states' climate change lawsuits against several large utilities

On a sweltering summer day at Georgetown University in 2013, President Obama alternated between wiping away sweat and announcing a series of new initiatives to address global warming. "Our planet is changing in ways that will impact all of humankind," the president remarked. "I refuse to condemn your generation, and future generations, to a planet that's beyond fixing."[1] He noted that 2012 was the United States' warmest year in recorded history, capping a fifteen-year period featuring twelve of the hottest years on record.[2] Obama pledged to achieve cuts in carbon dioxide (CO_2) and other greenhouse gases (GHGs) linked with rising temperatures in America and around the world. "We will be judged as a people, and as a society, and as a country on where we go from here."[3]

Obama's address is part of an unfolding story concerning the impact of climate change on the planet and how best to deal with it. Since the early 1980s, scientists have been concerned with the intensification of the greenhouse effect caused by emissions of certain gases into the atmosphere that trap the sun's energy and drive global temperatures upward. In the years since, lawmakers and environmental advocates have sought legislation to address air pollution contributing to this greenhouse effect. Efforts to combat climate change through legislative channels have proven an immense challenge, however, especially as congressional polarization on environmental issues has reached new highs. Following Obama's admonitions about the consequences of a warming planet, others warned of the economic effects of his plan to address them. "The future laid out by the president is one of economic stagnation, high unemployment, and an uncompetitive and uncertain economy," stated Senator Jim Inhofe (R-OK), a frequent Obama critic and the ranking Republican member of the Senate Environment and Public Works Committee. "We cannot allow this to happen."[4]

As the debate about the regulation of GHGs has heated up, splintering along the polarized lines of environmental protection versus economic growth, state litigation has played an increasingly important role in climate change policy. In his Georgetown University address, Obama cited a 2007 Supreme Court decision that declared CO_2 to be a pollutant for the purpose of the Clean Air Act (CAA), the main federal air pollution statute. This holding in *Massachusetts v. EPA,* considered by many as the most important court case in the history of environmental law,[5] set the stage for Obama to announce his climate change plans. This was a victory for the AGs and environmental advocacy groups, which had collaborated on a lengthy litigation campaign to force the federal government to address the issue of climate change.

This campaign, much like the acid rain lawsuits described in the previous chapter, featured a jumble of legal strategies that served as a challenge to Congress and an executive branch perceived as unwilling to address climate change. The key difference between the acid rain and climate change litigation was that while the CAA dealt with the issue of sulfur dioxide (SO_2) and acid rain after the 1990 amendments, Congress had specifically rejected the regulation of CO_2 when it enacted those amendments. To get around this purposeful omission, the AGs pursued parallel policy-forcing and policy-creating litigation strategies to force reductions in CO_2. With their victory in *Massachusetts v. EPA,* the AGs' litigation fundamentally reshaped the direction of America's climate policy. This chapter tells the story of these state-led litigation campaigns and their place within the broader climate change politics in America.

The Politics of Climate Change

Climate change first became a concern in the 1970s, when various studies indicated that worldwide emissions of CO_2 had rapidly increased in the atmosphere. In 1979, the National Oceanic and Atmospheric Administration estimated that CO_2 emissions would likely double by 2025, causing a greenhouse effect that could result in higher temperatures worldwide.[6] A number of scientific studies suggested that the best way to deal with this buildup of CO_2 and other GHGs would be to limit the total usage of fossil fuels worldwide.[7] Although most of the early attention to air pollution focused on problems of smog and acid rain, the EPA noted the potential dangers of the greenhouse effect as early as 1980.[8] By the end of the 1980s, environmental groups made climate change a policy priority. The Environmental Defense Fund, for example, issued a report in 1988 concluding that higher temperatures would bring about major flooding and changes to the world's animal and plant life.[9] Another EPA analysis followed this report, suggesting that global warming could destroy up to 80 percent of the nation's coastlines in the next century.[10]

The increasing political salience of climate change resulted in various legislative efforts to address the potential problem. Then-representative Albert Gore (D-TN) cosponsored the first congressional hearings to study the potential implications of global warming. The first major bill aimed at controlling GHGs was introduced in the Senate in 1988, with the bill calling for a 20 percent reduction in CO_2 emissions by the year 2000.[11] In 1990, the George H. W. Bush administration established the State and Local Climate Change Program, which provided grants and technical assistance to the states for developing the capacity to deal with climate change.[12] Congress also enacted the Global Change Research Act the same year, requiring periodic reports to Congress regarding the environmental and economic consequences of climate change.[13]

Despite these early efforts, legislative action on climate change was halting. Several groups had urged Congress to allow for the regulation of CO_2 and GHGs as part of the 1990 CAA amendments, but ultimately Congress declined to do so. In fact, the 1990 amendments did not mention GHGs at all except for one minor reference directing the EPA to "publish the global warming potential" of certain listed GHGs. This provision explicitly stated, however, that it "shall not be construed to be the basis of any additional regulation" of GHGs.[14]

However, the start of the 1990s looked promising for advocates of stricter curbs of GHGs. After initially withholding support for international climate change efforts, the George H. W. Bush administration joined negotiations for a United Nations Framework Convention on Climate Change in advance of the Earth Summit held in Rio de Janeiro in 1992 (known as the Rio Convention). President Bush signed and the Senate ratified the Rio Convention, which set schedules and standards for reducing GHGs on the part of the ratifying nations but contained no binding commitments.[15] Less than a year later, President Bill Clinton, fresh off his electoral victory, announced on Earth Day in 1993 that his administration would commit to significant reductions of GHGs by the year 2000.[16] Clinton began to implement several voluntary initiatives to control GHG emissions, and legislation in Congress proposed to create a GHG emissions trading scheme similar to the acid rain cap-and-trade program established by the CAA of 1990.[17] Al Gore, now vice president, continued to voice his long-standing concern about climate change by taking a highly visible role in promoting action on the issue, particularly through his best-selling book, *Earth in the Balance*, and his oft-repeated refrain that GHGs represented "the world's most important environmental threat."[18] Gore claimed that President Clinton was finally clearing the gridlock that occurred under the Bush administration on the issue of climate change.

The Rocky Road after Rio

Then came the 1994 elections. Riding a wave of voter discontent, Republicans swept into control of Congress and pledged to reduce the size and powers of the federal government. Republicans in the House quickly voted to freeze the implementation of most new regulations, and the House majority whip introduced legislation to repeal the CAA of 1990 and other air pollution regulations.[19] House Republicans also sought to cut the EPA's budget by one-third, eventually passing a 14 percent cut to the agency.[20] Most famously, battles over the budget led to a partial government shutdown, forcing the EPA and many other government agencies to furlough employees.[21] With a conservative Republican majority in Congress, the prospect of domestic action on climate change appeared dim.

With many of his legislative proposals meeting a hostile audience in Congress, President Clinton placed renewed emphasis on international diplomacy concerning climate change. The United States participated in a pair of meetings among the parties to the Rio Convention, and the Clinton administration endorsed the Berlin Mandates that called for the development of binding emission targets and new rounds of negotiation.[22] Amid international reports outlining the link between human activity and climate change and growing international pressure for nations to act on the issue, the Clinton administration proposed a new global agreement on climate change in January 1997.[23] In advance of the next major meeting of the parties to the Rio Convention in Kyoto, Japan, the administration called for an amendment to the earlier convention that would set up an international cap-and-trade system for GHGs.[24]

The Clinton administration's forays into international negotiations on climate change received increasingly negative responses in Congress. For example, Senator Frank Murkowski (R-AK), chairman of the Senate Energy and Natural Resources Committee, warned the administration that the Senate would not go along with any international protocol that would impose an economic hardship on the United States.[25] Other Republicans in the Senate expressed similar concerns, particularly to the extent that GHG cuts would be legally binding and hurt the economy.[26] Even Clinton's fellow Democrats expressed concerns about international climate change treaties. Robert Byrd (D-WV) took a leading role in the fight against additional pollution reduction targets, sponsoring a resolution with Senator Chuck Hagel (R-NE) declaring strong senatorial opposition to any international GHG emission cuts that did not include developing countries or that "would result in serious harm to the economy of the United States."[27] This Byrd-Hagel resolution unanimously passed the Senate 95–0, leading several senators to describe the resolution as a "treaty killer."[28]

The Clinton administration nevertheless pressed ahead with its international efforts, signing an agreement reached by the parties to the Rio Convention at Kyoto (known as the Kyoto Protocol) after several US concessions during negotiations.[29] For the first time, industrialized nations agreed to mandatory GHG emission reduction targets for six GHGs, including CO_2. These varied from country to country, with the United States pledging to meet a standard 7 percent below 1990 levels within the next ten to fourteen years.[30]

The Kyoto Protocol came under attack immediately from industry groups and legislators, who claimed that the treaty would devastate the economy and allow developing countries to avoid deep emission cuts. Senate leaders warned that the treaty would be "dead on arrival" if it reached the Senate.[31] Despite an effort by the Clinton administration to build support for the treaty, it became clear that Congress was not going to ratify it. Instead, several members of Congress emphasized voluntary mechanisms as the only politically possible approaches to climate change–related legislation.[32] Abandoning much of his attempt to build support for the protocol, Clinton left office without ever submitting the treaty to Congress.[33]

Clinton's Parting Shot: The Cannon Memorandum on CO2

The Senate had already expressed its displeasure with the Kyoto Protocol through the unanimously adopted Byrd-Hagel resolution in 1997, but several members of Congress were concerned that the Clinton administration would attempt to pursue the spirit of the protocol through administrative regulation. Congress enacted a budget rider that prevented Clinton from trying to implement any aspects of the treaty through administrative regulation, including one prohibiting the EPA from using funds to "develop, propose, or issue rules, regulations, decrees or orders for the purpose of implementation, or in contemplation of implementation" of Kyoto.[34] Additionally, Congress pressed EPA officials to fully reveal their approach to GHGs. During budget hearings on the EPA's fiscal year 1999 appropriations, Representative Tom DeLay (R-TX) asked Administrator Carol Browner whether the EPA believed it had authority to regulate GHG emissions under the CAA. The EPA responded a few weeks later with a memorandum from Jonathan Cannon, the EPA general counsel, concluding that CO_2 satisfied the definition of air pollutant under §302(g) of the CAA.[35] This section of the CAA defines "air pollutant" as

> any air pollution agent or combination of such agents, including any physical, chemical, biological, radioactive (including source material, special nuclear material, and by-product material) substance or matter which is emitted into or otherwise enters the ambient air. Such term includes any precursors to the formation of any air pollutant, to the extent that the Administrator has identified such precursor or precursors for the particular purpose for which the term "air pollutant" is used.[36]

Cannon noted that because this "broad definition" included "any" physical, chemical, biological, or radioactive matter that "enters the ambient air," CO_2 must fall within the statutory definition. He noted that this was the case even for substances like CO_2, which are naturally present in the air. Nevertheless, Cannon stated, the EPA could not regulate CO_2 emissions until it issued a finding that these emissions were "reasonably anticipated to cause or contribute to adverse effects on public health, welfare, or the environment" (a finding known as an endangerment finding).[37] This, Cannon noted, the EPA had declined to do to this point.

The Cannon memorandum displeased members of Congress who were worried that Administrator Browner would take the next step of issuing an endangerment finding for CO_2. Two key environmental subcommittees held a joint hearing in 1999, asking, "Is CO_2 a Pollutant and Does EPA Have the Power to Regulate It?"[38] In response to both these questions, the new EPA general counsel, Gary Guzy, answered in the affirmative. As did Cannon, Guzy noted that §302(g) defined air pollutant very broadly—broadly enough to encompass CO_2.[39] He went on to emphasize that the CAA does not limit itself to localized pollutants. In 1970, he noted, Congress stated in the act that consideration of a pollutant's effects on welfare "includes, but is not limited to, effects on soils, water, crops, vegetation . . . weather, visibility, and climate." "Thus, since 1970, the Clean Air Act has included effects on 'climate' as a factor to be considered in [EPA's] decision as to whether to list an air pollutant." Guzy emphasized, however, that despite this authority, the "Administration has no intention of implementing the Kyoto Protocol prior to its ratification on the advice and consent of the Senate."[40]

The Back Door to CO_2 Controls: *Massachusetts v. EPA*

Counsel Guzy made these comments before Congress on October 6, 1999. Exactly two weeks later, a group of eighteen environmental interest groups filed a rule-making petition to the EPA, arguing that the CAA obligated the agency to regulate GHGs because of the harm global warming presented to the environment and human health. Specifically, the petition claimed that the EPA had a nondiscretionary duty to regulate GHGs under §202 of the CAA, which pertains to emission standards for mobile sources such as cars and trucks.[41]

According to the petition, the EPA's mandatory duty was clear because the statutory language in §202 stated that the EPA administrator "shall by regulation prescribe . . . standards applicable to the emission of any air pollutant from [new motor vehicles], which in his judgment cause, or contribute to, air pollution which may reasonably be anticipated to endanger public health or welfare." The petition cited Cannon's memo and Guzy's testimony in arguing that the EPA itself considered CO_2 to be an air pollutant. Once the EPA makes that determination, the groups claimed, the "shall" language of §202 required the EPA to act following an endangerment finding.[42] The petition noted that an endangerment finding does not require proof of actual harm and instead allows the administrator to make such a precautionary finding under the "reasonably be anticipated" language of §202. The groups cited several prior reports and statements from the EPA and other agencies noting the potentially adverse effects of global warming. The petition claimed these previous statements constituted an endangerment finding, thus triggering the EPA's mandatory duty to regulate GHG emissions from mobile sources under §202.

The environmental interest groups threatened active litigation if the EPA did not make a decision on the petition within the statutorily imposed eighteen-month requirement.[43] With less than eighteen months before leaving office and Congress aligned against any attempt to regulate GHGs, the Clinton administration opted to leave this issue to the next administration and took no action on the petition. The groups' petition was thus still outstanding when the Clinton administration left office in January 2001, leaving the question of the EPA's duties under §202 in limbo. The results of the famously divisive 2000 presidential election, meanwhile, signaled that reducing GHGs emissions would remain on the national back burner. Despite his tapping of Christine Todd Whitman, who had overseen several climate change initiatives as governor of New Jersey, as the new EPA administrator, incoming president George W. Bush took a much different approach to climate change issues than had the previous Clinton administration.

The first indication of the new approach occurred in March 2001 when Bush announced his plan to remove the United States from any further international negotiations for the implementation of the Kyoto Protocol.[44] Bush also stated that he would not seek to regulate CO_2 emissions from power plants, reversing a campaign pledge his press secretary characterized as "a mistake."[45] The Bush administration also made it clear that its focus on the issue of climate change would be limited to continuing and modifying some of the voluntary initiatives developed earlier.[46] Congress, meanwhile, was considering a number of proposals to deal with climate change, including a CO_2 cap-and-trade bill introduced by senators John McCain (R-AZ) and Joseph Lieberman (D-CT).[47] These efforts, however, ran up against the common criticism that CO_2 regulation would be too expensive and would raise costs for consumers. With sentiment against GHG regulation still strong in Congress and the Bush administration signaling that it would not make the issue a priority, federal action remained unlikely.

State Litigation as a Regulatory Avenue

With action on climate change seemingly stymied on both the national and international levels, advocates for GHG emission reductions continued to seek other avenues for policy development. As documented by Barry Rabe in his study of state-based climate change policy in the late 1990s and early 2000s, the failure of the United States to ratify the Kyoto Protocol and the Bush administration's regulatory approach meant that the issue "devolved on a de facto basis in the United States to subnational units."[48] As Rabe documents, a number of governors and state legislatures in the early 2000s enacted climate change policy on the state level.[49] While this state action was occurring, AGs also became considerably involved in climate policy, building on their earlier efforts on acid rain. Unlike the actions of individual governors or state legislatures, however, AGs used their policy tools to accomplish national policy changes during an era in which national policy development on the issue was not forthcoming.

At the same time that they skirmished with federal policymakers concerning acid rain, several AGs entered the fray challenging the Bush administration's approach to CO_2. In July 2002, eleven AGs sent a letter to President Bush urging the administration to take stronger action on climate change, including backing CO_2 cap-and-trade legislation. Because climate change was the "most pressing environmental challenge of the 21st century," the AGs argued, the administration's "completely AWOL" approach to the issue would lead to "catastrophic" effects both environmentally and economically. The AGs also noted, "Continued federal inaction will inevitably lead to a wider range of state regulatory efforts," warning that "in addition, states and others are beginning to review their litigation efforts."[50] James Milkey, the head of the Environmental Protection Division of the Massachusetts AG's office, noted that there was not yet consensus on the mechanisms or time frame for such litigation. Nevertheless, he said, "there is power in numbers" and claimed that as more states took legal actions, they would be more likely to change national policy.[51] The Bush administration, for its part, denied that there was any leadership vacuum on climate change, pointing to the voluntary initiatives promoted by the administration.[52]

This voluntary approach did not satisfy the various environmental interest groups who had filed the original 1999 petition concerning GHG regulation under §202. The EPA had not yet acted on their petition by December 2002, and the groups sued the agency in an attempt to force the EPA to act on the petition.[53] The filing came a day after EPA administrator Whitman stated her position that "carbon dioxide is not a Clean Air Act pollutant" in the same way that criteria pollutants (including SO_2) involved in the administration's Clear Skies initiative "directly impact[ing] human health" were.[54] Once the groups filed this suit, the EPA claimed they were still working through the backlog of comments filed after the agency's public comment period on the issue, which had closed the previous May 2001.[55]

A few weeks after the environmental interest groups filed their suit, several AGs joined the effort to force the EPA to take on climate change. Initially, however, they took a different approach than the environmental groups did in their petition pertaining to mobile sources. In January 2003, the AGs of Connecticut, Maine, and Massachusetts announced their intent to sue the EPA to force it to add CO_2 to a list containing six pollutants (known as criteria pollutants) already regulated by the agency under the CAA. In §108 of the CAA, a provision similar to that of §202 for mobile sources, directs the EPA administrator to add new air pollutants to the list if "in his judgment" the pollution caused by emissions "may reasonably be anticipated to endanger public health or welfare."[56] The difference is that this endangerment finding triggers regulatory action under §109, which requires the EPA to set national ambient air quality standards (NAAQS) for each of the listed pollutants. The NAAQS specifies the maximum allowable emissions for each criteria pollutant, requiring states to create policies that will reduce the concentration of each pollutant in their states to the allowable level.

The AGs formally brought the suit, *Massachusetts v. Whitman,* in the US District Court for Connecticut in June 2003.[57] Quoting the earlier comments by Cannon and Guzy, the AGs claimed in the complaint that the EPA had already declared CO_2 to be an air pollutant and had subsequently made judgments that climate change harmed human health and welfare. Because of this, they claimed, §108 obligated the EPA to list CO_2 as a criteria pollutant. The AGs also identified specific harms to their states' economic and property interests due to the reasonably anticipated effects of global warming, including damage to coastal shorelines and beaches, water quality problems, and damage to agricultural and forestry resources.[58]

The AGs' strategy was explicitly based on a lawsuit by the Natural Resources Defense Council (NRDC) in 1976 that successfully forced the EPA to list lead as a criteria pollutant, which was the last time that a pollutant had been added to the list.[59] This approach differed from the mobile sources §202 strategy in that it directly sought to compel the EPA to regulate GHG emissions from a much broader range of sources, including stationary sources such as power plants. This complemented the litigation strategy several AGs were developing in the context of their acid rain and New Source Review litigation discussed in chapter 6. Because of the wide scope of the lawsuit, one environmental interest group attorney noted that *Massachusetts v. Whitman* represented "one of the boldest legal moves a state attorney general has ever made," likening the scope of the actions to the tobacco litigation of the 1990s.[60]

On August 28, 2003, however, the EPA filed a motion to dismiss the AGs' lawsuit and denied the long-pending petition brought by environmental interest groups asking the EPA to regulate CO_2 for mobile sources. Formally withdrawing Cannon's memorandum and Guzy's testimony, the agency argued that Congress had never intended for CO_2 to be an air pollutant under the CAA.[61] "Even if CO_2 were an air pollutant generally subject to regulation under the CAA," the EPA stated, "Congress has not authorized the Agency to regulate CO_2 emissions from motor vehicles to the extent such standards would effectively regulate car and light truck fuel economy." The Energy Policy and Conservation Act directs the Department of Transportation, and not the EPA, to set fuel economy standards for vehicles. In addition, the EPA argued such regulation is "not appropriate at this time" because the agency was already taking a number of actions to address climate change. These other programs, the EPA explained, made for better policy at this time than regulating CO_2 under the CAA. This was due to both the uncertainty of climate change research and to the broad economic impacts such regulation would have.[62]

The EPA's denial of the AGs' lawsuit and the environmental group's mobile sources petition led to a shift in the AGs' strategy. On September 3, 2003, only a few days after the EPA's denial and motion to dismiss *Massachusetts v. Whitman,* the three AGs involved in *Whitman* announced that they would file a lawsuit in the DC Circuit challenging the EPA's denial of the environmental groups' petition. The AGs filed a motion to voluntarily dismiss *Whitman* without prejudice the same day. According to the plaintiff AGs, "We are still focused on global warming as the problem, we just changed our approach to solving it and decided to take EPA head on" at the appellate level.[63]

This new approach marked the birth of *Massachusetts v. EPA*. On October 23, 2003, a large coalition of AGs, cities, and environmental advocacy groups joined forces to challenge the EPA's petition denial in the DC Circuit.[64] This included twelve AGs as well as the environmental interest groups that had filed the original petition in 1999. The twelve plaintiff AGs, eleven of them Democrats, included all but one of the AGs from New England—the notable exception being New Hampshire's Republican attorney general—as well those from New York, New Jersey, Illinois, New Mexico, Washington, Oregon, and California.[65]

The lawsuit contained many of the same arguments the environmental petitioners had presented in their original 1999 petition. The complaint argued that the "plain language" of the CAA authorized the EPA to regulate emissions of CO_2, and that the §202 mobile source provision obligates the EPA to regulate CO_2 as an air pollutant under the act. The AGs again cited the Guzy and Cannon memos as evidence that the EPA believed that it already had the authority to regulate GHGs.[66]

Coalitions in Climate Change Litigation

These AGs worked closely with several environmental advocacy groups during the early litigation process, with Connecticut AG Richard Blumenthal noting that, like the tobacco cases of the 1990s, gaining success in climate change litigation "will take perseverance and fortitude by State

Attorneys General and their allies, such as the National Resources Defense Council. . . . We form alliances that are greater than the sum of their parts."[67] A lead attorney from the NRDC likewise pointed to the benefits of working together with the AGs when he noted that the NRDC was "delighted to be working with the Attorneys General offices and really delighted with Dick's [Blumenthal] early leadership on these issues [including *Massachusetts v. EPA*]. We did have breakfast together and something did happen, because Dick went back and assigned a couple of his best staff to work on this and made contacts with other Attorneys General offices."[68] Massachusetts's lead brief in the case, authored by Georgetown Law professor and environmental advocate Lisa Heinzerling, came together only after multiple conference calls among representatives of the twenty-nine plaintiffs aligned against the EPA.[69]

During the time that the plaintiff AGs' case in *Massachusetts v. EPA* awaited DC Circuit review, opposition began to array against it. Ten AGs, all Republicans, intervened on the side of the EPA along with several automobile trade groups.[70] The AG intervenors, similarly to the EPA, argued that the court's analysis must be governed by the Supreme Court's seminal decision in *Chevron v. Natural Resources Defense Council*. *Chevron* requires courts, when engaging in review of agency actions, to "give effect to the unambiguously expressed intent of Congress" in the underlying statute. If the statute is ambiguous, "the court does not simply impose its own construction on the statute. . . . [Rather,] the question for the court is whether the agency's answer is based on a permissible construction of the statute."[71] If this were answered in the affirmative, the court would not disturb the agency's interpretation, reflecting *Chevron*'s aim of prodding courts to defer to administrative agencies. Because they claimed the EPA's interpretation of the CAA was a reasonable and permissible construction of the CAA, the intervenors and the EPA argued that *Chevron* required the court to defer to the agency's decision not to regulate GHGs under the CAA.[72]

To defend this interpretation, the intervenor AGs argued that the CAA's establishment of an ambient air approach did not and could not apply to GHG pollutants like CO_2. As noted in the previous chapter, the CAA's basic structure targets a much different type of pollution than either acid rain or climate change. The CAA dealt with pollution like smog, which results when emissions from nearby pollution sources enter the ambient air. The NAAQS, as the name implies, was designed to address this sort of ambient air pollution. By contrast, CO_2 mixes with the earth's atmosphere at much higher levels than that of the ambient air, which makes it difficult to separate CO_2 emitted from American sources as opposed to international sources. Because the states have no mechanisms available to affect CO_2 emissions from sources outside the United States, regulating CO_2 under the CAA would make it impossible for states to attain their required air quality standards under NAAQS. The intervenor AGs were thus concerned that the EPA's regulation of CO_2 under the CAA would trigger NAAQS requirements, inevitably resulting in states being in nonattainment status by no fault of their own, much as several AGs had argued was the case in the acid rain litigation of the 1980s.

In a decision issued in July 2005, a sharply divided three-judge panel of the DC Circuit sided with the EPA and upheld the agency's decision not to regulate GHGs under the CAA. The court did not, however, address the specific concerns highlighted by the intervenor AGs; nor did it decide the question of the EPA's authority to regulate GHGs under the CAA. Instead, Judge Arthur Randolph's short opinion decided that the EPA had valid reasons not to regulate GHGs. This included the EPA's judgment about the scientific uncertainty surrounding the effect of GHGs on climate change, as well as the agency's policy judgment that regulating GHGs under §202 would "result in an inefficient, piecemeal approach to the climate change issue."[73]

The other two judges on the panel offered their own opinions, though for opposite reasons. Judge David Sentelle concurred in the judgment but argued that the court did not need to reach the issue of whether the EPA had given adequate reasons for not regulating GHGs under the CAA. Instead, he concluded that the case was "not justiciable in its present form with its present champions in the present forum" because the "EPA is correct in its assertion that the petitioners have not demonstrated the element of injury necessary to establish standing." In particular, the alleged harms claimed by the plaintiffs were general harms to "humanity at large," rather than the particularized injury required by the Supreme Court's standing doctrine.[74] Judge David Tatel, on the other hand, provided a lengthy dissent on much different grounds. He first concluded that at least one plaintiff—the Commonwealth of Massachusetts—met the three elements of standing articulated in *Lujan v. Defenders of Wildlife:* "injury, causation, and redressability." Most importantly, Massachusetts had asserted a "particularized injury" with its claims that it faced the loss of its coastal lands, and that this injury was caused by climate change. Judge Tatel then went on to claim that a plain reading of the definition of air pollutant in §302(g) of the CAA requires the conclusion that GHGs are covered by this statutory definition. He then rejected each of the EPA's reasons for nevertheless not regulating GHGs under the statute, concluding that the "EPA has authority—indeed, the obligation—to regulate their emissions from motor vehicles."[75]

The AGs' role to this point in *Massachusetts v. EPA* followed a similar track as the acid rain policy-forcing litigation of the 1980s—an active petitioning and litigation strategy, followed by a loss in the DC Circuit. What changed from earlier acid rain litigation, and dramatically so, was that the DC Circuit did not have the final word in this case. After the DC Circuit's denial of en banc review, the plaintiff AGs sought Supreme Court review of the DC Circuit's decision.[76] In June 2006, the Court announced that it would grant certiorari in the case on two questions: first, whether the EPA has the authority under §202 of the CAA to regulate CO_2 and other GHGs from motor vehicles associated with global warming, and second, whether the EPA may decline to issue emission standards for motor vehicles on the basis of policy considerations not enumerated in that section of the CAA. In their opening briefs to the Court, the plaintiff AGs pressed their argument that the EPA conducted no "serious scientific inquiry" into the public health issues raised by global warming and instead adopted a "misguided" interpretation of the CAA, noting that only Judge Tatel's lengthy dissent addressed the EPA's authority to regulate GHGs under the statute in the DC Circuit.[77]

On the day that the AGs filed their briefs in the Supreme Court, lead Massachusetts attorney general Thomas Reilly held a press conference with representatives of several of the involved environmental interest groups to announce the actions of the "powerful coalition" that had now formed against the EPA.[78] In addition to the original plaintiffs, six additional AGs joined the suit against the EPA as amici along with a broad array of additional environmental and business groups, individuals, and others. A large coalition also formed on the side of the EPA, which included the intervenor AGs mentioned earlier as well as several industry groups.

So Long, Chevron*: The Supreme Court Responds to* Massachusetts v. EPA

On April 2, 2007, the Supreme Court announced its landmark decision reversing the DC Circuit's opinion by a 5–4 vote, marking a striking victory on every count for the plaintiff AGs. Though the question of the plaintiffs' standing was not explicitly in front of the Court, Justice Stevens's opinion devoted considerable length to this issue. The Court noted that only one of the several petitioners needed to have standing for the Court to review the case, and it confined its analysis only to the lead petitioner, the Commonwealth of Massachusetts. Stevens began by noting, "Well before the creation of the modern administrative state, we recognized that States are not normal litigants for the purposes of invoking federal jurisdiction." Relying on a citation to the 1907 case of *Georgia v. Tennessee Copper Co.*—a case not cited in any of the plaintiffs' briefs—the Court held that as a state with a "well-founded desire to preserve its sovereign territory," Massachusetts had a "special position and interest" in the case and was entitled to "special solicitude in [the Court's] standing analysis."[79]

The Court then proceeded to rule for the petitioners on both counts concerning the substantive questions in front of the Court. On the first question, the Court held that the phrase "any pollutant" in §302(g) of the CAA "embraces all airborne compounds of whatever stripe," including carbon dioxide, methane, nitrous oxide, and hydrofluorocarbons, rejecting the EPA's attempt to "read ambiguity into a clear statute."[80] The Court addressed the contention that Congress did not intend for the CAA to regulate CO_2 by stating, "While the Congresses that drafted §202(a)(1) might not have appreciated the possibility that burning fossil fuels could lead to global warming, they did understand that without regulatory flexibility, changing circumstances and scientific developments would soon render the CAA obsolete. The broad language of §202(a)(1) reflects an intentional effort to confer the flexibility necessary to forestall such obsolescence." Rather than focus on the intentions of Congress specifically as to the regulation of CO_2, the Court thus instead focused on what it saw as the intent of Congress to provide regulatory flexibility through broad statutory declarations.

On the second question, the Court rejected the EPA's argument that even if it had the authority to regulate, it could choose not to do so on the basis of policy considerations not specified in the statute. These considerations offered "no reasoned explanation for its refusal to decide whether greenhouse gases cause or contribute to climate change," as the statute requires. Under the "clear terms" of the CAA, the "EPA can avoid taking further action [to regulate GHGs] only if it determines that greenhouse gases do not contribute to climate change or if it provides some reasonable explanation as to why it cannot or will not exercise its discretion to determine whether they do."[81] Because of that, the EPA's judgment that regulating motor vehicle CO_2 emissions would represent "an inefficient, piecemeal approach to address the climate change issue" was irrelevant. Further, if the scientific uncertainty is "so profound that it precludes EPA from making a reasoned judgment as to whether greenhouse gases contribute to global warming, EPA must say so."

Several observers noted that the Court's decision in *Massachusetts v. EPA* was one of the most important cases in the history of American environmental law, an observation seconded by the victorious AGs.[82] Although the Court did not explicitly order the EPA to make an endangerment finding triggering the regulation of GHGs under the CAA, the decision placed the EPA in a position where it could only rely on scientific evidence and not policy considerations in its decision making. Because the Court found that GHGs "fit well within the Clean Air Act's capacious definition of air pollutant" under the CAA's statutory definition in §302(g), the EPA had to make an endangerment finding for mobile sources in §202 based only on whether GHGs "cause, or contribute to, air pollution which may reasonably be anticipated to endanger public health or welfare."[83] Without the ability to rely on policy considerations, the EPA was essentially compelled to make such an endangerment finding.

Common Law, Uncommon Lawsuits: *Connecticut v. American Electric Power*

As the AGs' policy-forcing litigation in *Massachusetts v. EPA* worked its way through the courts, several AGs worked on a parallel strategy to achieve stricter CO_2 regulations. This strategy, similar to the New Source Review (NSR) lawsuits examined in chapter 6, used policy-creating litigation in an attempt to create regulations directly upon industry. Although this strategy did not achieve the same level of successes as either the NSR lawsuits or *Massachusetts v. EPA*, this campaign illustrates the range of regulatory options the AGs have been willing to pursue since their landmark tobacco settlement in 1998.

New York attorney general Eliot Spitzer's September 1999 announcement of acid rain lawsuits against power plants, discussed in the previous chapter, marked the first time that an AG litigated directly against private utilities to reduce air pollution emissions. It also served as a precedent for "a new legal frontier in the fight against global warming" against several private utilities based on their CO_2 emissions.[84] In July 2004, a coalition of AGs announced that they would sue several private utilities in the US District Court for the Southern District of New York in an effort to force them to reduce their emissions of CO_2. The eight AGs, all Democrats, represented states in the Northeast as well as California, Iowa, and Wisconsin.[85] In this "groundbreaking" lawsuit, the AGs sought no monetary damages. Instead, they sought an injunction against the five named utility companies to "cap [their] carbon dioxide emissions and then reduce them by a specified percentage each year for at least a decade."[86] AGs selected these five power companies as defendants because they were, according to the EPA emissions data the AGs used in this case, the nation's five largest emitters of CO_2.[87] Not only were these five companies the worst polluters "by a substantial margin," according to Spitzer, but they "have been recalcitrant" in acting to address the problem of climate change.[88]

However, the AGs could not rely on the same provisions of the CAA that they did in their NSR lawsuits because the CAA did not explicitly provide for CO_2 regulation. To get around this problem—something they were addressing on the statutory side through their policy-forcing suit in *Massachusetts v. EPA*—the AGs used a creative new argument. Their complaint sought relief under the federal common law of public nuisance and, alternatively, under state public nuisance theories. The alleged public nuisance was global warming, which the AGs claimed was "injurious to the plaintiffs and their citizens and residents." These injuries included, among other things, "the right to public comfort and safety, the right to protection of vital natural resources and public property, and the right to use, enjoy, and preserve the aesthetic and ecological values of the natural world."[89]

The industry reaction to this suit, *Connecticut v. American Electric Power* (known as *Connecticut v. AEP*), was swift and negative. "This action brings new meaning to the term 'nuisance lawsuit,'" stated one industry source. "The idea that any one company's emissions are responsible for global climate change is more political science than environmental science."[90] US Chamber of Commerce president Thomas Donohue argued that the action was "a blatant end-around Congress" and federal and state agencies in setting US policy on climate change. Moreover, Donohue continued, not only is carbon dioxide "not a pollutant," but the AGs' complaint "is symptomatic of America's legal crisis and yet another example of unwarranted litigation that hurts American consumers and destroys jobs."[91] Another observer noted that the "sweeping, mandatory injunction" sought by the AGs "would require the court to be involved in the operations of the defendants for years."[92] Other industry sources noted that the suit was unnecessary because the companies had taken voluntary actions under President Clinton's Climate Challenge program to reduce CO_2 emissions, something that Eliot Spitzer nevertheless dismissed as "inadequate and inconsequential."[93]

The strong rhetoric from a variety of industry sources was a reflection of the potential breadth of the AGs' new strategy. Because the AGs based the suit on common-law legal theories rather than statutory hooks, they did not specify particular pollution sources contributing to the public nuisance. Instead, their complaint pointed to all of the defendants' CO_2 emissions "from any state where their electric generation operations may be located" as contributing to the public nuisance. Because the AGs' coalition included members from the Northeastern, Midwestern, and Western parts of the United States, they were able to identify a wide variety of alleged harms, such as beach erosion in Rhode Island, injuries to agriculture in Iowa and Wisconsin, and harm to "chinook salmon, coho salmon and steelhead trout species" in California.[94] *Connecticut v. AEP,* therefore, potentially reached a far wider range of industries than those specific plants identified in the earlier acid rain litigation campaign against industry.

The AGs explicitly noted they intended this lawsuit to have a broad impact across the entire electric generation industry. "We are seeking relief that includes no money damages. . . . We're trying to change the way the [electric power plant] industry does business," as Richard Blumenthal put it.[95] In response to concern about the plausibility of the public nuisance legal theory relied on in this case, Blumenthal noted, "Some may say that the states have no role in this kind of fight or that there's no chance of success. To them I would say: think tobacco."[96] As with tobacco and the AGs' other climate change litigation in *Massachusetts v. EPA,* the AGs worked with a number of advocacy groups in this litigation. Several environmental interest groups filed a similar common-law-based suit on the same day and in the same court as the AGs.[97] This private suit was eventually consolidated with the AGs' suit.

The Courts Respond to Connecticut v. AEP

At the same time that the *Massachusetts v. EPA* narrative was unfolding, the eight AGs who had brought the common-law nuisance suits in *Connecticut v. AEP* awaited Judge Loretta Preska's decision in the US District Court for the Southern District of New York. They received their answer in September 2005, when Judge Preska dismissed the AGs' action on the basis that the case represented a nonjusticiable political question. The court, Preska said, was essentially being asked to resolve a major policy question requiring balancing the benefits of GHG regulation against the economic impacts of such regulation. "In this case, balancing those interests, together with the other interests involved, is impossible without an 'initial policy determination' first having been made by the elected branches to which our system commits such policy decisions."[98] Congress or the executive branch can better balance these interests, and for that reason, the courts should and must decline to exercise jurisdiction. Because Judge Preska held that the

AGs' complaint involved nonjusticiable political questions, she dismissed the complaint without reaching any of the merits of the case.

The AGs immediately appealed the decision, noting that the Second Circuit "has historically been extremely favorable" to the arguments of pro–environmental group interests.[99] The plaintiffs were to wait quite some time before a Second Circuit ruling, however. Although the case was fully briefed by March 2006 and oral argument occurred that June, the three-judge panel of the Second Circuit did not decide the case until over three years later in September 2009. Several observers suggested that the delay was a direct result of the swirling (and accurate) speculation that one of the three judges on the panel—Sonia Sotomayor—was a potential Supreme Court nominee.[100]

The remaining two-judge panel decided the case on September 21, 2009. In a rather surprising and lengthy decision, the panel reversed the district court's decisions and reinstated the AGs' lawsuit. The panel, consisting of Republican-nominated judges Peter Hall and Joseph McLaughlin, held that all the plaintiffs had standing to pursue the injunctions that they sought in the case—an issue not addressed in the district court opinion. The court noted that the states were suing on behalf of their "quasi-sovereign interests" under the ancient common-law doctrine of *parens patriae,* which had been relied on in early twentieth-century cases such as *Georgia v. Tennessee Copper Co.*[101] The states' interest in protecting their property from damage satisfied the requirement that the plaintiffs demonstrate an identifiable injury. Citing *Massachusetts v. EPA,* the court noted that this injury need not already be occurring but merely needs to be imminent and relatively certain to occur. The court then held that these injuries were "fairly traceable to the actions of" the utility defendants. The fact that many other emitters were also contributing to climate change did not affect the causation analysis.[102]

The court then reversed Judge Preska's holding that the political question doctrine barred the AGs' claims. "It is error to equate a political question with a political case," the court held. "Given the checks and balances among the three branches of our government, the judiciary can no more usurp executive and legislative prerogatives than it can decline to decide matters within its jurisdiction simply because such matters may have political ramifications."[103] Further, nowhere in the plaintiffs' complaints do they "ask the court to fashion a comprehensive and far-reaching solution to climate change." Instead, they sought specifically to limit the GHG emissions from several distinct coal-fired electricity plants. A decision on the merits of the case would not establish a national or international emissions policy, which would be outside of the purview of the court.[104]

Finally, the court held that the plaintiffs had stated a viable nuisance claim under federal common law, which was another issue the district court below had not reached. After a lengthy review of precedents, the court held that both the AGs and other plaintiffs had adequately stated a claim that the defendants conduct caused "unreasonable interference" with "a right common to the general public." Further, although Congress has enacted laws affecting air pollution, none of those laws has displaced the federal common-law claims in this suit because those laws did not "actually regulate the nuisance at issue." "It may happen that new federal laws and new federal regulations may in time pre-empt the field of federal common law of nuisance. But until that comes to pass, federal courts will be empowered to appraise the equities of suits alleging creation of a public nuisance by greenhouse gases."[105] Richard Blumenthal, the lead AG on the case, commented, "This ruling vindicates our tenacious and tireless battle on behalf of a powerful coalition of states and environmental advocates—a battle that will now have its day in court."[106]

One of the main purposes of the suit, however, was not even to reach a day in court. Instead, the *Connecticut v. AEP* case was modeled on previous efforts to sue and settle with private industry. "This lawsuit is comparable to our fight against Big Tobacco, without the money," as Richard Blumenthal put it.[107] "Our goal is not money damages, but a change in company practices to stem the pollution and safeguard our environment and economy."[108] The case thus aimed not only to result in the regulatory changes in one specific settlement but also to have a ripple effect on members of the electric generation industry.[109] Perhaps the most important long-term purpose was to reach the discovery stage of the trial. As one former AG noted, if the energy industry possesses embarrassing e-mail messages and memorandums similar to those that proved devastating to tobacco companies, "it's a hammer" that could drive industries to the negotiating table.[110]

After the momentous Second Circuit decision in September 2009, the industry defendants unsuccessfully sought en banc review at the Second Circuit before appealing to the Supreme Court. The petition for certiorari generated substantial amicus curiae activity, including twelve AGs who filed an amicus brief urging the Court to accept the case and reverse the Second Circuit's decision. These states emphasized that the question of climate change regulation was a political question not appropriate for the courts, noting, "Allowing some states to seek common-law injunctions against industries in other states would undermine the entire state–federal regulatory scheme."[111]

This time, the plaintiff AGs encountered opposition to the suit from not only Republicans and industry groups but also from fellow Democrats. Five Democratic AGs joined eight Republican AGs on the petition for certiorari to the Supreme Court. A union-oriented group also filed an amicus brief against the plaintiff AGs' position, noting that the "jobs and economic well-being of [union] members will be critically impacted by cases regarding climate change" and that piecemeal efforts to deal with GHG such as *Connecticut v. AEP* threaten to fail to take workers' interests into account.[112] Most importantly, the Obama administration weighed in against the plaintiff AGs in a brief urging that the Court grant certiorari, a move that caused considerable consternation among environmental groups.[113] The government's brief noted that the EPA was already dealing with climate change and CO_2 controls, arguing that the Second Circuit decision "was predicated on the now-obsolete conclusion that EPA had not taken action under its CAA authority to regulate carbon-dioxide emissions from stationary sources. Stripped of that premise, the result reached by the court of appeals is no longer warranted (if indeed it was at the time of the decision)."[114] Further, the regulatory approach taken by the EPA "is preferable to what would result if multiple district courts—acting without the benefit of even the most basic statutory guidance—could use common-law nuisance claims to sit as arbiters of scientific and technology-related disputes and de facto regulators of power plants and other sources of pollution."[115]

On June 20, 2011, the Supreme Court unanimously reversed the Second Circuit's holding in a decision that was widely expected following the Obama administration's intervention in the case. The majority opinion, written by Justice Ginsburg, held that the CAA had displaced the AGs' federal public nuisance arguments. Because the CAA authorizes the EPA to address GHG emissions—the holding of the Court in *Massachusetts v. EPA*—this statutory route closes off the possibility of using federal common law to achieve the same objectives. "The expert agency is surely better equipped to do the job," Ginsburg wrote, "than individual district judges issuing ad hoc, case-by-case injunctions." The Court held further that this analysis did not change simply because the EPA had not yet exercised its regulatory authority.[116]

Despite their loss, however, *Connecticut v. AEP* resembled more of a speed bump in a larger litigation campaign than a major defeat. Indeed, it is not clear whether the Court would have ruled against the AGs if they had not already won in *Massachusetts v. EPA*. The Court's main holding was that the AGs' federal public nuisance arguments had been displaced by the CAA's regulation of CO_2, which was forced by the AGs' litigation in *Massachusetts v. EPA*. Further, the Court held that the AGs had standing to bring this case, upholding the Second Circuit's exercise of jurisdiction and indicating that the Court has not retreated from the broad state standing announced in *Massachusetts v. EPA*.[117] Finally, the Court left open the AGs' potential use of state common-law nuisance theories against CO_2 emitters, even with EPA action of climate change in process.[118] Although as of this writing the states have not pursued this strategy, largely because the Obama administration has taken regulatory actions to reduce CO_2 emissions, it could very well be part of a future effort under an administration less willing to institute regulatory controls on GHGs.

Conclusion

The AGs' climate change litigation throughout the George W. Bush administration, operating parallel to their efforts on acid rain, marked a dramatic expansion of previous efforts to litigate air pollution policy during the Reagan years. What these litigation campaigns had in common is that both arose when other political branches seemed unwilling or unable to enact stronger pollution controls. In the absence of new legislation addressing issues of acid rain and climate change, AGs turned to new methods of policymaking as well as existing federal statutes as a way to achieve similar goals. AGs learned from the tobacco litigation experience that the regulation-by-settlement approach could be a powerful way to influence air pollution policy. They used this approach to try to achieve industry regulations not explicitly provided under federal law. Although not all of these attempts were ultimately successful, it is clear that this tool has become a permanent part of the states' litigation tool kit. At the same time, AGs used litigation to advance innovative interpretations of existing federal statutes. This effort resulted in a series of courtroom victories concerning the regulation of acid rain and GHGs, helping reshape the entire American environmental policy regime.

The AGs' resort to these alternative means of policymaking is the result of a complex mix of factors and has created a web of reverberations throughout the federal air pollution regime. The litigation also raises a number of broader points about the operation of the modern American political system. I turn to these observations in the next chapter.

CHAPTER EIGHT

STATE LITIGATION AND NATIONAL ENVIRONMENTAL POLICY

A glorious mess . . .
Representative John Dingell (D-MI), referring to the "morass" of regulation and litigation concerning greenhouse gases after *Massachusetts v. EPA*

During periods in which congressional conflict combined with a deregulatory-minded executive branch to make action on emerging environmental issues unlikely, state attorneys general emerged as an alternative venue for national policymaking. Throughout the 1980s, AGs used coordinated litigation in an attempt to force the Reagan administration to address the issue of acid rain. A similar story unfolded two decades later during the George W. Bush administration, when activist AGs took to the courts to counter a lack of national policy development concerning climate change. Although both litigation campaigns used different strategies and addressed different issues, they sought the similar goal of expanding national regulation.

This chapter steps back from the specifics of the environmental litigation campaigns examined in the two preceding chapters to consider several broader aspects of this litigation. As with their pharmaceutical litigation, AG activism in this area has its origins in the structure of the underlying federal policy regime. The twin reliance on litigation and federalism in the implementation of federal air pollution policy granted AGs crucial opportunities to play major roles in shaping national environmental policy. AGs progressively took advantage of their greater entrepreneurial space to engage in a form of national policymaking, using lawsuits and settlements as a way to expand the national regulatory state. This effort, which has featured increasingly partisan coalitions of AGs and other like-minded actors, aimed to deal with emerging environmental problems that typical national policymaking institutions seemed unable or unwilling to address. Although this litigation achieved a measure of success, however, it has also served to complicate the operation of the federal policy regime in a way that will likely have consequences for years to come.

Regulating Air Pollution through Multistate Litigation

Similar to their interventions in national pharmaceutical policy, AGs' air pollution litigation arose amid a broader debate about how best to balance government regulation and economic growth. The American environmental policy regime built in the 1970s relied on a so-called command-and-control regulatory structure, which featured government mandates specifying how and when private industry would be required to accomplish pollution reductions. However, parallel to similar deregulatory efforts concerning transportation and telecommunications policy, this command-and-control approach increasingly came under fire at the end of the 1970s and into the 1980s. During the Reagan era, economists and conservative politicians alike criticized command-and-control environmental regulation as inefficient government meddling in the private sector, with negative consequences for economic growth. They advocated market-based solutions to environmental problems that would allow greater flexibility to private industry in determining how to reduce their emissions.

These arguments gained an increasingly receptive audience during the 1980s. By 1990, advocates of market-based solutions to environmental regulation had succeeded in dictating the terms of the latest major change to the Clean Air Act (CAA) through the introduction of a cap-and-trade system that critics of the command-and-control approach had advocated as the preferable approach to acid rain regulation. Yet while federal policymakers moved away from command-and-control regulation, AGs used coordinated policy-forcing litigation to shift environmental regulatory policy in the opposite direction. Leading up to the CAA of 1990, AGs pursued innovative interpretations of the original command-and-control statute, the CAA of 1970 and the subsequent amendments in 1977, to address emerging environmental issues that Congress had not contemplated at the time the statutes were enacted. Their goal involved forcing the agency to set strict mandatory limits for emissions from specific sources in the Midwest, using the National Ambient Air Quality Standards (NAAQS) originally designed in 1970 for local pollution problems such as smog. Two decades later, AGs once again used the original command-and-control structure of the CAA in an attempt to address a large-scale, complicated environmental issue.

In litigation against the George W. Bush administration, AGs sought to force the Environmental Protection Agency (EPA) to address global climate change by regulating carbon dioxide (CO_2) through regulatory tools originally designed to address localized pollution.

Also during this period, the AGs paired their policy-forcing strategies with policy-creating litigation that could serve as a method of command-and-control regulation able to bypass the EPA altogether. Although the New Source Review (NSR) program had been moving in a direction that provided greater flexibility to industry, AGs exploited ambiguities in the existing regulatory structure to force leading energy firms to reduce their emissions in exchange for avoiding years of costly litigation and bad publicity. The settlements, frequently containing hundreds of pages of detailed regulatory requirements on industry defendants, directly contradicted the EPA's attempt to clarify the NSR standards in a direction granting greater regulatory flexibility to the energy-producing sector. After their successes in winning settlements in the NSR context, AGs attempted an even bolder move by suing leading energy firms under federal common law, claiming that the firms' pollution contributed to the public nuisance of climate change. These policy-creating litigation campaigns, similar to the AGs' policy-forcing efforts, were attempts to expand strict controls on American industry in order to address emerging policy problems.

Much like in the pharmaceutical context, this state litigation is an exercise of federalism, but a federalism that operates differently from standard conceptions of how the system works. Rather than seeking judicial protection from a federal government that had exceeded its authority, AGs instead used tools of adversarial legalism to try to expand federal power and national regulation. This was akin to the policy-creating litigation against pharmaceutical firms examined in earlier chapters, which resulted in settlements effectively expanding the boundaries of the national regulatory state and empowering federal agencies beyond anything Congress had authorized. Additionally, the AGs' environmental policy-forcing litigation has called for the federal government to exercise greater regulatory authority over the states themselves. The plaintiff AGs demanded EPA regulation of CO_2 and sulfur dioxide (SO_2) emissions under the CAA that would trigger not only expanded regulation of industry but also additional regulatory requirements for the states themselves through stricter NAAQS requirements. The AGs, in other words, sought to use litigation to force an otherwise unwilling federal government to expand its regulatory power at the expense of state policy flexibility. At the same time, AGs pursued a parallel strategy that built on the policy-creating strategy that had worked so well in the tobacco context by attempting to create national regulation from the ground up.

These efforts to expand national regulation through policy-forcing and policy-creating litigation have attracted increasing collaborations among both the AGs themselves and other actors seeking regulatory expansion. What began as a regional policy dispute has become a partisan struggle that has expanded to include nearly all of the AGs and a bevy of interest groups. Particularly given the federal government's role in creating the basic conditions within which the AGs' nationally focused litigation campaigns could flourish, this dispute cannot be described as simply "the states versus the federal government." Instead, contemporary AG litigation features a dynamic of some states attacking the federal government while simultaneously seeking to expand its authority. This in turn has led to increasing divisions amongst the states themselves.

Federal Support for the AGs' Role in National Policymaking

Similar to the pharmaceutical context, the structure of the underlying federal regulatory regime granted AGs crucial avenues through which to pursue national environmental policymaking. Reflecting the fragmented distribution of power in the American political system, the federal air pollution control regime Congress developed in the 1970s fragmented responsibility for air pollution reduction among several political actors. Rather than solely empowering a centralized national bureaucracy to tackle air pollution control, Congress built a regulatory structure that emphasized cooperative federalism. Under the theory of this cooperative structure, federal and state governments would work together to help carry out the shared national goal of air pollution reduction. Congress also incorporated adversarial legalism into the structure of the regime by providing a citizen suit provision enabling lawsuits that demanded compliance with the provisions of the CAA. Both of these aspects created the regulatory environment in which AGs could use litigation to play a major role in the development of national environmental policy.

Since the creation of this basic policy structure, federal institutions have continued to support AGs' role in national environmental policy. Federal courts have opened the door to state-driven challenges to environmental regulation, most strikingly through the development of the special solicitude standard announced in *Massachusetts v. EPA*. Additionally, during

Democratic administrations, the EPA has also viewed AGs as helpful allies able to entrench the agency's more expansive approach to national regulation.

The American Air Pollution Regime and Cooperative Federalism

Since its creation, the federal regulatory regime adopted a cooperative federalism model, seeking to make states a major part in the implementation of federal policy objectives. The CAA of 1970 stressed the primary importance of state and local governments in the implementation process. The act's preamble stresses "that air pollution prevention . . . and air pollution control at its source is the primary responsibility of States and local governments," while also making clear that "federal financial assistance and leadership is essential for the development of cooperative [air pollution control programs]." This approach was built on previous federal law in this area and was compatible with the rhetoric of the New Federalism of the Nixon era that emphasized the importance of granting localities "leeway for local option" and "local innovation, providing a variety of experimentation."[1]

Building on the commitment to cooperative federalism, the drafters of the CAA chose an ambient air quality approach to air pollution control. This NAAQS approach meant that the federal government would set the air quality standards and that states would determine ways to implement them through state implementation plans (SIPs). Several of the air pollution control programs developed after the original enactment of the CAA maintained this focus on state implementation.[2]

The CAA's requirement that the states implement air pollution regulations quickly led to sharp multistate conflicts. The CAA now required states to meet certain NAAQS standards through their SIPs, but the original act said little about the problems engendered by cross-border air pollution. It was not clear how issues pertaining to pollutants generated in upwind states that drifted into the downwind states' ambient air would be addressed. As discussed in chapter 6, much of the conflict on acid rain involved Northeastern states claiming that Midwestern states were reaping unjust economic rewards by exporting their pollution elsewhere. This pollution was not only causing acid rain damage throughout the state but was also contributing to several state counties entering NAAQS nonattainment status. Midwestern states, on the other hand, claimed that much of the Northeast's problems were of their own making, and that they were just trying to get a free lunch by exporting the costs of cleanup to them. In the case of climate change, several AGs pointed to CO_2 emissions from mostly Midwestern pollution sources as contributing to a wide variety of damage in their states resulting from climate change, much of it with economic consequences.

These conflicts have not swayed the federal government from the original cooperative federalism model for environmental regulation. Both the major sets of CAA amendments in 1977 and 1990 maintained the basic cooperative federalism approach, keeping states closely integrated into the federal policy scheme. Much as it has in the context of the Medicaid program, this continuing commitment to cooperative federalism has provided AGs a pathway into the operation of national policy by granting them a plausible claim that state interests were at stake in the debate over the shape of federal policy. This was particularly true since the federal scheme gave rise to increasing conflicts among states as cross-jurisdictional pollution became a larger problem.

The American Air Pollution Regime and Adversarial Legalism

In addition to incorporating states into the federal policy regime, the CAA also made litigation a key element of its pollution control regime. Congress enacted the CAA in 1970 at a time in which groups were increasingly turning to the courts in pursuit of their policy goals. In part, the growth of this manifestation of adversarial legalism was a product of both a growing emphasis on broad rights claims and an increasing distrust of administrative agencies allegedly captured by industry-oriented interest groups. Congress encouraged adversarial legalism by enacting several statutes in the 1960s and 1970s containing provisions that allowed so-called private attorneys general to enforce the provisions of the statutes through litigation.[3]

The CAA was no exception. Over the objections of industry groups and President Richard Nixon, §304 of the CAA of 1970 became the first environmental statute to allow "any person" to enforce any emission standard or administrative order against polluters directly.[4] In addition to this provision, the CAA also reflected skepticism among Democrats in Congress over the Nixon administration's willingness to enforce the act, authorizing suits against the EPA administrator "where there is alleged a failure of the Administrator to perform any act or duty . . . which is not discretionary with the Administrator."[5]

Since its adoption of the citizen suit provision in the original CAA, Congress maintained and expanded this commitment to adversarial legalism. The 1977 CAA amendments built on this litigation regime by allowing "any state" to petition the EPA to abate cross-border pollution through the new §126 mechanism. As noted in chapter 6, this section proved to be a crucial legal hook for the AGs' acid rain litigation campaign throughout the 1980s. The 1990 CAA amendments, while establishing a market-based approach to acid rain, nevertheless maintained and even expanded the role of adversarial legalism in federal air pollution control policy. The amendments strengthened the citizen suit provision in the CAA, providing those suing under this provision to obtain new civil penalties that would be deposited in a special fund in the US Treasury or be used for "beneficial mitigation projects" that "enhance the public health or the environment." The amendments also clarified that such §304 citizen suits were available to enforce CAA provisions against alleged past violations in addition to enforcement against sources currently in violation.[6]

As Congress maintained a commitment to adversarial legalism through amendments to the basic air pollution control regime, federal courts further bolstered it as well. As several observers of environmental law and litigation have noted, the question of standing to bring lawsuits in court has long been one of the key issues in environmental cases.[7] Beginning with their acid rain litigation in the 1980s, AGs claimed that they had rather expansive standing to sue based on Congress's opening of the courthouse doors in the CAA. This included, for example, suing under the international abatement provisions of the CAA despite concerns that the AGs were simply serving as surrogates for the interests of the Canadian government. Courts were generally quite open to these expansive claims of state standing, even when the AGs faced resistance from appellate courts on their substantive legal claims.

The courts' sympathetic reading of state standing came to the fore in *Massachusetts v. EPA,* which opened the courthouse doors even wider for AG plaintiffs. Holding that "states are not normal litigants for the purposes of invoking federal jurisdiction," the *Massachusetts* majority held that states must be afforded "special solicitude" when courts analyze standing claims.[8] This appeared to be a shift in the Court's standing analysis in environmental cases, which, since the Court's key 1992 decision of *Lujan v. Defenders of Wildlife,* has required litigants to demonstrate a "concrete and particularized injury that is either actual or imminent, that the injury is fairly traceable to the defendant, and that it is likely that a favorable decision will redress that injury."[9] Although the Court went on to discuss how Massachusetts met the three aspects of injury, causation, and redressability, it did so with the understanding that the states have a stronger claim to use the legal process when the federal government allegedly fails to protect them.

It is not entirely clear how far the Court's special solicitude rule will reach, though several federal courts in the wake of *Massachusetts* have relied on it to grant AGs expansive standing in environmental cases.[10] Other lower courts have read the special solicitude doctrine more narrowly, emphasizing that the doctrine does not excuse AGs from proving that their state has suffered a concrete injury because of federal policy.[11] Regardless of how expansively courts interpret the special solicitude rule in the future, it provides an illustration of the continued vitality of adversarial legalism within the federal environmental policy regime. By making litigation a major part of policy implementation in environmental policy—a choice made parallel to the continuing commitment to cooperative federalism—federal policymakers opened additional avenues for entrepreneurial AGs to influence this national policy regime.

Colluding with the Enemy: AG Litigation and the Pro-Regulatory EPA

Another subtle but important form of federal support for AG litigation against the EPA has come from the EPA itself. Although the EPA served primarily as the AGs' adversary during Republican administrations, the agency under pro-regulatory Democratic administrations has provided legal ammunition for the AGs' litigation campaigns. One of the final actions of President Carter's EPA administrator before President Reagan took office was to issue a pair of statements suggesting that acid rain was endangering public health and welfare in Canada—an action that played a key role in the AGs' §115 litigation. Similarly, the memoranda from EPA general counsels Gary Guzy and Jonathan Cannon near the end of the Clinton administration provided key evidence in the AGs' climate change litigation under §202. It was no coincidence that these various memoranda were issued at the very end of presidential administrations when Republican presidents were looming. As President Clinton's EPA administrator, Carol Browner, put it in the context of the AGs' NSR litigation, "having Eliot Spitzer in the mix" was one way to make sure "that the things I cared about would continue even if there was a Republican administration."[12]

During Democratic administrations, the EPA has also appeared to rely on AG litigation as a way to generate political cover for regulatory expansions. As noted in chapter 6, for example, the Clinton administration's EPA apparently welcomed a coordinated AG lawsuit so it could enter a binding legal settlement forcing it to impose stricter regulations of emissions from Midwestern sources.[13] Similar activity has occurred during the

Obama administration, as the EPA has often chosen not to defend itself against AG lawsuits and instead entered settlements requiring the agency to impose additional pollution reductions.[14] This sue-and-settle strategy has increasingly gotten the attention of other AGs who oppose stricter environmental regulation. In July 2013, Oklahoma AG Scott Pruitt led eleven of his Republican colleagues in a lawsuit demanding records from the EPA that the plaintiff AGs claimed would demonstrate that the EPA encouraged friendly lawsuits against itself.[15] The EPA, not surprisingly, has denied that it encourages such lawsuits, but the potential motivation for such suits is clear. By entering into binding settlements requiring regulatory expansion, the EPA can claim that its regulatory actions are compelled by law rather than arising from political discretion.

AG Litigation and the Expansion of Coordination

Much as with their pharmaceutical litigation, deepening coordination both among themselves and with other like-minded actors has been an important aspect of the development of the AGs' environmental litigation. AGs have forged litigation alliances with several environmental advocacy groups such as the Natural Resources Defense Council and the Sierra Club, which have increasingly realized that AGs, by virtue of their position representing the states, are increasingly valuable allies in environmental litigation. Further, coordination among the AGs themselves has widened considerably since the earliest days of multistate litigation in the 1980s, as the battles have turned from largely regional ones to sharply partisan fights.

Environmental advocacy groups have been a frequent partner in the AGs' attempts to achieve air pollution regulation through litigation. Several of these groups, including the Natural Resources Defense Council and the Sierra Club Legal Defense Fund, have been no strangers to litigation. By relying on the citizen suit provisions in federal environmental statutes, advocacy groups have used litigation as an important part of their overall political strategy.[16] For these environmental advocacy groups, collaborating with like-minded AGs has presented an additional avenue to press claims in court. Much as in the context of pharmaceutical litigation, AGs have the advantage of linking their litigation with state interests, which is particularly important in a policy area built on a frame of cooperative federalism. As the Supreme Court's special solicitude holding in *Massachusetts v. EPA* illustrated, courts may be more sympathetic to litigators who can plausibly tie alleged harms caused by federal actions to fundamental principles of federalism. Environmental advocacy group litigators have greater incentive to ally with AGs who can rely on this additional federalism argument to get into court, as it provides a more secure fallback position for their policy goals if courts determine that only the states, but not the private groups, have standing.[17]

AGs opposed to expansions of national environmental regulations have also collaborated with like-minded interests. The efforts of the AGs who mobilized on behalf of the EPA in *Massachusetts v. EPA,* for example, ran parallel to those of a variety of antiregulatory conservative advocacy groups and industry litigants. As discussed further in the chapter 9, challenges to a range of regulatory expansions attracted close collaborations between conservative AGs and others seeking to block those policies in court.[18]

Partisan Collaboration in Multistate Environmental Litigation

In addition to increased collaborations with other actors, the AGs' environmental litigation campaigns have featured wider, and increasingly partisan, coalitions among AGs themselves. What stands out in AGs' earliest collaborations on acid rain issues is that these battles were fairly contained and fought more on regional rather than partisan lines. All of the AGs seeking stricter EPA regulation during the 1980s represented downwind Northeastern states, with the exception of Minnesota's Hubert Humphrey III. All the AGs who sided with the EPA's position against new air pollution controls represented upwind Midwestern or Southern states, with AGs from other regions sitting on the sidelines. The litigation was bipartisan, as Democratic and Republican AGs from the Northeast joined in all eight of the multistate acid rain cases during this period, while they were opposed in two cases by Democratic AGs representing Midwestern and Southern states.[19] As Connecticut AG Joseph Lieberman characterized the litigation at the time, "it's region against region," as opposed to a partisan fight.[20] This tracked the general trend in Congress. Democratic stalwarts from upwind states such as Senator Robert Byrd (D-WV) and Representative John Dingell (D-MI), for example, led the charge against stricter acid rain controls, while Republican Northeasterners such as Senator John Chafee (R-RI) and Representative Sherwood Boehlert (R-NY) called for greater national action on acid rain. The same was true of the parties outside of Congress. In 1988, for example, a substantial number of Republican delegates to the party's convention broke with the Reagan administration to support government action to reduce acid rain.[21]

By contrast, multistate air pollution litigation since the 1980s has become both more widespread and more sharply partisan. Figure 8.1 illustrates the

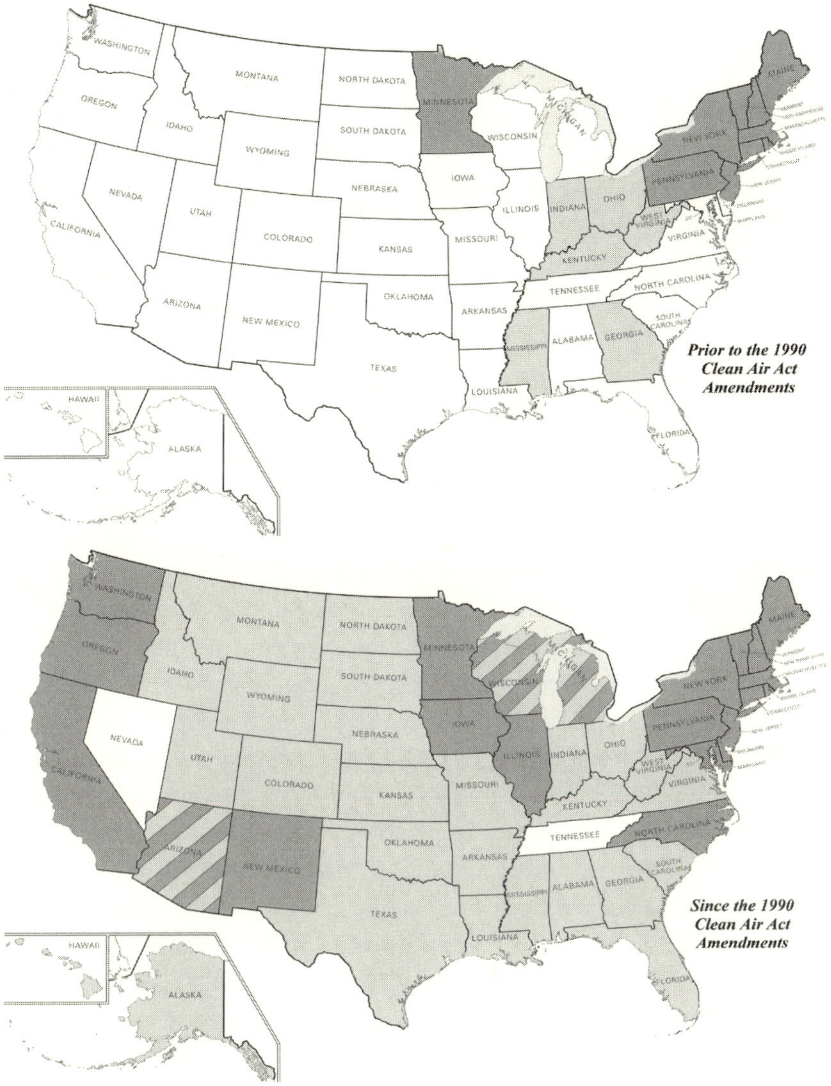

Figure 8.1. AGs involved in multistate acid rain and/or climate change litigation before and after the 1990 CAA amendments.

expansion of AG conflict in the period before and after the last time Congress overhauled the CAA in 1990. In figure 8.1, dark shading indicates that the state's AG participated in at least one lawsuit seeking stricter acid rain or climate change regulation, whereas light shading indicates AG participation in at least one lawsuit seeking less strict air pollution regulation. Striped shading indicates participation in at least one lawsuit in both categories. Finally, the states with no shading indicate the lack of their AG's participa-

Table 8.1. Partisan Appearances in Multistate Acid Rain and Climate Change Litigation, 1990–2013

No. of AG Appearances	Seeking More Regulation: Active Litigators	Seeking More Regulation: Amicus Filings	Seeking Less Regulation: Active Litigators	Seeking Less Regulation: Amicus Filings
Democrat	202	4	15	5
Republican	34	1	46	33

Source: Author's calculations.

tion in any coordinated acid rain or climate change lawsuits. As figure 8.1 indicates, most AGs sat out of what was largely a regional conflict in the earliest acid rain battles during the 1980s, but subsequent acid rain and climate change litigation attracted the involvement of nearly all AGs.

Although some scholars have noted that state governments have tended to feature less overt partisanship and more cross-party cooperation on environmental issues than their federal counterparts, it appears that the AGs' multistate litigation campaigns have more closely mirrored the partisan trends in Congress as opposed to those generally in state government.[22] In the early acid rain litigation, the conflict was more sectional, reflecting the interstate disputes generated by the CAA and the different economic incentives to join one side or the other. Now, however, the battles in Congress and among AGs alike are far more partisan than sectional. In acid rain and climate change litigation since 1990, AG involvement in lawsuits seeking regulatory expansion has been almost exclusively Democratic, while AGs opposing these efforts in court have been mainly Republican. Table 8.1 indicates how often Democratic and Republican AGs made appearances in the twenty-eight state acid rain or climate change cases since 1990, either as direct parties to the case or by filing amicus curiae briefs.

The highly partisan nature of state environmental litigation contrasts with litigation in the pharmaceutical context, which has featured considerably greater bipartisan cooperation among the AGs. Several features of this litigation likely account for this difference. First, most environmental litigation has involved policy-forcing lawsuits representing a direct challenge to the priorities of a particular presidential administration, which provides entrepreneurial AGs an excellent avenue to bolster their reputations among their fellow partisans. Attacking the Reagan or George W. Bush administrations on the environment was a good way to get ahead as a Democrat, particularly for AGs eying the possibility of running in a Democratic primary for other statewide positions, including senator and governor. Indeed, several of the leading AGs taking high-profile roles in both the acid rain and climate change litigation subsequently ran for other statewide positions, including Robert Abrams and Eliot Spitzer in New York, James Tierney in Maine, and Richard Blumenthal in Connecticut.

However, even AGs' policy-creating litigation, such as the NSR and climate change lawsuits against industry leaders such as American Electric Power, featured sharp partisan splits despite targeting business rather than a partisan administration. This is largely because air pollution settlements are a more explicitly political attempt to expand the regulatory state as opposed to efforts to fight so-called corporate fraud that are more subtly regulatory. Most importantly, pharmaceutical settlements typically involve a considerable amount of money flowing back to the states, giving AGs a clear incentive to sign on to settlements whether or not they agree with the underlying theories of the threatened case. Most environmental settlements, by contrast, do not involve large monetary settlements that benefit state coffers directly.

Finally, the increasing polarization in this area has occurred alongside a stronger relationship between region and party strength in American politics generally. A recurring theme in the acid rain and climate change disputes involved conflict among states claiming that the action of other states were harming their interests. It has been increasingly difficult, however, to separate this regional conflict from partisan conflict. In 1994, when Republicans captured both houses of Congress for the first time in fifty years, it accelerated partisan geographic trends that had been occurring for several years previously. States in the South and in portions of the Midwest shifted toward the Republican Party after decades of Democratic dominance, while the opposite occurred in the Northeast and on the West Coast. This shifting partisan alignment also appeared on the AG level, with Republican AG candidates achieving more political success in the South and Midwest while Democratic AGs increasingly represented Western and Northeastern states. As party increasingly overlapped with region, fewer AGs faced potential cross-pressures when the economic interest of their states came into conflict with the AGs' commitment to party loyalty.

AG Litigation and the National Environmental Policy Regime

Throughout the AGs' multistate litigation campaigns concerning both acid rain and climate change, the plaintiff AGs argued that they were taking action because federal policymakers had failed to address emerging environmental issues. However, even proponents of a stronger regulatory regime to address climate change viewed this regulation through litigation as a "distant second-best" solution compared to "tailor-made legislation as the best means of addressing carbon emissions."[23] The main reason was that the existing structure of the CAA was a mismatch for dealing with these emerging problems. When Congress originally designed the CAA in 1970, it did so with the assumption that pollution was a localized problem. The CAA focused on the sort of pollution bellowing out of dirty smokestacks and mixing with the ambient air in the same local area as the pollution sources. Until 1977, the CAA contained few provisions at all dealing with the complex issues of interstate pollution, and even then, Congress simply overlaid these provisions on top of the general ambient air approach established by NAAQS regulation.

Indeed, throughout the waves of multistate AG litigation during both the Reagan and George W. Bush administrations, the EPA stressed that the existing CAA was a poor way to deal with acid rain or climate change—and the agency had a point. On the acid rain issue, the attempt to use both the §115 and the §126 petition processes as a blunt instrument to force changes in upwind states' SIPs did not mesh well with the short statutory windows mandated by Congress in these provisions. This regulatory route, as the EPA noted at the time, would not only be time-consuming, costly, and perhaps ultimately impossible, but also would represent "a prescription for a decade's worth of court suits" over the new SIPs.[24] Stretching the CAA in such a way to deal with an acid rain issue that Congress had not anticipated in the CAA amendments of 1977 would create an uncertain regulatory environment and would be likely to drain agency resources away from other serious environmental problems.

Likewise, the regulatory structure of the CAA was a poor fit for the issue of climate change. Regulation of greenhouse gases under the CAA's ambient air approach is troublesome given that these gases are emitted from sources all around the globe, making it difficult to determine which sources are responsible for any environmental damage. Most importantly, using the existing CAA to address greenhouse gases, as the AGs sought to do in *Massachusetts v. EPA,* would trigger a new set of regulatory challenges because the structure of the existing statute was not designed to deal with greenhouse gases like CO_2. Although the AGs' litigation technically only involved greenhouse gases emitted from mobile sources such as cars and trucks, existing federal regulations require the EPA to subject stationary sources, such as power plants, to the same standard.[25] Under the CAA, stationary sources subject to regulation are any sources emitting more than 250 tons of "any air pollutant" per year. The problem is that this numerical threshold was designed to address pollutants like carbon monoxide that are typically emitted in much smaller quantities than CO_2. Because many stationary sources emit 250 tons of CO_2 each year—including schools, hotels, restaurants, and even some single-family residences—forcing the EPA to address climate change through the existing CAA would trigger the application of regulatory requirements meant for major power plants and factories to a range of sources Congress never intended to regulate under the act.[26] This would extend EPA regulation under the CAA well beyond its traditional scope and create an "enforcement nightmare" for the agency.[27]

Nevertheless, the same features of this litigation that made it problematic as a form of regulation made it desirable as a political strategy. The litigation would help maintain pressure on national policymakers and keep the issues alive in the national policy conversation. Further, the prospect of successful lawsuits and subsequent piecemeal regulation by the EPA was particularly distasteful to industry groups. Although the energy industry might prefer no additional regulation to a comprehensive congressional mandate, it would likely be more comfortable with a predictable regulatory environment as opposed to one constructed under a statute not designed for the problems the AGs were attempting to use it to solve. As Representative Edward Markey (D-MA) described the prospect of EPA regulation of CO_2, "We think this is a very helpful development that focuses the mind of industries and congressmen and senators all across the country. . . . Now you have a choice if you are in Congress: Do you want EPA to make that decision [about regulation] or would you like . . . to be in the room drafting the legislation?"[28] Indeed, the prospects of inefficient EPA regulation under the current federal statutory structure propelled several industry members to sign on to support national cap-and-trade legislation to address climate change and CO_2.[29] The common-law nuisance lawsuits against private industry, particularly *Connecticut v. AEP*, only ratcheted up the pressure on industry to support national legislation displacing these lawsuits.[30]

The strategy of using litigation to place pressure on federal policymakers to address an emerging environmental issue worked in the case of acid rain. Although the AGs' litigation ultimately failed in court, Congress enacted a new comprehensive regulatory structure that specifically dealt with the acid rain issue. The combination of the AGs' litigation failures and Congress's creation of a new comprehensive regulatory structure helped avoid potential regulatory problems that might have emerged had the original CAA been called on to apply to a problem it was not designed to address.

In the case of climate change, however, the situation has been reversed. Congress has been unable to agree on comprehensive climate change litigation—even when Democrats held both the presidency and substantial majorities in Congress—while the AGs' litigation has been far more successful. The combination of legislative failure and litigation success has meant that the admittedly distant second-best regulatory regime generated by litigation has become reality. When the Supreme Court voted 5–4 in favor of the plaintiff AGs in *Massachusetts v. EPA,* it spurred a regulatory cascade that, as Representative John Dingell (D-MI) put it, has created a "glorious mess" of regulatory policy. As previously noted, when the EPA issued a finding that categorized CO_2 as an air pollutant under the act in 2010—a finding essentially compelled by *Massachusetts*—it triggered EPA regulation of a much wider range of sources that were never meant to be subject to the regulatory regime.[31]

The problematic nature of this regulatory cascade has not gone unnoticed by federal policymakers. Several congressional proposals sought to prevent the cascading effect of *Massachusetts v. EPA,* either by revoking the EPA's authority to regulate CO_2 or establishing a cap-and-trade system of CO_2 regulation that would replace the system of direct EPA regulation.[32] The increasingly polarized Congress has failed to enact any such legislation, however, leaving it to the EPA to determine how to manage the fallout from *Massachusetts.* The agency's attempts to do so have served as an invitation for a new round of litigation and regulatory confusion, which I discuss further in chapter 9. These litigation efforts have been led by largely conservative AGs seeking to block new climate rules and have been opposed by similar coalitions of AGs who brought the litigation discussed in the previous two chapters.

The regulatory fallout from *Massachusetts* helps illustrate a problematic aspect of the AGs' use of litigation to force national policy development. Much as in the context of pharmaceuticals, AGs used litigation to achieve policy changes that federal policymakers were allegedly unable or unwilling to make. Such litigation, however, is a blunt instrument for regulation that, even if successful for one regulatory purpose, can nevertheless spur a host of new policy problems. The adjudicative process, as Donald Horowitz noted, is focused and piecemeal, and it provides no provision for policy review. Litigation focuses judicial attention on resolving unique cases with little consideration of how the resolution of the case affects the broader regulatory landscape of which it is a part.[33]

This basic dynamic appears repeatedly with contemporary multistate litigation, which has sought to create new national regulatory regimes that national policymakers are allegedly unwilling or unable to create through typical policymaking methods. The problem is that the nature of the adjudicative process makes it difficult for regulation through litigation to deal with subsequent policy consequences of any regulatory changes achieved through the process. Although the AGs successfully used litigation against the prescription drug industry as a form of price control, for example, it had consequences for health care providers threatened with decreased revenues. This in turn raised the unintended prospect of fewer providers participating in government health care provision for the poor and elderly. Similarly, while AG lawsuits forced the EPA to regulate greenhouse gases, it also generated a regulatory cascade that threatened problematic results such as single-family homes being regulated under a regulatory scheme meant for heavily polluting smokestacks.

In theory, Congress can step in to solve any of these sorts of regulatory problems spurred by the AGs' legal actions. Part of the political strategy behind this litigation, in fact, is to place pressure on Congress to adopt comprehensive regulatory regimes addressing alleged regulatory gaps identified by the AG plaintiffs. The problem with this strategy, however, is that it relies on subsequent action from the very institution whose inaction allegedly necessitated litigation in the first place. If Congress is unable to compromise on comprehensive policy solutions, the glorious mess of new policy problems left in litigation's wake remains.

CHAPTER NINE

THE RISE OF CONSERVATIVE STATE LITIGATION AND THE CHANGING SHAPE OF AG ACTIVISM

When the sun sets on this, one thing we know is that the Obama administration will scoff no more at the resolve and ability of state attorneys general.

Republican Texas AG Greg Abbott, referring to state lawsuits against the Affordable Care Act

Since President Obama's inauguration in 2009, conservative AGs have used coordinated litigation strategies to push back on several of the administration's policies. Most famously, several AGs initiated legal challenges to the Patient Protection and Affordable Care Act (ACA), popularly known as Obamacare, only minutes after the president signed it into law. This litigation campaign was the most prominent but hardly the only example of multistate AG activism against the Obama administration. By the end of Obama's first term in office, Republican AGs had filed over seventy lawsuits challenging the administration's policies. Texas AG Greg Abbott, who only half-jokingly described his average day as, "I go to the office. I sue the federal government. And then I go home," had by the middle of 2012 led twenty-four lawsuits against the Obama administration at a cost of over $2.5 million and thousands of hours of staff time.[1] AG challenges involved several policy areas from climate change and other environmental issues to immigration policy, financial regulation, and voting rights.[2]

This activity differs from the forms of contemporary AG litigation discussed earlier in this book in a couple of important ways. First, much of the activism during the Obama administration has sought to limit the exercise of national power through what I term policy-blocking litigation. Unlike policy-creating and policy-forcing litigation, both of which seek to expand the reach of the national regulatory state, policy-blocking litigation aims instead to constrain it. Second, policy-blocking litigation has a longer lineage in American politics than do the types of regulation-expanding litigation discussed in earlier chapters. AGs initiated policy-blocking challenges throughout the twentieth century, such as litigation against Progressive Era economic regulations and lawsuits challenging civil rights laws during the 1960s.[3]

Yet despite these differences, the conservative state litigation that has been so prominent during the Obama administration reflects broader trends in the nationalization of state litigation that are also apparent with other forms of contemporary AG activism. As with their policy-creating and policy-forcing strategies, AGs' policy-blocking litigation has sought to achieve national policy goals through increasingly coordinated and carefully orchestrated litigation campaigns. These campaigns have featured greater coordination not only among the AGs themselves but also between AGs and various like-minded interests. As this has occurred, AGs have used their positions in state government less to defend any unified conceptions of state interests and more to pursue divergent, and increasingly polarized, national policy goals.

This chapter examines these developments by first examining the most prominent policy-blocking campaign during the Obama administration: the litigation against the ACA. This effort, which began even before President Obama signed the ACA into law, was the result of close collaborations between Republican AGs and a variety of other conservative litigants. As the campaign proceeded and gained recognition from the courts, Democratic AGs joined the litigation conflict on the side of the national government and against their AG colleagues. I then turn to another important policy-blocking litigation campaign involving efforts to thwart the Obama administration's climate change regulations. Like the ACA litigation, these lawsuits were part of a concerted strategy featuring close collaboration between Republican AGs and other interests skeptical of government regulation. The conflict, as with the ACA lawsuits, generated sharp partisan conflicts between opposing groups of AGs.

After examining these case studies, I consider several broader points about AG activism during the Obama administration. First, polarization among the AGs has become increasingly apparent since President Obama's first inauguration. Compared to previous administrations, AGs' policy-blocking litigation efforts have become considerably more widespread and less bipartisan as AGs have pursued divergent policy goals. This trend is also apparent in other forms of AG activism, including the use of amicus curiae briefs as another method of influencing national policy across a wide range of issues. These trends reflect intensified activism on the part of conservative AGs who, after years of coordinated activism on the part of AGs seeking to expand the national regulatory state, for the first time have taken full advantage of this policymaking tool to push back against regulatory expansion. Feeding into this activity have been broader polarizing trends in American politics that have affected multiple political institutions throughout the United States.

A second aspect of contemporary AG activism, related to the first, is the increasing collaboration among AGs and various interests seeking national policy goals. The policy-blocking litigation examined in this chapter featured partnerships between AGs and advocacy groups critical of the ACA and environmental regulations, and AGs have supported various private party challenges to government policies through amicus briefs as well. In part, this development reflects the increased willingness on the part of conservatives to use the legal process for conservative policy goals. More broadly, however, it is a growing recognition on the part of outside groups and the AGs alike that such collaborations provide several benefits, including expanding the resources, legitimacy, and access to court for a broad litigation coalition seeking shared policy goals.

These aspects illustrate that while the methods conservative AGs have used to push back on Obama administration policies are not entirely new, this activity nevertheless reflects the changing shape of contemporary AG activism. Especially when considered in light of other forms of AG activity discussed in this book, the collaborative efforts on the part of Republican AGs since the start of the Obama presidency appear as the latest chapter in a broader story about the nationalization of state litigation.

Litigating Obamacare

Surrounded by a jubilant crowd of congressional leaders who punctuated his policy victory with cheers and applause, President Obama reflected on the long legislative journey leading up to his signing the Patient Protection and Affordable Care Act. "Today, after almost a century of trying; today, after over a year of debate; today, after all the votes have been tallied—health insurance reform becomes law in the United States of America," Obama remarked. "Today." In a nod to a tradition begun by earlier presidents signing historic legislation, Obama used multiple pens to place his signature on the most expansive social policy enacted in decades. After completing his signature with the twenty-second and final pen, Obama announced, "We are done."[4]

The president's signing of the ACA marked one of the most important developments in the American health care system since the enactment of Medicare and Medicaid in 1965. The final version of the ACA, enacted in early 2010 after months of legislative wrangling, contained several policy changes broadening health care coverage availability to millions of uninsured Americans. One policy change, the so-called individual mandate, requires most Americans to either carry some form of health insurance or provide an extra payment to the federal government.[5] The ACA also established several avenues through which individuals could obtain this required insurance. One such avenue increased access to government health care programs by expanding eligibility for Medicaid, the health care program for lower-income Americans. In return for continued federal funding of the states' Medicaid programs, the ACA required states to expand Medicaid coverage to people earning up to effectively 138 percent of the federal poverty level. According to Congressional Budget Office projections, this would extend Medicaid coverage to seventeen million additional Americans.[6]

Despite Obama's declaration that "we are done" after his signing of the ACA, the ACA's enactment was only the start of the story. Although the ACA's supporters hailed the legislation as an historic step forward for millions of Americans, its critics denounced it as big government run amok.[7] As soon as Congress enacted the final bill into law on a party-line vote, conservatives vowed to use all of their resources to stop the implementation of Obamacare. Several Republican legislators promised to introduce legislation to repeal the bill, and Republican state legislatures passed laws criticizing the ACA and threatening noncompliance with its provisions.[8]

AGs Enter the Partisan Conflict over the ACA

It did not take long for the AGs to join the broader partisan conflict over the ACA. Indeed, Republican AGs began organizing possible legal challenges even before the final ACA reached President Obama's desk. In September 2009, Florida AG Bill McCollum read an editorial in the *Wall Street Journal* by two of his former law partners, prominent conservative litigators David Rivkin and Lee Casey. The editorial, part of an early effort by several conservative lawyers to question the constitutional foundations of the ACA, argued that enacting the individual mandate exceeded congressional powers under Article I of the Constitution.[9]

These arguments caught McCollum's interest, and he reached out to several of his fellow AGs to discuss possible legal challenges if the bill became law. The initial collaborative efforts centered on the so-called Cornhusker Kickback, a provision in the version of the ACA passed by the Senate in

December 2009. Included to win the support of a crucial moderate Democrat, Senator Ben Nelson (D-NE), the provision guaranteed that the federal government would fund the cost of the Medicaid expansion for Nelson's state of Nebraska. This deal, however, applied only to Nebraska.[10]

Shortly after the Senate passed its version of the ACA, a coalition of thirteen AGs, all Republicans, publically denounced the Cornhusker Kickback. The group sent a letter to the Democratic leadership in Congress, arguing that having only Nebraska benefit from additional federal funding would lead to taxpayers in the remaining forty-nine states footing the bill. "In addition to violating the most basic and universally held notions of what is fair and just," the letter read, "we also believe this provision . . . is inconsistent with protections afforded by the United States Constitution against arbitrary legislation." The AGs called on Congress to either delete the provision or face litigation from the states on the matter.[11] A day after the AGs issued their litigation threat, Senator Nelson called South Carolina attorney general Henry McMaster, who had helped organize the AG coalition aligned against the Cornhusker Kickback. "What do I need to do to call the dogs off?," he asked McMaster.[12] Amid rising public outcry over what appeared to be an unseemly backroom deal, Senator Nelson agreed to remove the provision from the final version of the ACA.

The Cornhusker Kickback was not, however, the last of the AGs' concerns. The letter noted that by singling out the special treatment of Nebraska, "we do not suggest there are no other legal or constitutional issues in the proposed health care legislation."[13] The day before the AGs sent the letter to congressional leadership, McCollum contacted several of his colleagues asking them to review the proposed ACA and offer suggestions for a potential lawsuit.[14]

Active Litigation and Collaboration with Conservative Groups

This advance planning allowed the AGs to act quickly after the final enactment of the ACA. Just minutes after President Obama signed the legislation into law on March 23, 2010, Bill McCollum announced that, along with several of his fellow AGs, he was filing a lawsuit challenging the constitutionality of the ACA. The lawsuit, *Florida v. Department of Health and Human Services,* featured a coalition nearly identical to the group formed in opposition to the Cornhusker Kickback.[15] On the same day, but about 900 miles to the north, Virginia AG Ken Cuccinelli announced a separate but closely related lawsuit, *Virginia v. Sebelius.*

The choice of venue for both cases was no accident. Despite the availability of a federal court only a few blocks from his main office in Tallahassee, McCollum filed the case 200 miles away in federal district court in Pensacola. Unlike the court in Tallahassee, where a Democratic president had appointed the majority of judges, all three district court judges sitting in the Pensacola court were Republican appointees.[16] Further, McCollum had convinced his colleagues that the Eleventh Circuit in Atlanta, which hears appeals from the Florida district courts, would be one of the friendliest venues in the country for the AGs' argument.[17] Cuccinelli's lawsuit followed similar strategic concerns. Republican presidents had appointed all of the judges in the Richmond federal district court, and the Fourth Circuit that oversees appeals from Virginia had been regarded as "the boldest conservative appeals court in the nation."[18]

Although the Florida and Virginia cases both challenged the constitutionality of the ACA, they used different causes of action. The multistate lawsuit filed in Florida challenged several aspects of the ACA. The individual mandate provision, the states' complaint charged, "represents an unprecedented encroachment on the liberty of individuals living in the Plaintiffs' respective states." By enacting the mandate, Congress went beyond its constitutional power to regulate interstate commerce. The states also argued that the Medicaid expansion violated basic tenets of federalism. States that refused to implement the expansion were at risk of losing all federal funding for their Medicaid programs, which in most states represents nearly half of federal grants and a significant portion of the states' entire budgets. This not only represented an unfunded mandate, the states argued, but also violated the sovereignty of the states by "commandeering" the states' employees in violation of the Tenth Amendment.[19]

Virginia's lawsuit expressed similar concerns about the expansiveness of congressional power but used a different legal hook. In March 2010, Virginia became the first state to adopt a law prohibiting any governmental requirement that individuals carry health insurance within the state.[20] According to Cuccinelli's complaint, the individual mandate created an immediate "collision between the state and federal schemes." Although the Constitution's Supremacy Clause establishes federal law as the supreme law of the land, Cuccinelli claimed that the Virginia law remained valid because of the unconstitutionality of the ACA. In particular, the individual mandate was a congressional attempt to use the Commerce Clause to regulate an absence of commerce. "It has never been held that the Commerce Clause, even when aided by the Necessary and Proper Clause, can be used to require citizens to buy goods or services," the complaint read.[21] Because "the attorney general of Virginia has a duty to defend validly enacted Virginia laws from any challenge," Cuccinelli argued, he was the proper party to bring the lawsuit.[22]

Virginia v. Sebelius and *Florida v. HHS* also differed in terms of the lawyers conducting the litigation on behalf of the states. Lawyers within Cuccinelli's office, one of a growing number of AG offices with a state solicitor general position, handled Virginia's lawsuit. By contrast, the AG coalition behind *Florida v. HHS* retained private lawyers to assist their litigation. For McCollum, the choice of lawyers was easy. He turned to his former fellow law firm partners David Rivkin and Lee Casey, the two attorneys who had played an instrumental role in placing constitutional concerns about the individual mandate on the political agenda. The AGs agreed to pay them a heavily discounted fee of $250 an hour to serve as outside counsel for the states.[23]

The AG lawsuits were the first against the ACA, but they operated in tandem with several lawsuits by private employers and conservative advocacy groups. The Thomas More Law Center, a Michigan-based conservative advocacy group that "defends and promotes America's Judeo-Christian heritage and moral values," filed a lawsuit against the individual mandate on the same day as the state lawsuits.[24] Other interest groups soon followed, raising similar arguments as those in the states' coordinated complaint. Clint Bolick, the director of the libertarian Goldwater Institute who filed a constitutional challenge to the law a few months after the states, remarked, "You're going to see a thousand flowers bloom in terms of lawsuits. I'm hoping that this will die a death of a thousand cuts."[25]

The most important addition to the private groups' litigation campaign against the ACA came in the form of the National Federation of Independent Business (NFIB), which held a press conference in McCollum's office announcing that the conservative "voice of small business" was joining the AGs' lawsuit. The AGs had been in discussions with the NFIB about joining the lawsuit, a litigation strategy that came with a pair of major advantages. First, the NFIB represented employers directly affected by the ACA's provisions, which provided an additional premise for the coalition to claim standing to sue. Second, the NFIB pledged considerable resources for the lawsuit, taking some of the fiscal pressures off the state plaintiffs. NFIB retained the same lawyers representing the states, soliciting tax-deductible contributions to "help ensure we have the resources we need to mount a strong and successful legal challenge against this egregious law."[26]

Courtroom Successes and the Expansion of Partisan Conflict

Although cheered on by Obamacare's opponents, few observers gave the arguments against the ACA much chance of success. Liberal constitutional law scholar Erwin Chemerinsky argued that the arguments made by David Rivkin and others "had no basis in the law" and that "while there is much to argue about in the debate over health care reform . . . constitutionality is not among the hard questions to consider."[27] Other prominent attorneys suggested that the AGs' effort was so frivolous "the courts should also seek sanctions against the politically motivated attorneys general who filed them."[28] Conservative attorneys were likewise skeptical that the lawsuits would succeed. Even as he led the Goldwater Institute's litigation against the ACA, Clint Bolick remarked that the effort "faces very tough odds."[29] Charles Fried, a Harvard law professor and former US solicitor general under Ronald Reagan, declared shortly after the states' filings that he would "eat a hat which I bought in Australia last month made of kangaroo skin" if the courts overturned the ACA.[30]

However, it was not long before it became clear that the AGs' lawsuits were far from frivolous. In December 2010, three days before the start of oral arguments in *Florida v. HHS,* Judge Henry Hudson ruled in *Virginia v. Sebelius* that the individual mandate represented an unprecedented expansion of federal power unjustified by the Commerce Clause.[31] The following month, Judge Roger Vinson followed suit by ruling in favor of the multistate AG coalition in *Florida v. HHS.* Vinson's decision went even further than the decision in the Virginia case. Whereas Hudson had limited his holding of unconstitutionality to the individual mandate, Judge Vinson held that because the mandate and the ACA's other provisions "are all inextricably bound together in purpose and must stand or fall as a single unit," the entire ACA must fall—including the Medicaid expansion and the hundreds of other provisions in the act.[32]

The pair of district court decisions received praise from Republican legislators and criticism from Democrats, reflecting partisan battles over Obamacare occurring elsewhere in the American political system. As the AGs' litigation progressed, the Republican majority in the US House passed legislation repealing the ACA in its entirety.[33] The House Judiciary Committee invited Cuccinelli, who had become a rising star in Republican politics, to testify about constitutional defects in the ACA.[34] State legislatures were also active in the Obamacare debate, with several following Virginia's early strategy of passing laws and state constitutional amendments prohibiting the operation of the individual mandate within their states.[35]

Meanwhile, Democratic AGs countermobilized in support of the ACA and against their Republican colleagues. This included a group of AGs, all Democrats, who filed amicus curiae briefs in support of the ACA's constitutionality in several of the cases challenging the ACA, including in their fellow AGs' challenges in Virginia and Florida.[36] These AGs argued that "comprehensive national healthcare reform is urgently needed" in an era of skyrocketing medical costs, and they maintained that the ACA did so in a way that properly "continues a longstanding and necessary partnership" between the states and the federal government in the health care policy arena.[37]

Obamacare on Appeal

The pair of district court decisions in *Virginia v. Sebelius* and *Florida v. HHS* made the seriousness of the constitutional challenges clear. "There's been a big change in the conventional wisdom," said Randy Barnett, a Georgetown law professor and libertarian activist whose early scholarly work on the ACA's constitutionality contributed to the foundation of the AGs' litigation.[38] Helping bolster the legitimacy of the lawsuits, the coalition behind *Florida v. HHS,* which now included the NFIB and twenty-six states, hired Paul Clement to represent them on appeal. Clement, a conservative superlawyer who at the age of forty-five had already served as US solicitor general and argued fifty-seven cases before the Supreme Court, signed a contract for a flat fee of $250,000 after a process in which the AGs interviewed several conservative litigators.[39] Meanwhile, the NFIB continued serving as a valuable litigation ally for the AGs, providing significant resources for the lawsuit. The organization's financial records indicated that it spent nearly $1.2 million on the lawsuit in 2010 alone.[40] "They have dedicated a tremendous amount of resources to the lawsuit," said newly elected Florida attorney general Pam Bondi, who had enthusiastically taken over the lead role in *Florida v. HHS* after McCollum's failed bid for the states' governorship. "We're thrilled, because that's saving our state money. That's saving the 25 other states money as well."[41]

Initially, however, it appeared that appellate victories for the plaintiff AGs remained unlikely. As the Fourth and Eleventh circuits heard oral arguments in *Virginia v. Sebelius* and *Florida v. HHS,* respectively, the federal government had a string of victories in other ACA lawsuits. By May 2011, eight federal district courts had dismissed constitutional challenges to the ACA brought by private party plaintiffs.[42] Shortly after oral arguments in

Florida v. HHS, the Sixth Circuit dismissed the Thomas More Law Center's appeal in an opinion written in part by Judge Jeffrey Sutton, a prominent conservative.[43] In a decision joined by two George W. Bush appointees, the Third Circuit also rejected an appeal by a New Jersey physicians' group on procedural grounds.[44] The latter two cases meant that in the summer of 2011, the DOJ was undefeated in appellate court.

This changed when the Eleventh Circuit panel issued its decision in *Florida v. HHS* on August 12, 2011. The 207-page majority opinion characterized the individual mandate as "a wholly novel and potentially unbounded assertion of Congressional authority" unjustified under the Commerce Clause. The majority also held that the fine for noncompliance with the individual mandate was for constitutional purposes a penalty and not a tax, prohibiting Congress from citing its taxing power to justify the mandate.[45] Although the Fourth Circuit rejected AG Cuccinelli's claims a month later, holding that his lawsuit served "merely as a smokescreen for Virginia's attempted vindication of its *citizens'* interests" as opposed to the state's sovereign interests,[46] the Eleventh Circuit's earlier decision marked the first time an appellate court had agreed that the ACA was constitutionally vulnerable. The split among the circuits on the question of the ACA's constitutionality made it a near certainty that the Supreme Court would rule on the case.

Only about six weeks after receiving several petitions for certiorari from both the federal government and various lower court plaintiffs, the Supreme Court agreed to hear the appeals from the Eleventh Circuit, consolidating them in a case now formally titled *NFIB v. Sebelius*.[47] The Court scheduled an unusually lengthy five and a half hours of oral argument over three days in late March 2012, contrasting with the usual hour for most of the cases the Court hears. Paul Clement argued the case on behalf of the states, squaring off with Solicitor General Donald Verrilli. Many perceived the oral arguments to have gone poorly for the federal government, leading several observers to conclude that a decision striking down the ACA was a distinct possibility—a considerably different outlook than the one two years earlier, when the lawsuits were widely viewed as unlikely to succeed and even "frivolous."[48]

After months of speculation, the Supreme Court handed down its ruling on June 28, 2012. Many observers had expected a 5–4 decision following the oral arguments in March, but few if any predicted that Chief Justice Roberts would join the four liberal justices in upholding congressional power to enact key provisions of the ACA. Also surprising was the grounds for him doing so. The individual mandate, the Court held, was a valid exercise of

Congress's taxing and spending powers because the mandate was a tax and not a penalty. Although the threat of having to pay more to the government if one did not purchase health insurance clearly aimed to influence individual behavior, this was not unlike many other taxes that previously passed constitutional muster. "Because the Constitution permits such a tax, it is not our role to forbid it, or to pass upon its wisdom or fairness," Roberts concluded.[49]

However, the decision was far from a complete loss for the AG coalition that had initiated the case against the ACA. First, while the majority upheld the ACA as part of Congress's taxing power, Roberts's opinion rejected the claim that the Commerce Clause and the Necessary and Proper Clause supported this exercise of congressional power. Noting that Congress "has never attempted to rely on that power to compel individuals not engaged in commerce to purchase an unwanted product," Roberts characterized the individual mandate not as regulating existing commercial activity but instead as a device to compel commerce. "Construing the Commerce Clause to permit Congress to regulate individuals precisely *because* they are doing nothing would open a new and potentially vast domain to congressional authority," Roberts wrote. "That is not the country the Framers of our Constitution envisioned."

Even more significantly for the future of the ACA, the Court sharply limited the Medicaid expansion by a surprising 7–2 vote. Although Congress could use its spending power to provide "relatively mild encouragement" for the states to enact changes to their Medicaid programs, in this case "the financial 'inducement' Congress has chosen is much more than 'relatively mild encouragement'—it is a gun to the head." This marked the first time that the Court struck down a federal spending program as being unduly coercive on the states, which had a practical impact not lost on the Court. "States may now choose to reject the expansion; that is the whole point," the majority wrote.[50]

These elements of the Court's holding provided the AG plaintiffs with a significant silver lining. Florida AG Pam Bondi called the limits on the Medicaid expansion a "big win" for fiscal responsibility and states' rights, and she cited the Chief Justice's Commerce Clause opinion as illustrating that "there are real enforceable limits to the power of the federal government over the lives of the American people."[51] Bondi's predecessor, Bill McCollum, whose lawsuit marked the beginning of the ACA's long journey in the courts, invoked an argument made popular by conservatives who argued that the federal government's expansive reading of the Commerce Clause would justify it regulating virtually everything. "At least it's clear that they can't order you to buy broccoli," he remarked.[52] Meanwhile, several governors and state legislatures rejected the ACA's Medicaid expansion, an option made possible only because of the legal campaign against the policy.[53]

It's Never Over: The Continuing Obamacare Battle

Despite ample evidence to the contrary, scholarly and popular discourse frequently characterizes the Supreme Court as having the final word on constitutional matters. *NFIB v. Sebelius* provides another counterexample to this common claim. Despite the Court's decision, the constitutional and political questions surrounding the ACA continued. Partisan conflict over Obamacare led to a two-week government shutdown in October 2013, and by March 2014 the Republican-led House had voted fifty times to repeal part or all of the law since its original passage.[54] So many attempts to attack the law persisted after the Court's decision that, in a poll conducted in April 2013, over 40 percent of Americans thought that the ACA had already been repealed or were unsure whether it was still good law.[55]

Further, several AGs continued to bring legal challenges against other provisions of the ACA. A coalition of seven Republican AGs announced that *NFIB v. Sebelius* would not derail their lawsuit, claiming that the ACA's contraceptives coverage mandate violated the religious rights of employers who objected to abortion and contraception. Accompanying the states on the lawsuit were several antiabortion advocacy groups, including the Catholic Mutual Relief Society of America.[56] Republican AGs also filed amicus briefs supporting private party challenges to the contraceptives mandate, an effort opposed by Democratic AGs countermobilizing in support of the provision.[57] The Supreme Court ultimately addressed these various challenges in *Burwell v. Hobby Lobby Stores,* which in June 2014 held that the contraceptives mandate violated the religious rights of closely held corporations under the federal Religious Freedom Restoration Act.[58]

In still another challenge to the ACA, Oklahoma Republican AG Scott Pruitt initiated a lawsuit claiming that a rule the IRS promulgated to help implement health care exchanges violated the terms of the ACA itself.[59] Indiana's Republican AG, as well as individuals in Virginia and the District of Columbia, filed similar lawsuits following Pruitt's challenge.[60] In July 2014, the DC Circuit decided one of the challenges in favor of the plaintiffs, holding that the IRS could not provide tax subsidies to individuals in states that had not established their own health care exchanges.[61] Meanwhile, Texas AG Greg Abbott organized a coalition of twenty Republican AGs who filed an amicus brief supporting a lawsuit claiming that the ACA violated the Constitution's Origination Clause by starting in the Senate instead of the House.[62] Regardless of the ultimate outcome of these challenges, which remained ongoing when this book went to press, they illustrate AGs' continued activism against the ACA's implementation even after *NFIB v. Sebelius* upheld most of the law.

Litigating Climate Change Policy

The AG litigation campaign against the ACA constituted the most prominent policy-blocking challenge to the Obama administration, but it hardly stood alone. Republican AGs have also orchestrated litigation campaigns seeking to block a range of Obama administration's environmental policies, including a sustained effort to block climate change regulations adopted in the wake of *Massachusetts v. EPA*. Like the ACA litigation, this was part of a concerted strategy involving wide collaboration among Republican AGs and conservative interests to push back on national regulatory expansion. Also similar to the ACA cases, this effort spurred an opposing coalition of Democratic AGs and liberal interests to defend the federal government's position.

Climate Change Regulation after Massachusetts v. EPA

As discussed in chapter 7, *Massachusetts v. EPA* was a successful multistate AG challenge to the George W. Bush administration EPA's decision to decline regulating carbon dioxide (CO_2) and other greenhouse gases under the Clean Air Act (CAA).[63] By rejecting the EPA's reasoning for refusing to regulate greenhouse gases, the Court's decision effectively compelled the agency to begin addressing climate change. The EPA took little action to implement the decision in the final months of the Bush administration, but under the direction of new EPA administrator Lisa Jackson, the agency made reducing greenhouse gases a top priority at the start of Obama's presidency.[64]

The first step was the agency's announcement of its so-called endangerment finding on April 24, 2009, determining that CO_2 was a pollutant endangering human health. This finding, eventually finalized on the first day of a major international climate change conference in December 2009, triggered the EPA's duty under §202 of the CAA to issue greenhouse gas emission standards for new motor vehicles. The EPA finalized these motor vehicle standards, collectively known as the Tailpipe Rule, in May 2010.[65]

As chapter 8 noted, however, the endangerment finding and subsequent regulation of greenhouse gas emissions from motor vehicles triggered a regulatory cascade applying EPA regulation to a broader range of pollution sources. In addition to directing the agency to regulate emissions from motor vehicles, the CAA also extends EPA regulation to emissions of "any air pollutant" from stationary sources, such as factories and power plants.[66] Under a long-standing interpretation dating to 1980, the agency defined "any air pollutant" in this section as including any pollutant otherwise regulated under the CAA.[67] The Obama administration's EPA reaffirmed this interpretation in its Timing Rule (also known as the Triggering Rule) issued in March 2010, which specified that when the Tailpipe Rule went into effect as planned in 2011, it would trigger broader greenhouse gas emissions controls for stationary sources as well.[68]

The problem, however, is that this decision effectively prompted EPA regulation of a much wider range of sources never meant to be subject to the regulatory regime. The CAA's stationary source provisions apply to facilities emitting more than 250 tons of "any air pollutant" per year. Only large facilities emit 250 tons of pollutants traditionally regulated under the CAA, such as carbon monoxide, but many stationary sources emit 250 tons of CO_2 each year—including schools, hotels, restaurants, and even some single-family residences. To avoid the CAA's application to these smaller sources, the EPA issued an additional regulation to try to control this regulatory cascade. In October 2009, the agency proposed a rule specifying that only pollution sources emitting over 25,000 tons of CO_2 per year would be subject to stringent agency regulation under the CAA (the Tailoring Rule).[69] After strong concerns from industry groups and comments from state permitting agencies, the EPA raised the regulatory threshold in its final rule. The revised Tailoring Rule specified that sources already required to obtain EPA pollution permits for other pollutants would be subject to the new greenhouse gas regulations if they emitted over 75,000 tons of CO_2 per year. Sources not already required to obtain pollution permits would be subject to the rules if they emitted over 100,000 tons of CO_2.[70]

These new climate change rules received heavy criticism from Republicans and industry leaders. Because the science of climate change was still contested, critics claimed, the rules would have an uncertain effect on the environment yet would be "certain to come at a huge cost to the economy."[71] Further, critics suggested that the rules represented administrative overreach. One former EPA assistant administrator argued, for example, that the agency's Tailoring Rule was attempting to solve the problem of overregulation "simply by changing the 250 ton number [in the CAA] to 25,000 tons. Normally, it takes an act of Congress to change the words of a statute enacted by Congress."[72]

Opponents sought to block the rules in several venues. Shortly after the EPA announced the endangerment finding, eighty-six House Republicans signed on to a resolution urging an end to the EPA's regulations.[73] Members of both the House and Senate introduced legislation seeking to delay EPA action on climate change or prohibit the agency from regulating greenhouse gases altogether.[74] Several state legislatures adopted resolutions expressing concerns with the EPA's approach, and other states considered bills prohibiting state efforts to reduce greenhouse gas emissions.[75] Meanwhile, lobbyists for several industry groups discussed coordinating possible legal challenges to the rules, including the possibility of pooling resources to hire counsel.[76] Only about two weeks after the endangerment finding became official, the Coalition for Responsible Regulation (CFRR), a newly formed nonprofit group whose members included several energy and mining firms, filed a DC Circuit lawsuit contesting the finding. On the same day, the conservative Southeastern Legal Foundation filed a petition for reconsideration of the rules on behalf of several Republican members of Congress.[77]

AGs Enter the Partisan Conflict over the Climate Regulations

As Congress and states debated legislative responses to the EPA's new climate change program and private litigants initiated legal actions to block the new rules, several Republican AGs intervened in the conflict. Shortly after the EPA finalized its endangerment finding, the lawyer representing the Texas-based CFRR, Eric Groten, approached Texas AG Greg Abbott with a proposition. In an e-mail to Abbott, Groten noted that the CFRR had been the first to file a lawsuit against the new regulations and asked if Texas planned to get involved. "I'd like to begin the coordination process," he stated. "Plus of course we would like to see state petitioners involved, and Texas is an obvious candidate."[78]

This early contact presaged Abbott's active involvement in the lawsuit. On February 16, 2010, a few weeks after this initial meeting, Abbott filed a petition for review of the finding in DC Circuit Court. On the same day, several other parties filed similar challenges to the rule in the DC Circuit. Alabama's Troy King and Virginia's Ken Cuccinelli, both Republican AGs, filed their own lawsuits, as did the US Chamber of Commerce, several Republican members of Congress, and various conservative public interest groups.[79]

Although the initial petitions were not required to specify the legal basis for the requested review, the AGs' statements during press conferences following the filing mirrored other Republican officials' concerns about the economic impact of the climate rules. The AGs also referred to a controversy involving leaked e-mails sent by climate scientists that seemingly suggested manipulation of data in studies linking greenhouse gas emissions and climate change. Because the EPA had relied on these studies to justify its endangerment finding, the AGs argued that this controversy undercut the agency's scientific basis for its regulations.[80] Cuccinelli would soon build on this legal strategy by issuing a civil investigative demand to University of Virginia climate scientist Michael Mann, claiming that Mann's "use of manipulated data to apply for taxpayer-funded research grants in Virginia is potentially fraud."[81] Although this lawsuit was eventually dismissed,[82] it signaled that AGs were prepared to push back on climate change regulation with several different strategies.

A month after the initial lawsuits in February, the litigation battlefield expanded when a coalition of sixteen AGs sought to join Texas's lawsuit against the EPA's endangerment finding. As the EPA finalized its other rules throughout 2010, including the Tailpipe, Timing, and Tailoring rules, AGs and other industry and conservative interest group allies filed additional petitions seeking to block each of the new regulations. Faced with increasing pressure from Congress and the courts, the EPA announced that it would delay implementation of the new rules until the following year.[83]

Much as with the Obamacare litigation, Democratic officials criticized the plaintiff AGs' litigation and supported the federal government. Representative James Moran sent a letter to Cuccinelli suggesting that the lawsuit against Mann would have a "chilling effect on future academic freedom and scientific inquiry," and Democratic state legislators in Virginia introduced legislation that would remove the AGs' ability to issue civil investigative demands.[84] Meanwhile, Democratic AGs mobilized to defend the Obama administration's climate change rules. Massachusetts AG Martha Coakley organized a coalition of sixteen AGs who defended the endangerment finding by intervening on EPA's side in the existing lawsuits, arguing that the finding "marked the end of an era in which the federal government refused to acknowledge that anything could or should be done about global climate change."[85] Similar coalitions of AGs would later intervene in support of the other challenged climate change rules.

Table 9.1 provides an overview of the AGs involved in challenges to the Obama administration's climate change regulations, either in support or in

Table 9.1. Parties Supporting and Opposing the Obama Administration EPA's Climate Change Rules

AGs Involved in Challenges			
Against EPA		Supporting EPA	
Republican	AL, AK, FL, GA, HI*, IN, [KS], LA, MI, [MT], NE, ND, [OH], OK, SC, SD, TX, UT, VA, [WV], [WY]	Republican	ME, WA
Democrat	KY	Democrat	AZ*, CA, CT, DE, IL, IA, MA, MD, MN, NC, NH, NM, NY, OR, RI, VT

Selected Other Groups Involved in Challenges	
Against EPA	Supporting EPA
• American Chemistry Council	• [Washington Legal Foundation]
• Coalition for Responsible Regulation	• [America's Great Waters Coalition]
• National Association of Manufacturers	• Center for Biological Diversity
• [Pacific Legal Foundation]	• Earthjustice
• Senator McConnell and other members of Congress	• Environmental Defense Fund
• Southeastern Legal Foundation	• National Wildlife Federation
• US Chamber of Commerce	• Natural Resources Defense Council
• Utility Air Regulatory Group	• Sierra Club
	• [Union of Concerned Scientists]

Note: Parties in brackets submitted amicus briefs and were not direct parties to the litigation. Asterisks indicate states that shifted positions during the course of the litigation. Hawaii originally opposed the EPA, but the state withdrew from the litigation when a Democrat replaced its Republican AG. Arizona supported the EPA until a Republican AG replaced the Democratic AG.

opposition to the EPA. Also included in table 9.1 are several of the dozens of industry and public interest groups also involved in the litigation. As the table indicates, the litigation operated along sharply partisan and ideological lines.

Obama's Climate Change Regulations in Court

By the middle of 2010, the EPA faced many AG and private-party challenges to various aspects of its climate change policy, several of which the DC Circuit consolidated under the caption *Coalition for Responsible Regulation v. EPA*. Abbott served as the lead AG for the multistate coalition aligned against the rules. Helping craft Abbott's legal arguments was David Rivkin, the same conservative attorney who was also serving as a lead counsel on the Republican AGs' litigation campaign against the ACA.[86]

After the DC Circuit refused the AGs' request for a stay delaying the EPA's climate change rules, Abbott filed briefs on behalf of the states detailing the substantive legal arguments against the challenged rules. The first brief, filed in May 2011, argued that the endangerment finding was "arbitrary and capacious" because the EPA had neither articulated a satisfactory explanation for its action nor considered voluntary adaptation and mitigation of climate change.[87] The second brief filed a month later challenged the Timing and Tailoring rules, claiming that the EPA was attempting to "impose unilaterally a drastic new regulatory regime without the congressional authorization or input required by the Clean Air Act."[88] A few months later, the coalition of AGs and allied environmental interest groups supporting the EPA's rules filed their briefs in the case. Emphasizing the "massive foundation of scientific evidence" supporting the EPA's rules, the group urged the court to allow the agency's climate program to continue.[89]

On June 26, 2012, a three-judge panel of the DC Circuit unanimously upheld all four of the major elements of Obama's climate change program, including the endangerment finding as well as the Tailpipe, Timing, and Tailoring rules. The court refused to question the EPA's reliance on existing scientific research on climate change, stating that the evidence the agency relied on for the endangerment finding was "substantial" and that the court ought to provide "an extreme degree of deference to the agency when it is evaluating scientific data." Because the CAA required the EPA to regulate emissions from new motor vehicles following the endangerment finding (which itself was required after *Massachusetts v. EPA*), the Tailpipe Rule was also a valid exercise of agency power. The court did not reach the merits of the Timing and Tailoring rules, however, holding instead that neither the AGs nor the industry plaintiffs had standing to challenge the regulations.[90]

The DC Circuit's decision was a major victory for the Obama administration's EPA, but the various plaintiffs vowed to continue challenging the regulations. The AG plaintiffs petitioned for certiorari in the Supreme Court concerning all four rules, and the Court agreed to hear part of the challenge in October 2013. While allowing the DC Circuit's decision on the endangerment finding and the Tailpipe Rule to stand, the Court agreed to decide whether the EPA's regulation of greenhouses gases from stationary sources was permissible. The Court held oral arguments on this question in February 2014, with David Rivkin again arguing on behalf of the multistate coalition.

The Court announced its decision in the now-captioned *Utility Air Regulatory Group v. EPA* on June 23, 2014. In a complicated opinion written by Justice Scalia, the Court held that the EPA had exceeded its statutory authority by promulgating the Timing Rule. Characterizing the EPA's rule as "the single largest expansion in the scope of the [Act] in its history," the Court determined that the agency's interpretation of the term "air pollutant" in the CAA was unreasonable "because it would bring about an enormous and transformative expansion in EPA's regulatory authority without clear congressional authorization." Allowing the EPA to rewrite unambiguous statutory terms "would deal a severe blow to the Constitution's separation of powers." Although the Court invalidated the EPA's greenhouse gas regulations as applied to newly regulated sources, however, it held that the agency could apply its new CO_2 limits to sources that were already subject to regulation for the emission of other pollutants. Unlike the EPA's attempts to regulate new sources based solely on CO_2 emissions, applying CO_2 limits to sources already regulated by the EPA "is not so disastrously unworkable, and need not result in such a dramatic expansion of agency authority, as to convince us that EPA's interpretation is unreasonable."[91]

The Court's decision provided a partial victory for both sides of the dispute. Although in practice the decision succeeded in blocking only a relatively small portion of the Obama administration's new climate rules, Republican Texas AG Greg Abbott called the decision "a great victory for the rule of law and for the Constitution" and "a resounding defeat for those, like the President, who would use unelected bureaucracies to override the will of the people."[92] Meanwhile, Democratic Massachusetts AG Martha Coakley emphasized that the Court upheld CO_2 regulation for already regulated sources, which allowed the EPA to continue regulations for the bulk of the sources it had initially intended to regulate.[93] Regardless of the characterization of *Utility Air* as either a victory or defeat for the plaintiff AGs, the decision serves as only the latest instance of AG involvement in climate change policies—involvement that will undoubtedly continue as the Obama administration continues to pursue new regulations addressing CO_2 emissions.

Nationalized Activism during the Obama Administration

Policy-blocking efforts against the ACA and new climate change regulations were different from other forms of AG activism because they sought to constrain the scope of national policy. The ACA litigation challenged the individual mandate as an unconstitutional assertion of Congress's power to regulate interstate commerce and the Medicaid expansion as a federal attempt to coerce the states. The climate change litigation challenged the very basis of the Obama EPA's attempts to regulate CO_2 and other greenhouse gases, thereby attempting to reverse the victories other AGs had won in *Massachusetts v. EPA*.

Much like other campaigns examined in this book, however, both of these litigation campaigns relied on the fundamental lynchpin of contemporary AG activism: the use of the legal process to dictate the shape of national policy. This mirrors what AGs have done to expand the scope of national regulation through earlier policy-creating and policy-forcing strategies. These campaigns also help to illustrate another crucial development: the increasing tendency of AGs, collaborating among themselves and like-minded outside interests, to use their positions to pursue partisan and ideological goals that stretch beyond unified conceptions of state interests. Both of these elements are key components of the broader nationalization of state litigation.

AG Partisanship and the Rise of Republican AG Activism

After a 2012 press conference of nine Republican AGs who highlighted their various lawsuits against the Obama administration, Texas AG Greg Abbott remarked, "There seems to be, in addition to the size, an intensified cohesion and collegiality among the [Republican] AGs. Part of it is based on personality. Part of it is based on sense of purpose."[94] In one sense, the intensified Republican activism to which Abbott referred is not particularly surprising. After all, Democratic AGs aggressively challenged the Bush administration in several policy areas, and the Obama administration presented Republican AGs with a similar opportunity to push back against a president of the opposite party.

Nevertheless, Republican AGs are far more active now than they were the last time that a Democrat occupied the White House. During the Clinton administration, Republican AGs participated in policy-blocking challenges, but they typically did so as part of a broader bipartisan coalition. Multistate AG challenges to federal environmental regulations and new laws such as the Driver's Privacy Protection Act drew support from AGs of both parties.[95] When partisan conflict over federal laws allegedly violating state sovereignty entered the courts, as it did with the National Voter Registration Act of 1993, it tended to be Republican governors and not AGs leading the charge.[96] Few Republican AGs became involved even in the most important cases of the

Supreme Court's federalism revolution throughout the 1990s. *New York v. US* (1992), which involved a challenge to a federal law regulating state radioactive waste management as a violation of the Tenth Amendment, was led by liberal New York AG Robert Abrams and supported mainly by Democratic AGs.[97] Only three AGs became involved in the major federalism case of *US v. Lopez* (1995)—and all three supported the federal government's position.[98] Likewise, a large bipartisan AG coalition supported the United States' position in *US v. Morrison* (2000), with only one Republican AG, Alabama AG William Pryor, arguing that the federal law at issue violated principles of federalism.[99]

Litigation during the Obama administration, by contrast, was both broader and more partisan. With the ACA litigation, as one of Cuccinelli's briefs in the litigation put it, "It became possible for the first time in American history to count a clear majority of states in litigation with the federal government, each claiming that the federal government has exceeded its enumerated powers."[100] This litigation proceeded on partisan grounds, with Republican AGs initiating the challenge and Democratic AGs opposing them. A similar dynamic was apparent in the policy-blocking challenges to the administration's climate change rules. Unlike the regional battles between AGs apparent in earlier policy-forcing suits concerning acid rain policy in the 1980s, AG participation in this environmental litigation has become broader and more partisan.

The increased coordination among conservative AGs and overall polarization of AG activism during the Obama administration is apparent in other AG activities as well. As with policy-blocking litigation, AGs have long used amicus curiae briefs to signal to the Supreme Court issues important to the states.[101] Nevertheless, their use during the Obama administration reflects a sharp intensification of polarization among AGs. As discussed earlier in this chapter, Democratic AGs filed several amicus briefs in their Republican colleagues' health care and environmental lawsuits in order to assist in the defense the federal laws. In many other areas, partisan coalitions of Republican AGs have used amicus strategies to oppose both the federal DOJ and the administration's Democratic AG allies. In addition to supporting or opposing their fellow AGs in state-initiated cases involving immigration and voting rights, AGs have used this strategy to pursue social issue agendas in private party challenges concerning gay rights, gun control, abortion, religion, and affirmative action.[102] The expansion of partisan AG involvement into various high-profile political disputes resembles similar trends in the office of the US solicitor general, which, as Michael Solimine has noted,

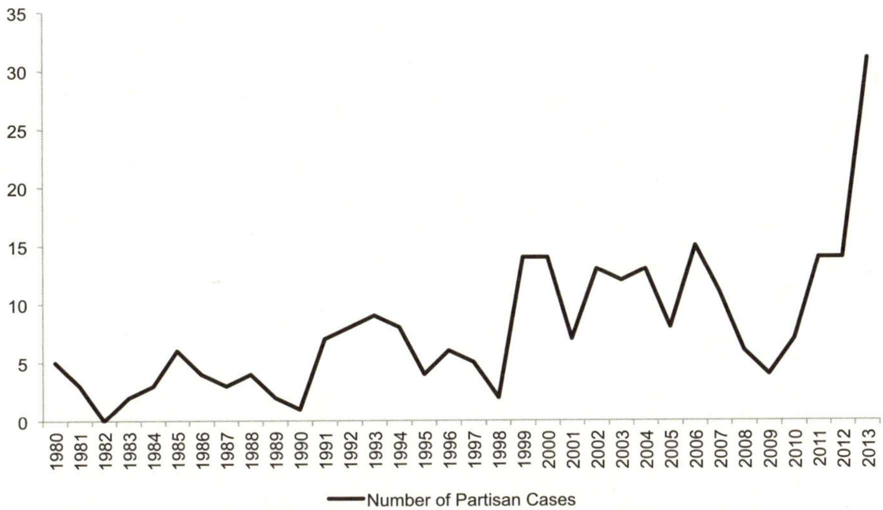

Figure 9.1. Number of partisan multistate amicus briefs, 1980–2013. Source: Author's calculations from data collected on Lexis-Nexis.

has been increasingly willing to involve the federal government in litigation with only attenuated connections with executive branch interests.[103]

Figure 9.1 illustrates partisan trends in coordinated AGs' amicus strategies over time and during the Obama administration, using original data collected on all cases in the US Supreme Court from 1980 to 2013 in which multiple AGs collaborated on an amicus brief.[104] Each of the approximately 1,200 Supreme Court cases in this data set were coded as attracting either bipartisan or partisan AG involvement. For the purposes of this analysis, partisan briefs were those in which Republican or Democratic AGs constituted at least 80 percent of the AGs participating on the brief.[105] The results suggest a strong upward trend in partisan behavior over time, and particularly during the Obama administration.

The large spike in polarization during 2013 reflects that many of the cases that had been percolating in the lower courts finally reached the Supreme Court during this year. Overall, seventy-five cases involved partisan participation among AGs during the first five years of the Obama administration. This total is already greater than the total for the entire Reagan and Clinton presidencies (twenty-three and sixty-eight cases, respectively) and approaches the total through eight years of the George W. Bush administration (eighty-nine cases).

As with policy-blocking litigation, the partisan shape of AGs' amicus activity is different from the previous Democratic presidential administration. In nearly all of the cases (96 percent) in which Republican AGs joined amicus briefs taking a position opposing the Clinton administration, they did so as part of a bipartisan AG coalition. In fact, of all of the partisan briefs AGs filed during the Clinton administration, most involved Democratic AGs taking a position opposing the administration. Only five cases during the entire Clinton administration featured multiple Republican AGs collaborating on a partisan brief, compared to fifty during the first five years of the Obama administration alone.[106] Further, the scope of the conflict is also different. In previous administrations, most cases involving even controversial topics such as gay rights and religion attracted little attention from AGs.[107] Now, however, such high-profile issues are nearly certain to attract wide and partisan AG amicus participation.

What has contributed to the intensification of polarization among the AGs? Why have Republican AGs, who as a group were relatively muted the last time a Democrat occupied the White House, taken on more activist roles? Several broader factors have contributed to this trend.

First, and most directly, AG activism has reflected intensifying polarization apparent elsewhere in the political system. Although polarization increased after Republicans captured control of Congress in 1994, there has been a considerable surge in polarization throughout the political system since 2000.[108] State governments have been no exception, as state-level political conflicts increasingly mirror national-level partisan splits. As late as George W. Bush's second term, one could speak of a distinction between the polarized national environment and a less polarized state-level politics.[109] Reflecting a similar development among governors and other state-level institutions, however, the polarization on the national level has trickled down to the AGs.

This trickle-down polarization is apparent in the way that national electoral patterns have become more apparent in the results of state level elections. Several observers have noted how divided control of state governments has become quite uncommon as state-level electoral results reflect the national voting patterns of their electorates.[110] This partisan sorting is true of the AGs as well, and particularly so in recent years. In 2010 and 2012, for example, Republicans were successful in capturing AG seats in relatively conservative states long represented by Democratic AGs, including Oklahoma, West Virginia, and Georgia. Figure 9.2 provides a broader look at the state-level partisan sorting over time by indicating the number of states from 1981 to the present in which (1) one party controlled the governor's office and both chambers of the state legislature, (2) the AG was of

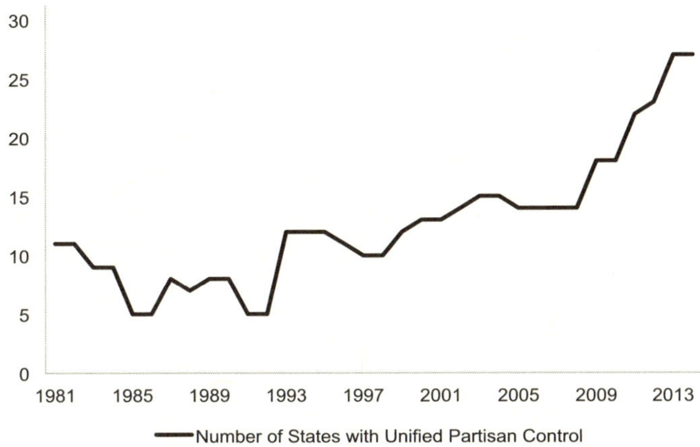

Figure 9.2. Number of states with unified partisan control, 1981–2013. Source: Author's calculations.

the same party as the rest of state government, and (3) the state voted for the president of that party in the previous election. As figure 9.2 illustrates, more AGs than ever before represent their expected state from a partisan point of view, suggesting the closing gap between national and state-level partisanship.

Voters' increasing tendencies to vote for state-level offices similarly as they do in national elections has in turn contributed to greater Republican AG electoral success. Democrats had long dominated this position, maintaining a significant majority of the AG positions since at least 1980.[111] The 1992 elections served as a high point for Democratic AGs when they won thirty-eight AG positions, and they continued to hold a strong majority of the nation's AG seats throughout the Clinton and George W. Bush administrations. Since then, however, Republican AGs have seen an influx of new members to their ranks. After Louisiana AG Buddy Caldwell's switch to the Republican Party in early 2011, Democrats no longer held a majority of the AG seats for the first time in decades.

Parallel to these electoral developments, AGs created new institutions reflecting increasing partisan splits. In response to what he viewed as his Democratic colleagues' increasing willingness to engage in regulation through litigation, particularly in the tobacco litigation of the late 1990s, Republican Alabama AG William Pryor helped establish the Republican Attorneys General Association (RAGA) in 1999.[112] Democrats responded by founding the Democratic Attorneys General Association in 2002, which, like RAGA, serves as a way to elect more party members and as a forum to discuss partisan policy priorities.[113] These developments marked a significant departure from AGs' traditional practice of meeting only under the auspices of the National Association of Attorneys General and regional nonpartisan groups.[114] This mirrored what was happening with other state-level institutions. The Republican and Democratic governors associations, for example, have become increasingly important relative to the bipartisan National Governor's Association.[115]

It is notable that in contrast to the polarization that has grown prominent in other national and state-level venues, much of the AGs' partisanship had its origins in Democratic activism. In her study of growing polarization within Congress in the 1980s and 1990s, Barbara Sinclair noted that polarization in Congress was spurred largely by a rightward ideological shift among Republicans and an increasing willingness of Republican leaders to use unorthodox lawmaking to achieve conservative goals.[116] The opposite has been true in the case of AG litigation. The establishment of RAGA and the subsequent conservative AG collaborations during the Obama administration were a reaction to earlier Democratic AG activism seeking liberal goals. This coordinated Democratic AG activism had begun with battling the regulatory priorities of the Reagan administration, but it intensified after the tobacco litigation and during the George W. Bush administration. Although individual Republican AGs occasionally initiated challenges against the Clinton administration, more aggressive and coordinated conservative state litigation emerged only after state litigation matured as a method of unorthodox policymaking, particularly after the tobacco settlement and lawsuits against the George W. Bush administration. For the first time since the emergence of nationalized state litigation, Obama's election provided Republican AGs a target.

Coordination with Outside Groups

Another crucial aspect of the nationalization of state litigation has been increased AG coordination with outside interests that share similar policy goals. The AGs' ACA and climate change lawsuits, for example, operated in tandem with several lawsuits by private industry and conservative advocacy groups. The AGs themselves retained prominent conservative litigators, including David Rivkin and Paul Clement, to represent their position in court.

The emergence of this coordinated litigation is related in part to the increasing willingness and capacity among conservatives to use the courts to achieve conservative policy goals. As Steven Teles traces in his study of the development of the conservative legal movement, it was only after liberals had come to dominate the law and American legal institutions that conservatives realized that successes in electoral politics were insufficient for the advancement of conservative policies. Although criticism of judicial activism was (and still is) an important element of conservative rhetoric, conservatives have increasingly warmed to the tools of non–electoral party mobilization, including litigation. Since the 1980s, conservative public interest law has become increasingly sophisticated, learning from previous mistakes to use strategic lawsuits more effectively for mobilizing and challenging newly adopted policies.[117] One of the most recent signals of this increasing sophistication has been conservative advocacy groups enlisting sympathetic AGs as litigation partners.

Nevertheless, relationships between ideological interest groups and AGs are hardly limited to conservatives. As discussed in this and previous chapters, Democratic AGs have frequently allied with liberal advocacy groups and private class-action attorneys in litigation aimed at influencing national policy. Massachusetts's lead brief in *Massachusetts v. EPA*, for example, was authored by Georgetown law professor and environmental advocate Lisa Heinzerling, and it came together only after multiple conference calls among representatives of the twenty-nine state and advocacy plaintiffs aligned against the EPA.[118] In policy-creating litigation against pharmaceutical companies, AGs worked in tandem with a coalition of various unions, private class-action attorneys, and progressive advocacy groups.[119]

The flowering of these partnerships between AGs and outside parties on both the political right and the left reflects the realization by both groups that collaboration offers several benefits. For the AGs, collaborating with outside groups helps the states expand the resources available to engage in lengthy, large-scale litigation campaigns. In the ACA litigation, for example, the NFIB served as a valuable ally for the AGs, providing significant resources for the lawsuit. Similarly, as discussed in earlier chapters, interest group plaintiffs in environmental cases and class-action attorneys in pharmaceutical litigation helped to provide legal expertise and financial resources for AG litigation.

These collaborations also benefit the AGs' advocacy group and private litigator allies in part because AG participation helps add legitimacy and publicity to the political concerns underlying their litigation. In a passage that Teles also highlights in his work on the conservative legal movement, Jack Balkin has suggested that

> the question of what is "off the wall" and what is "on the wall" in law is tied to a series of social conventions that include which persons in the legal profession are willing to stand up for a particular legal argument. In law, if not in other disciplines of human thought, authority, and particularly institutional authority, counts for a lot. The more powerful and influential the people who are willing to make a legal argument, the more quickly it moves from the positively loony to the positively thinkable, and ultimately to something entirely consistent with "good legal craft."[120]

The AG coalition aligned against the ACA, which eventually included a majority of the states, brought considerable institutional authority to this litigation. The AGs' position as legal representatives of their states allowed them to portray the ACA court battle as not simply a part of new ideological conflicts concerning health care but rather as fundamentally about one of the oldest conflicts in American politics: federalism. State plaintiffs were in a more legitimate position to advance this argument than advocacy groups explicitly seeking ideological goals or corporations seeking to avoid new regulatory obligations. Their lawsuits further helped publicize new legal arguments, forcing other political actors to react. Other groups of AGs, for example, sought to defend the ACA by filing amicus briefs in favor of the law. However, much as how briefs in opposition to petitions for certiorari counterproductively increase the likelihood of the Court taking the case because they signal its importance,[121] this opposition merely assisted the movement of previously frivolous arguments against the ACA closer to being "on the wall."

Conservative AGs' use of lawsuits to move ideas from off the wall to on the wall built on earlier AGs' attempts to achieve something similar to extend the national regulatory state. As chapter 3 illustrated, the states' pharmaceutical pricing litigation helped move legal arguments previously viewed as outside the realm of possibility to the foundation of one of the most important contemporary attempts to influence drug company behavior. Likewise, the notion that provisions of the Clean Air Act originally drafted in the 1970s could address environmental problems like climate change that emerged only years later was unlikely. By building broader coalitions and continuously pressing their arguments in boardrooms and courtrooms, AGs helped legitimize legal ideas that were previously off the wall. Conservative AGs' policy-blocking litigation during the Obama administration is the latest chapter in the development of this dynamic.

In addition to adding legitimacy to legal arguments, AGs also brought another valuable resource along with them: the ability to get into court. The AGs' claims of standing to sue have, much as in other contexts, largely relied on the model of cooperative federalism that federal policymakers adopted in modern social policy. The states in *Florida v. HHS* based their standing claims on the impact that the expansion of Medicaid provisions would have on state budgets—a claim that would not exist if Medicaid, like Medicare, was a fully nationalized program. Likewise, AG challenges to the Obama administration's EPA are based on regulatory changes affecting states that are part of the cooperative environmental federal policy regime. Like other instances of modern state litigation, partnering with AGs grants advocacy groups a way in to court by adding an element of standing that they alone could not claim. Ironically, given the very different regulatory ambitions of the AGs who had brought the ACA litigation, *Massachusetts v. EPA*'s announcement that states ought to have "special solicitude" in the courts' standing analysis served to strengthen Republican AG arguments that they had a special claim to challenge federal policy.[122]

AGs and the Representation of State Interests

The increasing polarization among the AGs and collaboration with a broader range of interests is part of a larger story of the nationalization of state litigation. As the line between national and state politics became increasingly blurred, AGs began defining their states' interests in increasingly partisan and nationalized terms. This has left fewer issues in which there are clearly discernible and unified state interests conflicting with those of the federal government. Instead, AGs have alternated between broadly describing state interests as either the necessity of protecting state policy autonomy or upholding the interests of their individual citizens against government (state or federal) overreach, depending on the nature of the underlying policy dispute.

Consider AGs' involvement in several recent high-profile cases in the Supreme Court. In *Hollingsworth v. Perry* and *US v. Windsor*, two prominent gay rights cases decided in 2013, separate Democratic and Republican AG coalitions filed amicus briefs taking an opposite position from one another. While both groups of AGs claimed that their status as their states' legal representatives gave them an interest in these cases, the AGs' respective positions appeared to be more about the policy merits of the cases and less about federalism. While Massachusetts AG Martha Coakley and her fellow

Democratic AGs argued in *Windsor* that the federal Defense of Marriage Act "represents an unprecedented intrusion into an area of law that has always been controlled by the states," she simultaneously led a Democratic coalition in *Hollingsworth* urging a federal court to intervene and strike down California's Proposition 8 banning same-sex marriages.[123] Meanwhile, a Republican AG coalition claimed that striking down Proposition 8 would "undermine the ability of states to define and regulate marriage" but on the same day many of the same Republican AGs filed a brief in *Windsor* defending a federal statute regulating an area of family law that had traditionally been under state control.[124]

Recent cases concerning abortion, gun control, and affirmative action illustrate a similar dynamic of AGs taking positions in favor of limiting state policymaking authority. In *McCullen v. Coakley,* a challenge to Massachusetts's thirty-five-foot buffer zone around abortion clinics, twelve Republican AGs filed an amicus brief urging the Court to strike down the state law because the law "exempts speakers likely to express favorable views about abortion."[125] Similarly, a group of AGs urged the Court to strike down a local law in *McDonald v. Chicago,* involving a challenge to Chicago's strict gun control law. Their interest in the case, they claimed, flowed from the AGs' status as fundamental "guardians of their citizens' constitutional rights." The AGs, in other words, advocated for increased federal authority over state policymaking, all in the name of ensuring that "millions of Americans" are not "deprived of their Second Amendment right to keep and bear arms."[126] This trend of AGs arguing in favor of a result that would effectively constrain state authority has also appeared in recent cases such as *Schuette v. Coalition to Defend Affirmative Action,* which featured a group of Democratic AGs opposing Michigan AG Bill Schuette's defense of the state's constitutional ban on affirmative action.[127]

The lack of consistency in these arguments suggests that AGs are using their structural independence and nearly exclusive control over shaping their state's position in litigation to pursue their own, and increasingly partisan, conceptions of good public policy. These developments are not to say that AGs cannot or will not work together across party lines. As discussed in earlier chapters, policy-creating litigation against corporations tends to attract bipartisan AG participation, even if Democrats are more active in initiating these cases. AGs' amicus brief filings in criminal procedure cases have attracted largely bipartisan support for decades, including during the Obama administration.[128] Yet this latest chapter of AG activism reveals increasing tensions among the AGs. Throughout the contemporary era discussed in this book, AGs have used national collaboration among themselves and like-minded interest groups for the increasingly divergent ends of partisan involvement in conflicts over national policy and the American regulatory state. In short, AGs have been at the center of a new form of intergovernmental conflict—one that does not represent the familiar conflict between unified state interests against federal power but rather one that involves states using the courts to pursue interests defined in divergent and increasingly partisan ways.

What are the implications of the nationalization of state litigation for American democracy? Although contemporary AG activism has created new avenues for policy change in an increasingly stultified national political system, are there reasons to be concerned? I address these questions in the concluding chapter.

CHAPTER TEN

STATE ATTORNEYS GENERAL AND THE NATIONALIZATION OF STATE LITIGATION

The question of the relation of the states to the federal government is the cardinal question of our constitutional system. . . . It cannot, indeed, be settled by the opinion of any one generation, because it is a question of growth and every successive stage of our political and economic development gives it a new aspect, makes it a new question.
Woodrow Wilson, *Constitutional Government in the United States*

We are talking about the new frontier of federalism.
Michael Leavitt, former governor of Utah, on the states' modern regulatory roles

Many Americans describe their political system as slow and inefficient. Particularly when viewed in contrast to hierarchically organized European democracies, the American system appears resistant to policy change. Many scholars have attributed this to the numerous veto points lodged throughout the United States' institutional structure.[1] These veto points include specific institutional developments such as the Senate filibuster as well as broad organizing principles including the diffusion of governmental authority established by separation of powers and federalism. Some observers view this as a great virtue of the system, harkening back to James Madison's famous argument in *Federalist* No. 51 about how "ambition must be made to counteract ambition."[2] To others, this is a dysfunctional state of affairs. America's institutional structure too frequently prevents necessary policy change, except perhaps in rare critical junctures witnessed during the New Deal era or in the work of the Eighty-Ninth Congress during the mid-1960s.[3] Particularly when combined with the emergence of intense political polarization in contemporary politics, institutional fragmentation appears to be a significant barrier to American political development.

However, the debate over the desirability of the system's many veto points too often loses sight of a key feature of the diffusion of power in America's fragmented constitutional system. Rather than inevitably leading to political gridlock, this fragmentation also spurs new points of entry for political entrepreneurs and institutional innovation. The very institutions designed and assumed in practice to work to stymie policy change, including separation of powers and federalism, work to create new opportunities for national political development. The AGs examined throughout this book serve as prime examples of this dynamic. Many of their coordinated litigation campaigns that have become commonplace in recent years—whether pertaining to prescription drugs, climate change, financial regulation, tobacco control, or health care—represented entrepreneurial innovations that followed policy failures in other venues.

In this concluding chapter, I consider several broader aspects concerning the role of contemporary AG activism in the shaping of national policy. First, I suggest that the various forms of activism examined throughout this book illustrate a fundamental shift in the nature of state litigation. Propelled by continuing commitments to cooperative federalism and adversarial legalism in federal policy, state litigation has become increasingly nationalized. Equipped with wide discretion to represent the legal interests of their states, AGs have defined their role in increasingly divergent terms, leaving fewer activities that involve clearly discernible state interests. This in turn has led to increasing conflicts both among the AGs themselves as well as between AGs and other state institutions.

I then turn to a pair of questions that have lurked in the background throughout this book, one normative and another speculative. First, to what extent is the rise of modern AG activism a positive development in American politics? How does it fit with the purported benefits of a robust American federalism? Although few scholars have specifically considered the AGs' role in the system, several have argued in favor of a vision of contemporary American federalism that promotes interaction between multiple institutions in the policymaking process. I suggest, however, that the addition of AGs' voices to national policymaking is problematic in several respects. Although AG litigation serves as a method of breaking policy gridlock, it also raises fundamental issues about democratic governance. The second question is whether, regardless of the normative merits or demerits of this form of national policymaking, the rise of modern state litigation is likely to continue. I suggest that it is, driven by several incentives of various actors in the American political system. The AGs themselves, along with members of industry, advocacy groups, and federal policymakers, have reasons to support the continuation of this new form of national policymaking.

The Nationalization of State Litigation

The backdrop for contemporary AG activism, as I have argued, has been two key developments in America's system of separation of powers since the latter half of the twentieth century: the increased importance of both states and litigation in the process of policy implementation. Rather than grant administration of new federal programs exclusively to federal agencies, implementation of many aspects of federal policy shifted to the states in the 1960s and 1970s. At the same time that the vertical separation of powers between the states and federal government became increasingly blurred, the same was becoming true of the horizontal separation of powers. Particularly since the 1960s, American policy underwent a process of juridification as courts and litigation became much more important in resolving complex questions of public policy.[4] Congress played a key role in this development, building a litigation state that opened the courthouse doors for litigants to enforce key elements of federal policy.[5]

The increased role of states and litigation in American national policy provided new opportunity points for AGs to influence policy development. These opportunity points widened even further as policymakers across the three branches of the federal government provided AGs additional legal resources. Congress bolstered AGs' enforcement capacities through federal grants and by allowing states to enforce federal laws. Federal courts provided AGs enhanced standing to sue even as they began adopting restrictive standing rules for private litigants. Federal agencies provided AGs with resources they could use to bring litigation against private industry and even encouraged state policy-forcing lawsuits as a method of providing political cover for regulatory expansions.

The long-term effect of the federal government's invitation for AGs to influence national policy has been to encourage AGs to define state interests much differently than in the past. A crucial element of this shift is that while AGs have traditionally acted as representatives of their states, they have increasingly claimed the ability to represent a broader range of interests. This includes representing the interests of individuals as opposed to the states themselves. When challenging the individual mandate provision of the Affordable Care Act (ACA), for example, which operated on individuals and not states, the AGs' briefs claimed that the states were rightfully vindicating the "rights of their citizens" in the litigation.[6] Similarly, AGs have advocated for individual rights in areas such as same-sex marriage, abortion, and guns—even if this argues for a restriction of the states' own policymaking authority. This represents a shift away from the concept of the AGs as serving as guardians of their states' constitutional rights and reflects a shift in institutional purposes that has been years in the making. This shift began in the 1970s when, as discussed in chapter 2, state *parens patriae* authority expanded to encourage AGs to represent not just their states but also the interests of large classes of consumers and other individuals harmed by corporate conduct. AGs, in short, became a type of class-action litigator whose concerns stretched beyond the mere interests of states as states.

Further, AGs have pursued increasingly partisan and divergent agendas that reflect nationalized conflicts elsewhere in American politics. Policy-forcing litigation, as discussed in chapters 6 through 8, began largely as a regional dispute in which AGs' positions aligned closely with their states' economic interests. More recently, however, policy-forcing efforts are increasingly partisan rather than regional, reflecting national polarization on issues of environmental protection and climate change. Likewise, policy-blocking litigation was once a bipartisan affair that pitted states unified against federal encroachment, but it has increasingly become a tool for Republican AGs to articulate a conservative vision of federal regulatory power. AGs' use of amicus curiae briefs, as noted in chapter 9, reveals a sharp turn toward greater polarization, and especially so during the Obama administration.[7] Although the policy-creating litigation examined in chapters 3 through 5 features far more bipartisan AG activity, largely because the monetary rewards of joining settlements are too significant for AGs to forgo, partisan tensions exist even there. Faced with AG policy-creating activism led by liberal Democratic AGs, conservative AGs have pushed back against their colleagues' regulation through litigation.[8]

The increasing split between state interests and AG activism is also at work behind another recent trend of AGs refusing to defend their own state laws against constitutional attack. Texas AG Greg Abbott, for example, refused to defend his state's affirmative action policy before the Supreme Court in *Fisher v. University of Texas*.[9] Other recent examples include Pennsylvania's AG declining to defend the state's voter ID law on appeal and the California AG's decision to refrain from defending the state's ban on same-sex marriage.[10] After taking office after conservative AG Ken Cuccinelli's failed bid for Virginia's governorship, Democratic AG Mark Herring announced that federal courts ought to strike down his own state's same-sex marriage ban.[11] Several observers, including other AGs, have criticized these litigation vetoes as examples of AGs allowing ideological concerns to trump constitutional duties to defend state laws.[12]

As AGs have defined their defense of state interests in increasingly polarized terms, it has led to growing conflicts between AGs and other state institutions. In the ACA litigation, for example, several governors and state legislatures attempted to influence their AGs' decisions either to join or refrain from joining the ongoing litigation. Idaho's state legislature became the first of several to pass legislation purporting to require the AG to file a lawsuit against the ACA, and the Georgia legislature even introduced articles of impeachment against the state's Democratic AG for refusing to join the litigation.[13] The Republican governors of Nevada and Mississippi both announced that they were hiring special outside counsel to represent their states after the states' Democratic AGs had declined to do so, an action both AGs claimed violated their right to exclusive control over litigation in the name of their state.[14] Meanwhile, Democratic legislators criticized their states' Republican AGs for joining the challenge to the ACA. In Washington State, for example, the Democratic legislature moved to reduce Republican AG Rob McKenna's budget, and Seattle's city attorney initiated a lawsuit seeking to force McKenna's withdrawal from the litigation.[15]

With AGs pursuing policy goals increasingly divorced from state prerogatives, they have increasingly coordinated their efforts with other actors seeking similar policy goals. Progressive critics of corporate practices have found collaborating with AGs on policy-creating and policy-forcing litigation to be an effective way of achieving regulatory controls on the private sector that they had failed to achieve through typical policymaking avenues. Conservative advocacy groups have come to realize that partnering with AGs on policy-blocking lawsuits can boost the legitimacy of legal challenges and make it easier to get into court. In short, AG litigation has become an additional avenue for political contestation not only for the AGs themselves, but also for a wide range of litigants seeking national policy goals.

Ultimately, by creating and expanding opportunity points for AGs to influence national policy, the ironic result is that the federal government has encouraged significant challenges to its own authority. The AGs' policy-creating litigation explicitly sought to create new regulatory standards for private industry that conflicted with and even supplanted existing federal policy. Policy-forcing litigation served as a major roadblock for deregulatory-minded administrations to implement their policy visions. Particularly during the Obama administration, policy-blocking litigation has become an increasingly important policy tool for conservative AGs seeking to challenge national regulatory expansion. This development highlights the unexpected consequences of creating additional room in which political entrepreneurs can operate. By widening the entrepreneurial space available for AGs, federal institutions have encouraged the growth of national policymaking rivals whose actions frequently complicate the operation of national policy.

AG Litigation and Contemporary American Federalism

Although the nationalization of state litigation has generated new political conflicts, there is reason to believe that the emergence of AGs as national policymakers is nevertheless a welcome one. For one, AG activism has been a way to overcome the seemingly insurmountable barriers to policy change in America. In an era in which gridlock and inaction beset our national political institutions, the AGs' involvement in national policy provides a potentially productive way forward.

In this sense, AG activism may represent simply the latest chapter in the healthy development of American federalism—one with appeal across the political system. Conservatives have long celebrated federalism as a method of constraining state power, and AGs' policy-blocking litigation during the Obama administration illustrates how it can be a powerful method to reach this goal. After all, AGs helped transform seemingly frivolous legal arguments against the ACA into a litigation campaign that limited and nearly dismantled President Obama's signature domestic program.

Liberals have as many reasons, and probably more, to support expansion of AGs' national policymaking. In an era in which "private class actions are on the ropes," AGs' role in bringing consumer protection litigation may be more important than ever (a point I return to below).[16] More fundamentally, the AGs' version of federalism can and has served as a mechanism to achieve a larger and more energetic regulatory state. As noted in chapter 1, several contemporary scholars have celebrated a polyphonic conception of contemporary federalism that "consists of independent state and federal voices that interact together" to bring their powers to bear on common problems.[17] This conception of federalism as empowerment rather than federalism as constraint is valuable for the way it spurs regulatory dialogue among multiple actors, prevents the existence of "regulatory gaps" through overlapping regulation, and promotes policy experimentation.[18]

Nevertheless, the emergence of modern state litigation raises cause for concern. The AGs' voice in this polyphonic system, after all, has a much different tone than that of other state and federal actors. Rather than relying on typical policymaking processes such as legislation or rule making, the AGs use the tools of adversarial legalism to influence policy. By doing so, the AGs' coordinated activism differs in crucial ways from that of other policy actors. These differences, I suggest, raise some important difficulties in the AGs' exercise of states' rights.

Regulatory Dialogue in Practice: Polyphony, Cacophony, or Just Phony?

Among the purported benefits overlapping federal–state regulatory authority is the way in which "the concurrence of federal and state authority provides a valuable opportunity for dialogue."[19] Regulators on the state and federal levels can learn from one another through the informal feedback loops developed between different institutions working on the same problem.[20] This process of dialogue "facilitates regulatory innovation" and promises to develop "the optimal regulatory scheme" over time.[21] In addition, this process of dialogue is a fundamental part of the federalist regime. As David Shapiro put it, "The true genius of American federalism lies in the continuing and constitutionally assured basis for dialogue—for moral, political, economic, and social debate over the merits of the allocation of power."[22]

The ability of states to request and negotiate waivers from federal requirements, which has occurred with policies such as Aid to Families with Dependent Children in the 1990s and more recently with the ACA, represents a form of federal–state dialogue. To what extent, however, does AG litigation spur such dialogue? In one sense, such litigation does produce the potential for healthy regulatory conversation between governments. In several instances, Congress has enacted new regulations inspired by provisions in multistate settlements. The congressional changes to the prescription drug pricing scheme sparked by multistate litigation provide one such example. If only one regulator had a voice in the process, then these regulatory innovations may never have seen the light of day.

Nevertheless, the suggestion that polyphonic federalism promotes regulatory dialogue remains problematic in the context of the AGs' litigation. Initially, it might seem that the most important issue would be the potential for cacophony rather than dialogue. Numerous observers have broached the problem of corporations struggling to comply with a patchwork of state regulatory regimes in addition to federal requirements. Frequently, industry prefers a single comprehensive regulatory regime than a patchwork of confusing regulations. As Pietro Nivola stated, companies believe it is "better to have one 500-pound gorilla in charge of regulating the industry . . . than to deal with 50 monkeys on steroids."[23] In the case of multistate litigation, however, the problem is rarely one of regulatory balkanization. As chapter 2 illustrated, AG coordination has increasingly involved larger numbers of AGs, reducing the specter of dozens of "monkeys on steroids" operating separately.

Instead, the real issue is not that this coordinated activity is balkanizing policy but rather that the AGs' main source of influence—the legal process—is largely incompatible with the production of healthy dialogue. At the heart of the adversarial legal system is legal formality, which encourages participants to "invoke and insist on conformity to written legal procedures and preexisting legal rights and duties."[24] The end goal is to compel the opposing side to act in a certain way. In this sense, the legal process is designed to promote certain values, including uniformity and finality, which stand in contrast to the flexible value of dialogue.

When AGs use policy-forcing and policy-blocking litigation in an attempt to force the federal government to act, the end goal is not negotiation and compromise. Instead, litigation is a way to promote one particular vision of proper regulation at the expense of the other. AGs bringing Clean Air Act litigation against the Reagan and George W. Bush administrations were not interested in sparking intergovernmental dialogue; rather, they used the legal process to impose strict and formalistic legal requirements on the federal government. Unlike state governors who have worked with federal regulators to negotiate the implementation of Medicaid expansions contained in the ACA, AGs challenging the law were not interested in compromise. Instead, they invoked claims of legal rights that they hoped would trump the entire law. To continue the aural metaphor, AGs' use of multistate litigation in a polyphonic system is the equivalent to using a bullhorn to express one's position in a crowded room: it aims to drown out other voices, not add to them.

The AGs' policy-creating litigation would seem more compatible with the value of dialogue. After all, this litigation typically ends in negotiated settlements that avoid the winner-take-all nature of active litigation. Nevertheless, this form of state policymaking limits dialogue more than it promotes it.

One of the purported advantages of overlapping regulation is to gain input from a greater number of voices, but the AGs' settlement process includes only those voices that the AGs themselves invite to the negotiating table. Settlements often affect interests beyond the parties to the document, such as the doctors affected by changes to the average wholesale price system discussed in chapter 3, but those interests have little or no voice in the negotiations over the shape of settlement regulations.

The notion that dialogue helps lead to optimal regulatory policies is further complicated by the fact that legal settlements provide less opportunity for revision and less flexibility than other forms of regulation. Because settlements create legally enforceable rights for all of the parties involved, any subsequent amendments to the settlements require unanimity. Because any signatory can hold out in favor of the settlement status quo, it can make beneficial regulatory feedback loops more difficult. Rather than spurring innovative policies through dialogue, in other words, settlements can instead lock regulatory choices into place.

All three forms of AG litigation are thus likely to contribute to less, not more, regulatory dialogue. Unlike other forms of state policymaking such as legislation and rule making, coordinated litigation uses a process emphasizing values at odds with the vision of a properly functioning polyphonic federalism. Indeed, the entire point of these litigation strategies is to sidestep and avoid politics by circumventing a typical policymaking process alleged to be deadlocked and either unable or unwilling to act. In describing the juridification of American policy, Gordon Silverstein notes how legalistic approaches increasingly "substitute for, displace, and even undermine or kill the ordinary political processes."[25] This dynamic captures the rise of multistate litigation well. Such litigation might avoid ordinary political processes and the messiness and frustration that so frequently accompany them, but at the expense of the very values that federalism aims to promote.

Minding the Regulatory Gaps in Modern State Litigation

In several of their litigation campaigns, AGs have defended their activism as necessary to address regulatory gaps left open by federal inaction. Eliot Spitzer, for example, frequently cited this rationale as he led various lawsuits against private industry.[26] Likewise, AGs justified nationwide settlements imposing new regulatory requirements on pharmaceutical firms, tobacco manufacturers, electric companies, and many other industries as part of a fight for consumers when federal institutions could not or would not regulate corporate conduct. Other scholarly observers have similarly suggested that AGs serve to fill regulatory gaps left open by federal inaction.[27]

This rationale resonates with several contemporary scholarly defenses of federalism. Multiple, overlapping sources of authority also create regulatory redundancy, which can be advantageous in a couple of ways. First, even if a state policy cannot become legally binding, "state law can provide an important protest, a powerful criticism of the federal approach."[28] Similarly, Judith Resnick suggests that "these multiple sites for conflicts about social norms" allow the opportunity "to permit problems to be argued in more than one forum and more than once."[29] Second, redundancy also "constitutes a fail-safe mechanism, an additional source of protection if one or the other government should fail to offer adequate safeguards."[30] This gap-filling role is all the more important because federal agencies "are often confronted with information gaps, bureaucratic inertia, intransigent companies, resource constraints, political interference, and other handicaps that limit the capacity of the agency to act in the public interest."[31] This notion might implicitly find support in James Madison's remark in *Federalist* No. 46 that "the federal and State governments are in fact but different agents and trustees of the people, constituted with different powers and designed for different purposes."[32] Thus, if one level of government is not adequately representing the public interest on a particular issue, the people can then approach the other level for relief.

The AGs' contemporary activism, however, has occurred chiefly not in areas ignored by other regulators but rather in areas that are among the most heavily regulated, such as pharmaceuticals, advertising, and the environment. Although AGs may often characterize Congress's or a federal agency's decision not to regulate as a regulatory gap or a regulatory failure, such failures may in fact be a reasoned decision to reject the particular (stricter) approach sought by AGs. The regulatory schemes established by Congress in the area of pharmaceutical policy intended to balance a variety of competing concerns that AG litigation intended to disrupt, for example. Likewise, a Federal Trade Commission decision that a particular advertising campaign does not constitute false and deceptive advertising may reflect the view that the advertising actually enhances competition. AGs' regulation through litigation, in short, often does not fill gaps in regulation but displaces a regulatory scheme already in operation.

Further, when evaluating claims that AGs are filling regulatory gaps via multistate litigation, a reasonable question becomes: filling them with what, exactly? Although multistate litigation may attempt to achieve alternative national regulations, it frequently leaves in its wake a "glorious mess" rather than a coherent regulatory regime. The successful agency-forcing litigation in *Massachusetts v. EPA* left unclear how to apply the thirty-year old Clean Air Act to a new global problem of climate change. The AGs' litigation contributing to the fall of the AWP benchmark may have suggested an alternative prescription drug pricing mechanism, but it did not solve the related problem of how Medicaid providers would be fairly compensated upon adoption of this alternative pricing scheme. Much of this litigation, while achieving reformers' goals of stricter regulation, thus leaves open considerable questions about how the litigation's side effects would be resolved. In this way, the AGs' litigation may simply replace one regulatory regime with another one that is riddled with several regulatory gaps of its own.

(Over-)Regulating through Litigation

Even when AG litigation results in a stable and coherent regulatory regime, AG settlements filling alleged federal regulatory gaps frequently trump various concerns identified by Congress or agencies and may produce too strict or even "mindless regulation."[33] This is a particular danger with policy-creating litigation because it operates as a regulatory ratchet moving only in one direction: toward greater regulation. States cannot reach settlements containing looser regulatory requirements than what federal law requires because regulated industries must adhere to federal requirements whether or not they are a party to a multistate settlement. Settlements can and do contain stricter regulatory requirements than federal law does, however, because federal law sets a floor but not a ceiling on regulation.

This stricter regulation may have a variety of unintended negative side effects. As chapters 3 through 5 illustrated, stricter regulation of pharmaceuticals through litigation may result in fewer Medicaid providers, a decline in pharmaceutical innovation, and less information for consumers. Meanwhile, agency-forcing litigation aimed at directing the agency's attention to particular regulatory issues may lead to agency resource misallocations and the agency overlooking more serious problems.[34] If the dangers certain environmental problems pose are overstated, for example—much as acid rain may have been less a problem than originally believed—then overregulation in that area may lead to underregulation in others.

Providing a comprehensive cost–benefit analysis of AGs' form of regulation through litigation is beyond this book's scope. It is frequently difficult, if not impossible, to evaluate the full measure of beneficial intended consequences against the negative unintended consequences of any particular policy choice. Nevertheless, the possibility of overregulation is particularly problematic in the context of multistate litigation because AGs do not have the same sort of expertise to evaluate regulatory complexities as government agencies do. Although many AG offices have large staffs of attorneys, they do not have the levels of scientific and expert knowledge available to federal and state regulatory agencies. Nor do AGs have a consistent relationship with most of the targets of their multistate investigations, which is commonly the case with regulatory agencies. When litigating a case or negotiating a regulatory settlement, AGs also do not engage in the lengthy rule-making process that federal agencies do to gain an additional perspective on a problem.

Multistate litigation is also often conducted ad hoc, with one industry leader negotiating a regulatory settlement with the AGs separately from other firms and focused on that particular company's conduct, rather than being part of an administrative scheme that looks at the operation of an entire industry as a whole. Yet the result of these settlements is national regulation. The result is that, unlike federal regulators, AGs regulate on a national basis even as they have little working knowledge of how industries operate nationally and how particular regulatory solutions affect the industry as a whole. These problems complicate the view that multiple, overlapping sources of authority work to achieve the optimal regulatory regime.

The nature of coordinated state litigation as a regulatory ratchet potentially leading to overregulation illustrates a certain political irony about the nature of the AGs' federalism. Federalism and states' rights are most frequently associated with conservatives and limits on government, but coordinated AG litigation illustrates that decentralization is not inevitably a way to constrain regulatory expansion but can in fact promote it. Although conservatives may cheer coordinated AG litigation brought against the ACA and other policy priorities of the Obama administration, they are encouraging the continuation of an avenue of state policymaking that is institutionally more likely to lead toward regulatory expansion.

Regulatory Experiments without Borders

One of the most widely cited benefits of federalism is its ability to allow for a diversity of approaches to contemporary problems. The pithiest version is still Justice Louis Brandeis's famous observation, written as part of a dissent in a 1932 case: "It is one of the happy incidents of the federal system that a single courageous state may, if its citizens choose, serve as a laboratory; and try novel social and economic experiments without risk to the rest of the country."[35] Contemporary defenders of federalism as empowerment similarly highlight the federalist value of plurality, which suggests that the different geographical scope of the states and the federal government may give them varying perspectives on common problems and allows "differing approaches to address particular issues."[36] A number of AGs rely on this regulatory experimentation argument to defend the benefits of multistate litigation. Referring to his involvement in multistate consumer protection and antitrust litigation, for example, former Maryland AG Joseph Curran defended his involvement by arguing that "the states are good laboratories. Let us do our thing, and if it's a good solution, make it federal law."[37]

However, it is not clear that the states as laboratories analogy works as well with multistate litigation as it might for other state regulatory actors. Erwin Chemerinsky, in his defense of what he terms empowerment federalism, notes that "national action may be desirable to prevent spillovers and externalities." He offers the classic example of pollution originating in one state but ending up in another. He also suggests that lax state regulation resulting in a "race to the bottom" is a reason for national action, as in the case of one state gaining a competitive advantage by allowing child labor.[38] Policy externalities, however, can also occur in the opposite direction and toward stricter regulation. In what David Vogel described as the California Effect, states adopting strict regulations, especially those representing large consumer markets, can effectively project their regulatory standards nationwide. Because of the impracticality of differentiating products and practices to comply with the stricter regulatory schemes in these jurisdictions, companies are likely to adjust all of their products and practices to accede to the strictest state's regulations.[39]

Although any form of policymaking can conceivably contribute to the California Effect, it is particularly an issue with multistate litigation. It may be easier for a state legislature or administrative agency to "implement [a] rule within their boundaries,"[40] but multistate litigation implements rules that apply nationally—whether or not all of the affected states agree. The problem becomes even clearer when recalling that state law, particularly state consumer law, is the basis for a number of multistate lawsuits. Because the states so often work together to investigate and use threats of litigation to achieve multistate settlements with corporations, it is the broadest and vaguest state statutes that tend to have the most influence in negotiations since any settlement needs to satisfy the requirements of those laws. Although regulatory provisions in multistate settlements technically apply only to corporate practices in the jurisdictions that are signatories to the agreement, it is impractical if not impossible to differentiate company products and practices across the country. The result is that the laws of the strictest jurisdictions are effectively nationalized, trumping those in less strict jurisdictions. In other words, it shifts the regulatory floor upward. As Samuel Issacharoff and Catherine Sharkey have described it in a different but related context, this "backdoor federalization" results in "one state encroach[ing] upon the decisional autonomy of another."[41] Federal preemption may shut off state experiments by producing a single regulatory standard applying nationally, but multistate litigation often has the same effect.

The Buck Stops Where? The Problem of Democratic Accountability

These regulatory spillovers raise another important concern about contemporary AG litigation: it muddies the waters of democratic accountability. Although most AGs are elected officials, each is accountable only to his or her own state electorate. If voters do not like the regulatory experiment pursued by their state legislature, then they have some recourse at the voting booth. If voters do not like the regulatory results of an AG-led settlement, on the other hand, there is no similar recourse at the polls. Residents of Kansas, for example, have no opportunity to vote for or against the AG of New York, regardless of the national policy effects of a settlement reached by that official.

The accountability problem also becomes apparent when AGs' policy choices conflict with those of other state-level elected officials. When Alexander Hamilton argued against a plural executive in *Federalist* No. 70, he noted that their existence "tends to conceal faults and destroy responsibility." Multiple actors are able to engage in credit claiming and blame avoidance for any given policy in such a way that "public opinion is left in suspense about the real author."[42] As AGs become more aggressive in using litigation to achieve policy goals in the name of the state, it has become more difficult for voters to know who to hold responsible for these policy decisions. This is particularly true when multiple actors simultaneously claim the right to represent the legal interests of the state, as occurred when governors and AGs in several states took different positions on the legal challenges to the ACA. This problem would be less problematic with a clear separation of executive duties between the governor and AG. However, as AGs go beyond their traditional law enforcement role and instead use their position to make policy, the divide between gubernatorial and AG responsibilities has increasingly blurred.

Finally, and perhaps most fundamentally, the rise of coordinated AG litigation as a form of policymaking reinforces a trend of contemporary governance oriented around policies that are both invisible to and insulated from the public. America's "submerged state," as Suzanne Mettler characterizes it, consists of various government programs serving to obscure US governance from public view.[43] Mettler's analysis focuses on various social welfare programs that operate by granting incentives and transferring money through the tax code, but the notion of the submerged state captures much of contemporary regulatory governance in America. Whether through litigation or the tax code, more of American governance occurs through avenues that are mostly imperceptible to the American public and are difficult to displace. These avenues, by becoming more separated from traditional avenues of policymaking, make it more difficult for the public to identify what government policy actually is, never mind understand which actors are responsible for it.

Earlier in the chapter, I noted that political conservatives have particular reason to be concerned about modern state litigation because of the way it operates as a regulatory ratchet. At the same time, the accountability issue raises concerns for political liberals. Progressive advocates of good governance often quote Louis Brandeis's line that "sunshine is the best disinfectant," arguing that transparency is the best way to ensure that government is working for the public interest rather than for the elites' interests.[44] By placing public policymaking behind closed doors and in highly technical legal forums, the AGs' litigation has done precisely the opposite. It raises the prospect that policymaking will reflect the private interests of the parties involved rather than the broader public interest. When several prominent liberals criticized the AGs' $26 billion foreclosure settlement with national banks in 2012 as "letting the corporations off the hook," for example, it reflected the concern that the public interest is perhaps not best served in the settlement negotiating room.[45]

To a great degree, the accountability problem is inherent in the growth of cooperative federalism and adversarial legalism that has helped encourage modern AG litigation. Although this polyphonic system exhibits innovation and serves as a way of overcoming roadblocks in the typical policymaking process, it also blurs lines of policymaking authority to such a degree that it further submerges the American state from public view.

The Continuing Incentives for Multistate AG Activism

If contemporary AG activism is so problematic, why does it continue? One possibility, of course, is that while I have highlighted the downsides of coordinated AG activism, the benefits may well outweigh the negatives. Coordinated AG activism is, after all, a way to achieve policy development in an era of intensifying polarization and seemingly endless gridlock in national political institutions. Despite a rise in polarization among the AGs, they still often work together to efficiently address problems affecting multiple states. By focusing on the problematic features of modern AG litigation in this chapter, I do not deny the possibility that a full accounting of this litigation's benefits would make clear that this development is a net positive in contemporary American policymaking.

Nevertheless, I would suggest that the prospects of a continuation of AGs' contemporary nationalized activism have little to do with whether it is an ultimately positive or negative development in American politics. Instead, I would argue that this form of coordinated policymaking through litigation is likely to continue because at least four sets of key actors have an incentive for it to do so: the AGs themselves, their industry targets, private litigators including advocacy groups and class-action attorneys, and federal policymakers.

AG Incentives

The most obvious beneficiaries of the AGs' rise to national prominence have been the AGs themselves. Coordinated litigation allows AGs to pool their resources and put them in better position to litigate against large, multinational firms. In several settlements, AGs have augmented their own power by granting themselves additional regulatory oversight of targeted industries. Additionally, portions of the monetary recoveries in many settlements help to fund future litigation efforts and reduce the costs of litigation for the AGs.[46]

The freedom that the AGs possess in choosing how to direct their litigation efforts also provides excellent opportunities for political entrepreneurship, as multistate litigation is a good way to raise one's profile for future political campaigns. Policy-forcing and policy-blocking litigation challenging federal agencies under the ostensible control of one's political opponents serves as a fine way to signal one's partisan bona fides to primary election voters. Running on a record of being tough on corporate fraud is likely to be a political positive among most voters in a general election. It is no surprise that coordinated press releases among the AGs involved typically accompany the resolution of policy-creating litigation because participating in settlements with so-called corporate wrongdoers is an excellent opportunity for credit claiming.

Further, as noted in chapter 2, AGs have a strong incentive to join policy-creating litigation even if they disagree with this approach to regulate industry. If an AG refuses to participate in a settlement because of its regulatory effect on the private sector, as former Alabama AG William Pryor initially did in the case of the tobacco Master Settlement Agreement in the 1990s, it is unlikely to scuttle settlements with other states. Instead, all that occurs is that the dissenting AGs' state is left out of the settlement proceeds while the regulatory provisions of the settlement nevertheless go into effect. This dynamic helps explain why participation in policy-creating litigation tends to be bipartisan, despite settlements serving as a regulatory ratchet inevitably working in the direction of strengthening government intervention in the private sector.

Finally, the very success of previous multistate litigation campaigns itself provides an incentive for future lawsuits. As public policy and organizational scholars have noted for some time, organizations learn from experience.[47] Positive feedback reinforces later activity, creating public policy cascades in which "each change begets another even larger change."[48] Major litigation successes, especially the tobacco litigation that concluded in 1998, helped generate a cascade in which each successful settlement provided momentum for further settlements. This is especially true when previous litigation generates information the AGs can use to assist in future litigation campaigns. Even previous collaborations that do not lead to direct success in the courts—the acid rain litigation in the 1980s, for example—can serve as blueprints for future collaboration.

Industry Incentives

In the early days of multistate litigation, an attorney for Mobil Chemical predicted that while "most companies settle and go about their business. . . . Eventually there will be a revolt. Some companies will say they've had enough, and someone will make a vigorous defense."[49] In large part, however, this prediction has not been borne out. This is because most companies have several incentives to reach multistate agreements quickly.

One of the largest enemies of corporate practice is uncertainty. Multistate settlements allow companies, particularly publically traded companies, a way to manage this uncertainty. By placing a set value on payments in a settlement, the companies save on potential litigation expenses and eliminate the possibility of even greater losses in court. The risks of proceeding to trial often outweigh the benefits of settling, especially when, as in the pharmaceutical context, losing in court can result in exclusion from a major market of consumers. Further, for other companies in the process of business reorganizations or acquisitions, settling AG litigation allows them to make their future obligations concrete and allows them to move on with mergers and other business ventures.

Multistate settlements also serve as a way for businesses to manage public relations. Rather than fighting law enforcement efforts and risking an image as an incorrigible lawbreaker, settling a case can help a corporation avoid unwanted bad publicity. Most multistate settlements contain provisions denying any legal violations on the part of the defendant, which can serve as an additional protection against negative publicity. Targeted companies also drive larger multistate settlements by pushing for more inclusive agreements. The more AGs that sign on to a settlement, the more protection the company has from future liability.[50] This dynamic is similar to that involved in private class-action litigation, in which targeted corporations seek to consolidate similar claims.[51]

Finally, targeted industries face collective action problems in fighting policy-creating litigation. Unlike with AGs, who have incentives to collaborate as a way to gain leverage over corporate defendants, coordination among individual corporations is more problematic given that they are marketplace competitors with one another. Corporation A has little incentive to spend resources to fight lawsuits against its competitor, Corporation B. This remains true even as successful settlements with Corporation A generate positive feedback effects making subsequent litigation against Corporation B more likely. Because most of the AGs' litigation campaigns strategically target individual market leaders as part of a settlement-by-settlement approach to regulating entire industries, coordination and cooperation among industry defendants remains more difficult to achieve than coordination among their AG plaintiff adversaries.

Private Litigator Incentives

For advocacy groups and class-action attorneys frustrated in other political forums, AGs serve as valuable allies in achieving their policy goals. This is in part because AGs can use their institutional position as legal representatives of the states to raise the profile of legal arguments. The very act of litigating a claim, as Scott Barclay and Shauna Fisher note in the context of same-sex marriage lawsuits, can help transform the underlying goals "from the ridiculous to the possible."[52] Involvement of the states' chief law enforcers in these litigation efforts can provide a boost to the legitimacy of the underlying legal arguments, moving formally off-the-wall ideas onto the wall.[53] Not only do AGs have access to additional avenues of press influence, but also their involvement adds constitutional principle to arguments that otherwise might be dismissed as merely political. The suggestion that the ACA violated fundamental tenets of federalism became more plausible when the arguments moved from the far reaches of the conservative legal movement to AGs representing half of the states. On the opposite side of the political spectrum, Eliot Spitzer and other Democratic AGs' claims of states' rights helped overlay the constitutional principle of federalism over arguments made by liberal advocacy groups such as the Sierra Club and the Natural Resources Defense Council.

Related to the notion that AGs help provide a veneer of fundamental principle to otherwise ideological litigation, AGs' role as prosecutors enables them to create what Eugene Lewis terms an "apolitical shield" around activities that are actually very much political.[54] Unlike advocacy groups whose purposes are explicitly tied to ideological goals, AGs have the advantage of claiming that they work for the public interest by neutrally prosecuting illegal activity. By characterizing long-standing practices in the pharmaceutical industry as fraud, for example, AGs were able to achieve long-sought regulations of the prescription drug industry while seemingly taking politics out of the process altogether. In many ways, AGs have been prime beneficiaries of the turn in American policymaking toward "governing through crime."[55] In an era in which "popular entertainment celebrates such enforcers of criminal law,"[56] prosecutors are in a stronger position to gain public sympathies than are many other litigators—an advantage that interest groups can exploit by allying with AGs.

AGs serve as an invaluable ally to interest groups and private parties in another way as well. In recent years, private groups seeking to use the courts to pursue either monetary or policy goals have run into a variety of roadblocks. Efforts to reduce private litigation have taken various forms, from the Reagan administration's strategies to "defund the Left" by reducing federal resources available for liberal public interest groups to more recent tort reform proposals limiting damage awards in civil cases.[57] Recently, several of these efforts have been successful. The most significant federal effort, the Class Action Fairness Act of 2005 (CAFA), made several changes to civil procedure making private class-action litigation more difficult.[58] The federal courts have also presented significant roadblocks to private litigation. A pair of Supreme Court cases both decided in 2011, *Wal-Mart v. Dukes* and *AT&T Mobility v. Concepcion,* made maintaining class-action lawsuits more difficult by complicating certification of class actions and by preempting state laws enabling private litigation.[59] These efforts mirror other recent attempts of the federal courts to limit private litigation through restrictive interpretation of standing requirements and the wording of federal statutes.[60]

Even as Congress and the courts made it more difficult for interest groups and private class-action attorneys to get into court, however, both institutions were making it easier for AGs to bring lawsuits. As chapter 2 described, Congress has continued to expand AGs' enforcement jurisdiction in new and increasingly wider areas of national policy. Additionally, even those legislative efforts that aimed at reducing litigation have served to empower AGs. The same CAFA that sought to reduce private class actions contained provisions allowing state litigators access to information that they could use to launch independent investigations into allegedly harmful corporate conduct.[61] The same Supreme Court that had previously made it more difficult for groups to challenge federal agency regulations granted AGs "special solicitude" to bring challenges to such regulations and have been skeptical of federal attempts to preempt state prosecutorial efforts.[62]

As Congress and the courts made private litigation more difficult while clearing the path for AGs to bring additional cases, many interest groups and private class-action attorneys have latched on to AGs to help them get into court. Private class-action attorneys would have had difficulty gaining standing in court to demand future changes in pharmaceutical advertising, but AGs were able to by virtue of representing states allegedly harmed by corporate conduct. The Sierra Club would have had a difficult time convincing the court that the EPA's failure to regulate CO_2 harmed them directly, but the AGs entered the courthouse doors by virtue of ostensibly representing a state rather than a private group. That AGs are able to use law enforcement as a way to achieve political change through court decisions and multistate settlements provides a key tactical advantage that has not gone unnoticed by private litigators.

Federal Policymaker Incentives

Federal policymakers' support for expansions of AG capacity, as noted earlier, has in essence authorized and subsidized challenges to their own authority. So why do they continue to do it? For one, bolstering AGs' capacity has been a way for federal policymakers to supplement federal enforcement authority at relatively little cost to the federal government. In this sense, AG litigation reflects the broader contemporary dynamic of Congress harnessing nontraditional avenues for building bureaucratic power. Sean Farhang's analysis of the "litigation state," which has involved Congress encouraging private lawsuits as a crucial part of building national administrative capacity, is a prime example.[63] Particularly during an era in which Congress is ostensibly concerned about the federal debt, farming out enforcement powers to AGs may seem a particularly good deal. If AGs take on more enforcement authority, it can free budget hawks in Congress to advocate for cost savings in federal agency budgets. As AGs bring in money from settlements—some of which, at least in Medicaid fraud cases, flows to the federal government—granting AGs additional enforcement powers may bring in more revenue than the costs involved.

Just as importantly, the same mechanism that provides benefits to federal policymakers when it operates in its intended cooperative way also provides opportunities for challenges to federal policy. As Kenneth Shepsle famously noted, Congress is a "they," not an "it."[64] Many congressional enactments, and certainly many compromises, face significant levels of opposition. Multistate litigation may serve to unravel previous congressional deals, but at least some members of Congress are likely to cheer on this litigation even if it contradicts what Congress as a whole has done. Further, federal agencies may even encourage AGs lawsuits against themselves in order to provide political cover for regulatory expansion. As the AGs' air pollution litigation illustrated, the EPA welcomed such lawsuits during Democratic presidential administrations in order to place the agency under a legal obligation to expand regulation. AGs' litigation was something of an insurance policy to ensure, as former EPA administrator Carol Browner put it, "that the things I cared about would continue even if there was a Republican administration."[65]

Much of modern policymaking in the contemporary polarized climate is about preserving and creating pathways for policy influence. This is, for example, a major reason why the Senate filibuster has persisted despite frequent calls for its elimination. In a closely contested political environment in which party control of national institutions remains fluid, partisans have an incentive to preserve avenues granting the minority party significant policy influence. This is true even if, as in the case of the filibuster, these avenues serve to frustrate policymaking when those partisans constitute the majority. By maintaining AG litigation's influence in national policy, partisans in national political institutions preserve an important avenue for policy influence even in the wake of electoral losses in traditional venues for national policymaking.

As Woodrow Wilson suggested, the "cardinal question" of federalism "is a question of growth and every successive stage of our political and economic development gives it a new aspect, makes it a new question." The AGs' modern role in national policymaking reflects this mercurial nature of American federalism. It also serves as a reminder not to lose sight of the many paths of American political development in the United States. Important policy change in America does not only occur in short bursts of lawmaking or through landmark constitutional decisions of the United States Supreme Court. The process of statutory interpretation and enforcement, seemingly prosaic shifts in procedural rules, and the actions of political actors and institutions outside of Washington, DC, can all lead to significant national policy developments. Contemporary AG litigation provides another indication of how America's separation of powers regime, while perhaps making certain large-scale policy changes more difficult, also creates additional opportunities for national policymaking and state development. At the same time that these opportunities seek to solve certain perceived dysfunctions in national policymaking, however, they also raise new problems and challenges for democratic governance.

Understanding the contours of the AGs' role in national policymaking and the implications it has for contemporary American politics has become increasingly important as AGs' interventions in national policy, once rare, have become politics as usual. For better or worse, this is likely to remain true into the future given the various incentives existing for various actors to maintain the AGs' new national policymaking role. Eliot Spitzer, the activist New York attorney general who best exemplified the rise of the AGs at the start of the twenty-first century, perhaps put it best: "We're not going anywhere, we're going to hang around—so get used to it."[66]

APPENDIX

Data Collection for the Multistate Litigation Data Set (Chapter 2)

Data Sources

Given that much of the multistate litigation discussed in chapter 2 was resolved in out-of-court settlements rather than in reported court decisions, obtaining information on these cases required searching several sources. The main resource used for compiling this data set was the Lexis-Nexis "United States News Verdicts, Settlements & Decisions" database. This database contains news reports concerning decisions and out-of-court settlements from a large number of US newspapers, magazines, and wire services. My search of this database began by first adding "attorneys general" as an index term. I then used the following search string in all my searches of each year from 1980 to 2013: [(attorney! pre/2 general!) and (litigation or "settlement & compromise" or "suits & claims" or verdicts or "decisions & rulings" or "consent decrees & orders" or investigations)]. I proceeded to examine the search results for all sources relevant to AG settlements, judgments, and other litigation.

The resolution of AG litigation during this period typically had multiple news reports associated with each case, so I was able to find most multistate settlements and judgments using this Lexis-Nexis search. However, I supplemented this resource with a search of a number of publications issued by the National Association of Attorneys General, including *AG Bulletin, Consumer Protection Report, Antitrust Report, Telemarketing Fraud Bulletin, Medicaid Fraud Report,* and the *NAAG National Environmental Enforcement Journal.* In addition to these sources, NAAG's compilation of antitrust litigation (http://app3.naag.org/antitrust/search/) proved to be an invaluable source for identifying multistate antitrust litigation. The Environmental Protection Agency's collection of consent decrees (list of civil cases and settlements; http://cfpub.epa.gov/compliance/cases/) also provided information concerning a handful of multistate environmental settlements with private industry.

The news reports and settlement documents obtained from the above sources typically noted the participating and lead states involved in the litigation. When this information was unavailable from these sources, I conducted more targeted searches of each case. Individual AG websites proved to be the most helpful resource to find this missing information because AGs frequently identify the participating and/or lead states in press releases associated with the resolution of lawsuits or investigations.

Data Set Inclusions and Exclusions

The multistate litigation data set covered the period from 1980 to 2013. A few isolated examples of coordinated multistate litigation occurred before 1980, but I chose this period to cover all, or nearly all, of the modern period of multistate AG litigation. To be included in the data set, the case had to meet the following four criteria. The case had to:

- Involve "litigation," broadly defined as including both filed lawsuits or prelitigation investigations.
- Involve coordinated activities by at least two AGs.
- Share the same defendants and at least one common issue of fact.
- Conclude in a judicial decision, an out-of-court settlement, or another similar agreement.

Because of these inclusion criteria, two difficult-to-identify forms of multistate litigation are not included in this data set. First, the data set excludes investigations or lawsuits not definitively resolved, even if initial cross-state collaboration was involved. Multistate investigations ultimately ending in no finding of wrongdoing or that the AGs otherwise voluntarily ended without further action are not included. The main reason for excluding these actions is that these early-stage investigations are particularly difficult to discover. The details of most multistate investigations reside outside the public eye until the AGs file a suit, achieve a settlement, or otherwise reach a point in the investigation where some final action is likely. Further, many unresolved cases are technically still open, as AGs could potentially continue a voluntarily terminated investigation in the future.

Second, this data set does not include cases in which multiple AGs file similar suits but that involve separate investigations and resolutions rather than coordinated activity. These suits may include some level of coordination among the AGs, but they are closer to single-state cases rather than the coordinated litigation efforts that are this book's focus. In 2007, for example, a number of AGs expressed concern about the marketing of an energy drink named Cocaine, claiming that the producer was illegally marketing the drink as a street drug alternative and a dietary supplement. Ultimately, AGs from Connecticut, Illinois, and Texas reached settlements or court judgments prohibiting Cocaine from being marketed in those states, though each AG reached the settlements separately.[1] These actions likely involved some level of multistate collaboration during the course of the investigations, but the level of public coordination between AGs did not reach the level necessary to label these actions definitively multistate for the purposes of the statistics reported in chapter 2.

Further, the data set focused on multistate litigation efforts within the four broad policy areas in which nearly all AG multistate litigation occurs: consumer protection, antitrust, environmental, and health care litigation. I omitted a fifth potential policy area in which AGs have been active in multistate litigation, securities litigation, because only five AGs have full jurisdiction over their state's securities laws. In most states, the state insurance commissioner or the secretary of state handles multistate securities litigation.[2] Further, much of the securities litigation that became especially prominent during the George W. Bush era involved only a single AG—New York's—as a result of the concentrated presence of the financial industry in the Empire State.

It should be stressed that excluding these types of cases understates the broader contemporary influence of AGs in matters of public policy and regulation. My focus in the data set and in the book more broadly is on multistate activity, but single-state litigation can have national consequences as well. Perhaps the most prominent example is New York AG Eliot Spitzer's litigation against several large insurance and securities firms in the early 2000s, which had significant effects throughout the entire American financial sector as a result of the terms of the settlements negotiated between Spitzer and the firms involved.[3] Another example was California AG Bill Lockyer's single-state settlement with Pepsi in 2006 regarding Mexican-made soda bottle labels allegedly containing an unsafe quantity of lead. Following the settlement, the company agreed to shift to lead-free labels in California, but as a result of California's large consumer market and the impracticality of differentiating product labels in and outside of the state, this change affected Pepsi's product lines nationwide.[4] Occasionally, single-state lawsuits by states smaller than California and New York can have a nationwide impact as well, particularly if the suits target in-state businesses operating nationally.[5]

Additionally, this data set does not include coordinated AG activities apart from litigation, such as sign-on letters to congressional committees and coordinated testimony before administrative agencies. These other forms of coordinated AG activism can have an influence on national public policy outcomes as well, but they are not examined in this book.

Data for the Supreme Court Amicus Curiae Brief Data Set (Chapter 9)

Data Sources

I derived the data on multistate amicus curiae brief filings in the US Supreme Court chiefly from a search of the "US Supreme Court Briefs" database available through Lexis-Nexis. I used the following search string for each year of the study in order to identify briefs filed by AGs: COUNSEL ((attorney! w/2 general!) or (state! w/2 attorney!) or "Atty. Gen." or "Attorney Gen." or "Atty. General" or "solicitor general") or (amici pre/1 plural(states)). Because the Lexis-Nexis database includes only a limited number of briefs concerning petitions for certiorari in cases that the Court ultimately declines to review, I supplemented this search with a list of such cases provided by the Supreme Court Counsel for the National Association of Attorneys General, Dan Schweitzer.

Data Set Inclusions and Exclusions

The data include AG participation during both the pre-certiorari and merits stages of each case from 1980 through 2013. The more limited inclusion of pre-certiorari briefs in both the Lexis-Nexis database and NAAG compilation from 1980 to 1992 means that it is likely some of these briefs for this period are missing from this data set. However, because of the low level of partisan conflict apparent in merits cases during these years, it is unlikely that inclusion of any missing pre-certiorari briefs from this period would alter the trends identified in figure 9.1 in any significant way.

I constructed and organized this data set by case, as opposed to individual brief filings. Figure 9.1 therefore reflects the number of cases involving partisan activity, rather than the sheer number of partisan briefs filed. Therefore, when in a single case states first filed a brief at the certiorari stage and again during the merits stage, these briefs were counted only once. Additionally, I treated two other sets of cases as only one for the purposes of this analysis: cases in which states filed separate sets of briefs but on the same side of the case, and cases involving the same legal question that were later consolidated into a single case by the Court.

NOTES

CHAPTER 1. STATE LITIGATION AND THE STRUCTURE OF CONTEMPORARY AMERICAN POLICY

1. Martha Derthick, *Up in Smoke: From Legislation to Litigation in Tobacco Politics* (Washington, DC: CQ Press, 2005); Michael S. Greve, "Compacts, Cartels, and Congressional Consent," *Missouri Law Review* 68, no. 2 (Spring 2003): 285–388.

2. Nelson D. Schwartz and Shaila Dewan, "$26 Billion Deal Is Said to be Set for Homeowners," *New York Times*, February 9, 2012.

3. Woodrow Wilson, *Constitutional Government in the United States* (New York: Columbia University Press, 1911), 173.

4. E. E. Schattschneider, *Politics, Pressures, and the Tariff* (New York: Prentice-Hall, 1935), 288.

5. Paul Pierson, "The Study of Policy Development," *Journal of Policy History* 17, no. 1 (2005): 34–51.

6. Theda Skocpol, *Protecting Soldiers and Mothers: The Political Origins of Social Policy in the United States* (Cambridge, MA: Harvard University Press, 1992), 59.

7. Jacob S. Hacker, *The Divided Welfare State: The Battle over Public and Private Social Benefits in the United States* (Cambridge: Cambridge University Press, 2002).

8. Paul Pierson, *Politics in Time: History, Institutions, and Social Analysis* (Princeton, NJ: Princeton University Press, 2004), 5.

9. Robert A. Kagan, *Adversarial Legalism: The American Way of Law* (Cambridge, MA: Harvard University Press, 2001).

10. See, for example, Elisabeth S. Clemens and James M. Cook, "Politics and Institutionalism: Explaining Durability and Change," *Annual Review of Sociology* 25 (1999): 460: "In the United States, the combination of federalism and the division of authority among the branches of the federal government presents obstacles to the establishment of new national policies and fragments constituencies."

11. R. Kent Weaver and Bert A. Rockman, "Assessing the Effects of Institutions," in *Do Institutions Matter? Government Capabilities in the United States and Abroad*, ed. R. Kent Weaver and Bert A. Rockman (Washington, DC: Brookings Institution Press, 1993), 26.

12. Barbara Sinclair, *Unorthodox Lawmaking: New Legislative Processes in the US Congress*, 4th ed. (Washington, DC: CQ Press, 2012).

13. Gordon Silverstein, *Law's Allure: How Law Shapes, Constrains, Saves, and Kills Politics* (New York: Cambridge University Press, 2009); Steven M. Teles, *The Rise of the Conservative Legal Movement* (Princeton, NJ: Princeton University Press, 2008).

14. Alexis de Tocqueville, *Democracy in America*, trans. Harvey C. Mansfield and Delba Winthrop (Chicago: University of Chicago Press, 2000), 257.

15. Seymour Martin Lipset, *American Exceptionalism: A Double-Edged Sword* (New York: Norton, 1996), 270.

16. Kagan, *Adversarial Legalism.*

17. Silverstein, *Law's Allure.*

18. 347 US 483 (1954).

19. Sean Farhang, *The Litigation State: Public Regulation and Private Lawsuits in the US* (Princeton, NJ: Princeton University Press, 2010).

20. Kagan, *Adversarial Legalism.*

21. Lawrence M. Friedman, *Total Justice* (New York: Russell Sage Foundation, 1985).

22. Jeffrey M. Berry, *The New Liberalism: The Rising Power of Citizen Groups* (Washington, DC: Brookings Institution Press, 1999).

23. Farhang, *Litigation State.*

24. Arnold W. Reitze Jr., *Air Pollution Control Law: Compliance and Enforcement* (Washington, DC: Environmental Law Institute, 2001), 599–600.

25. See, for example, Peter H. Schuck, *Agent Orange on Trial* (Cambridge, MA: Harvard University Press, 1987); Jeb Barnes, *Dust Up: Asbestos Litigation and the Failure of Commonsense Policy Reform* (Washington, DC: Georgetown University Press, 2011).

26. Thomas Burke, *Lawyers, Lawsuits, and Legal Rights* (Berkeley: University of California Press, 2003), 171.

27. See, for example, Class Action Fairness Act of 2005, Pub. L. No. 109-2, 119 Stat. 4 (codified at 28 USC §§1332(d), 1453, 1711–15 (2006)); AT&T Mobility v. Concepcion, 131 S. Ct. 1740 (2011); Ledbetter v. Goodyear Tire & Rubber, 550 US 618 (2007); CompuCredit Corp. v. Greenwood, 132 S. Ct. 665 (2012).

28. Dodd-Frank Wall Street Reform and Consumer Protection Act, Pub. L. No. 111-203, 124 Stat. 1376 (2010).

29. Two recent examples from the US Supreme Court are Massachusetts v. EPA, 549 US 497 (2007), and Cuomo v. Clearing House Association, 557 US 519 (2009).

30. Gerald Rosenberg, *The Hollow Hope: Can Courts Bring About Social Change?*, 2nd ed. (Chicago: University of Chicago Press, 2008).

31. Robert H. Mnookin and Lewis Kornhauser, "Bargaining in the Shadow of the Law: The Case of Divorce," *Yale Law Journal* 88, no. 5 (1979): 950–997.

32. Charles Epp, *Making Rights Real: Activists, Bureaucrats, and the Creation of the Legalistic State* (Chicago: University of Chicago Press, 2010).

33. Daniel J. Elazar, *American Federalism: A View From the States,* 3rd ed. (New York: Harper & Row, 1984), 2.

34. Morton Grodzins, "The Federal System," in US President's Commission on National Goals, *Goals for Americans, The Report of the President's Commission on National Goals* (New York: Columbia University Press, 1960), 265.

35. Philip Kurland, *Politics, the Constitution, and the Warren Court* (Chicago: University of Chicago Press, 1970), 96.

36. John Kincaid, "From Cooperative to Coercive Federalism," *Annals of the American Academy of Political and Social Science* 509 (1990): 139–152.

37. New York v. United States, 505 US 144 (1992); Printz v. United States, 521 US 898 (1997).

38. Samuel H. Beer, "The Adoption of General Revenue Sharing: A Case Study in Public Sector Politics," *Public Policy* 24 (1976), 131.

39. James Madison, "Federalist #51," in *The Federalist Papers,* ed. Clinton Rossiter (New York: New American Library, 1961).

40. Alexander Hamilton, "Federalist #28," in *The Federalist Papers,* ed. Clinton Rossiter (New York: New American Library, 1961).

41. See, for example, Evelyne Huber and John D. Stephens, *Development and Crisis of the Welfare State: Parties and Policies in Global Markets* (Chicago: University of Chicago Press, 2001); David Brian Robertson, "The Bias of American Federalism: The Limits of Welfare-State Development in the Progressive Era," *Journal of Policy History* 1, no. 3 (1989): 261–291; Jacob S. Hacker and Paul Pierson, "Business Power and Social Policy: Employers and the Formation of the American Welfare State," *Politics and Society* 30, no. 2 (2002): 277–325.

42. William H. Riker, *Liberalism against Populism* (San Francisco: W. H. Freeman, 1982); Barry R. Weingast, "The Economic Role of Political Institutions: Market-Preserving Federalism and Economic Development," *Journal of Law, Economics, and Organization* 11, no. 1 (1995): 1–31; Michael S. Greve, *The Upside-Down Constitution* (Cambridge, MA: Harvard University Press, 2012).

43. Timothy Conlan, *From New Federalism to Devolution: Twenty-Five Years of Intergovernmental Reform* (Washington, DC: Brookings Institution Press, 1998), 8.

44. Ibid., 297; Printz v. United States, 521 US 898 (1997).

45. Theda Skocpol and Vanessa Williamson, *The Tea Party and the Remaking of Republican Conservatism* (New York: Oxford University Press, 2011).

46. Stephen Gardbaum, "New Deal Constitutionalism and the Unshackling of the States," *University of Chicago Law Review* 64, no. 2 (1997): 483–566.

47. Ibid., 486.

48. Robert A. Schapiro, "From Dualism to Polyphony," in *Preemption Choice: The Theory, Law, and Reality of Federalism's Core Question,* ed. William W. Buzbee (New York: Cambridge University Press, 2009), 42.

49. Robert A. Schapiro, *Polyphonic Federalism: Toward the Protection of Fundamental Rights* (Chicago: University of Chicago Press, 2009), 97–104.

50. New State Ice Co. v. Liebmann, 285 US 262, 311 (1932) (J. Brandeis, dissenting).

51. Renee M. Jones, "Dynamic Federalism: Competition, Cooperation, and Securities Enforcement," *Connecticut Insurance Law Journal* 11, no. 1 (2005): 107–131.

52. Erwin Chemerinsky, "Empowering States: The Need to Limit Federal Preemption," *Pepperdine Law Review* 33, no. 1 (2005): 69–75.

53. Robert B. Ahdieh, "From Federalism to Intersystemic Governance: The Changing Nature of Modern Jurisdiction," *Emory Law Journal* 57, no. 1 (2007): 11–12.

54. Ann E. Carlson, "Iterative Federalism and Climate Change," *Northwestern University Law Review* 103, no. 3 (2009): 1097–1162.

55. David E. Adelman and Kirsten H. Engel, "Adaptive Federalism: The Case against Reallocating Environmental Regulatory Authority," *Minnesota Law Review* 92, no. 6 (2007): 1796–1850.

CHAPTER 2. THE EMERGENCE OF MODERN STATE LITIGATION

1. Celia Cohen, "Bill Clinton's 'State of the World' Address," *WBOC News (Delaware)*, November 12, 2009, http://www.wboc.com.

2. Kim Hart, "Facebook Executive Leverages Friends in Attorney General Bid," *The Hill*, November 5, 2009, http://thehill.com.

3. Arlen C. Christensen, "The State Attorney General," *Wisconsin Law Review* 1970 (1970): 298, 300.

4. Emily Myers and Lynne Ross, *State Attorneys General: Powers and Responsibilities*, 2nd ed. (Washington, DC: National Association of Attorneys General, 2007), 12–14.

5. Paul Nolette, "Litigating the 'Public Interest' in the Gilded Age: Common Law Business Regulation by Nineteenth-Century State Attorneys General," *Polity* 44, no. 3 (2012): 373–399.

6. Steven Andersen, "Power of the State: The Rise of State Attorneys General," *Corporate Legal Times*, August 2003, 38.

7. William J. Baxley, "The State's Attorney," *Alabama Law Review* 25 (1972): 19.

8. Lynn Mather, "The Politics of Litigation by State Attorneys General: Introduction to Mini-Symposium," *Law and Policy* 25, no. 4 (2003): 425; Stefanie A. Lindquist and Pamela C. Corley, "National Policy Preferences and Judicial Review of State Statutes at the United States Supreme Court," *Publius: The Journal of Federalism* 43, no. 2 (2013): 151–178.

9. Eric N. Waltenburg and Bill Swinford, "The Supreme Court as a Policy Arena: The Strategies and Tactics of State Attorneys General," *Policy Studies Journal* 27, no. 2 (1999): 242–259.

10. Sean Nicholson-Crotty, "State Merit Amicus Participation and Federalism Outcomes in the US Supreme Court," *Publius: The Journal of Federalism* 37, no. 4 (2007): 599–612; Eric N. Waltenburg and Bill Swinford, *Litigating Federalism: The States Before the Supreme Court* (Westport, CT: Greenwood Press, 1999); Lindquist and Corley, "National Policy Preferences."

11. For example, NAAG frequently adopts policy resolutions and sends sign-on letters to Congress and federal agencies. NAAG archives these materials on its website (http://www.naag.org).

12. The Appendix provides further information about the data collection methods used for this chapter.

13. W. Kip Viscusi, ed., *Regulation through Litigation* (Washington, DC: Brookings Institution Press, 2002); Andrew P. Morriss et al., *Regulation by Litigation* (New Haven, CT: Yale University Press, 2009).

14. Mnookin and Kornhauser, "Bargaining in the Shadow of the Law."

15. For an excellent analysis of the tobacco Master Settlement Agreement, see Derthick, *Up in Smoke*.

16. Greve, "Compacts, Cartels," esp. 346–364.

17. Colin Provost, "State Attorneys General, Entrepreneurship, and Consumer Protection in the New Federalism," *Publius: The Journal of Federalism* 33, no. 2 (2003): 37–53; Colin Provost, "The Politics of Consumer Protection: Explaining State Attorney General Participation in Multi-State Lawsuits," *Political Research Quarterly* 59, no. 4 (2006): 609–618.

18. See, for example, National Association of Attorneys General, "States Settle with Household Finance," *Consumer Protection Report*, November 2002, 1.

19. Nelson Schwartz and Shalila Dewan, "States Negotiate $26 Billion Agreement for Homeowners," *New York Times*, February 8, 2012.

20. New York v. Microsoft Corp., No. 1:98CV1233 (D.D.C. May 15, 1998).

21. See, for example, "Chubb Agrees to $17 Million Settlement, Ban on Contingent Commissions," *BestWire*, December 21, 2006, http://www.tmcnet.com.

22. The NAICS "is the standard used by federal statistical agencies in classifying business establishments for the purpose of collecting, analyzing, and publishing statistical data related to the US business economy." US Census Bureau, "Introduction," http://www.census.gov. The NAICS separates the American economy into several numerical categories, with two-digit codes describing the twenty broad industry sectors and longer codes providing differentiation within each of these sectors. For corporations listed under more than one code, I used the code most closely related to the substance of the litigation at issue.

23. Specifically, 587 of the multistate cases in the data set (85.6 percent) involved AGs from more than one census-defined region of the country.

24. The US Census Bureau produces reports classifying industries by concentration ratios, which specify the percentage of output generated by the largest companies within each industry. US Census Bureau, "Concentration Ratios," http://www.census.gov. According to the 2007 Economic Census, the top twenty companies accounted for 99 percent of total output in the tobacco industry and 71 percent in the pharmaceutical industry. The top-twenty concentration ratios were 96 percent, 86 percent, and 63 percent for the telecommunications, petroleum manufacturing, and health and personal care industries, respectively.

25. Michael S. Greve, "States' Rights on Steroids," *AEI Outlook Series*, September 2002, http://www.aei.org.

26. Patricia A. Conners, "Current Trends and Issues in State Antitrust Enforcement," *Loyola Consumer Law Review* 16 (2003): 57.

27. "Interview with Patricia Conners," *Antitrust Source*, May 2002, 5.

28. Oregon's AG, for example, was the fourteenth most active multistate participator during this period. Iowa placed nineteenth and Vermont twenty-third.

29. Colin Provost, "An Integrated Model of US State Attorney General Behavior in Multi-State Litigation," *State Politics and Policy Quarterly* 10, no. 1 (2010): 17.

30. For Pryor's criticism of what he viewed as his fellow AGs' harmful activism, see William Pryor, "Litigators' Smoke Screen," *Wall Street Journal*, April 7, 1997.

31. Clean Air Act, Pub. L. No. 91-604, 42 USC §7604(a)(1)–(2) (1970). Citizen suit provisions were also used in the Clean Water Act (33 USC §1365) and the Safe Drinking Water Act (42 USC §§300f(12), 300j-8).

32. Farhang, *Litigation State*.

33. See, for example, South Carolina v. Katzenbach, 383 US 301 (1966); Massachusetts v. Mellon, 262 US 447 (1923).

34. See, for example, South Carolina v. Katzenbach, 383 US 301 (1966).

35. Waltenburg and Swinford, "Supreme Court as a Policy Arena," 245.

36. Cornell W. Clayton and Jack McGuire, "State Litigation Strategies and Policymaking in the US Supreme Court," *Kansas Journal of Law and Public Policy* 11, no. 1 (2001): 18.

37. David Lauter, "States Strive to Win High Court Favor," *National Law Journal,* January 28, 1985, 22.

38. Clayton and McGuire, "State Litigation Strategies," 22–23.

39. Cornell Clayton, "Law, Politics, and the New Federalism: State Attorneys General as National Policymakers," *Review of Politics* 56, no. 3 (1994): 542.

40. Clayton and McGuire, "State Litigation Strategies," 23.

41. National Association of Attorneys General, "NAAG Standing Committees," http://www.naag.org.

42. An overview of some of these task forces is available on the American Bar Association's website (http://www.abanet.org).

43. Pryor, "Litigators' Smoke Screen."

44. See the website of the Democratic Attorneys General Association (http://www.democraticags.org).

45. DAGA, for example, holds policy conferences throughout the year. See DAGA, "Events," http://www.democraticags.org.

46. Derthick, *Up in Smoke,* 192–198.

47. Leah Godesky, "State Attorneys General and Contingency Fee Arrangements: An Affront to the Neutrality Doctrine?," *Columbia Journal of Law and Social Problems* 42, no. 4 (2009): 589.

48. Chris Rizo, "AGs Look to Outside Counsel Amid States' Budget Woes," *Legal Newsline,* August 6, 2009, http://legalnewsline.com; Nora Lockwood Tooher, "Plaintiffs' Lawyers Tackle Drug Price-Fixing Litigation for States," *Lawyers USA,* June 4, 2007, http://lawyersusaonline.com.

49. Kagan, *Adversarial Legalism.*

50. Ibid.

51. National Association of Attorneys General, *Selected Statistics on the Office of Attorney General* (Washington, DC: National Association of Attorneys General, 1978), 495.

52. "State Prosecutors Crack Down on Business," *Business Week,* May 15, 1978, 53.

53. Alan D. Maness, "State Antitrust Enforcement: Its Evolution and Future Direction," *Antitrust Bulletin* 27, no. 1 (1982): 831.

54. Myers and Ross, *State Attorneys General,* 323–325.

55. John Miles, "Current Trends in State Antitrust Enforcement," *Antitrust Law Journal* 47, no. 4 (1979): 1353.

56. Office of the Inspector General, "Medicaid Fraud Control Units, Fiscal Year 2013 Annual Report," http://oig.hhs.gov.

57. Myers and Ross, *State Attorneys General,* 146–147, 331–332; Joseph F. Zim-

merman, "Interstate Cooperation: The Roles of the State Attorneys General," *Publius: The Journal of Federalism* 28, no. 1 (1988): 77–78.

58. ABA Section of Antitrust Law, *State Antitrust Enforcement Handbook,* 2nd ed. (Chicago: ABA Publishing, 2008), 51.

59. Robert T. Stephan, "National Consumer Protection Enforcement," *Antitrust Law Journal* 58, no. 1 (1990): 250–251.

60. Margaret H. Lemos, "State Enforcement of Federal Law," *NYU Law Review* 86, no. 3 (2011): 710–711.

61. Cuomo v. Clearing House Association, 557 US 519 (2009).

62. Dwight Carswell, "CAFA and *Parens Patriae* Actions," *University of Chicago Law Review* 78, no. 1 (2011): 345–376; Mississippi v. AU Optronics Corp., 134 S. Ct. 736 (2014).

63. Massachusetts v. EPA, 549 US 497, 518 (2007).

64. Pub. L. No. 110-314, 122 Stat. 3016 (2008).

65. Pub. L. No. 111-203, 124 Stat. 1376-2223 (2010).

66. US Department of Justice, "Financial Fraud Enforcement Task Force," http://www.stopfraud.gov.

67. Richard P. Ieyoub and Theodore Eisenberg, "State Attorney General Actions, the Tobacco Litigation, and the Doctrine of Parens Patriae," *Tulane Law Review* 74, no. 5 (2000): 1859–1883.

68. Louisiana v. Texas, 176 US 1 (1900); Missouri v. Illinois, 202 US 598 (1906); Georgia v. Tennessee Copper, 206 US 230 (1907).

69. Pennsylvania v. New Jersey, 426 US 660 (1976).

70. Hearing Before the House Subcommittee on Monopolies and Commercial Law, "Antitrust Parens Patriae Amendments: Hearings on HR 12528 and HR 12921," 93rd Cong., 2nd Sess. (1974).

71. Hearing Before the House Committee on the Judiciary, "Antitrust Parens Patriae Act," 94th Cong., 1st Sess. (1975). At several points in the congressional testimony over the Hart–Scott–Rodino amendments, the proposed state powers were described as "class actions by the state" (for example, see "Antitrust Parens Patriae Amendments," 61).

72. Hearing Before the Senate Committee on the Judiciary, "Antitrust Improvements Act of 1976," 94th Cong., 2nd Sess. (1976), 6.

73. Ibid., 124.

74. In the legislative history of the thirty-two statutes containing provisions empowering states to enforce federal law, few contained comments critical of an expanded role for state enforcement. State empowerment provisions typically received either unanimous positive or neutral treatment or generated no commentary in the legislative history at all.

75. Alfred L. Snapp & Son, Inc. v. Puerto Rico, 458 US 592 (1982); Maryland v. Louisiana, 451 US 725 (1981).

76. Pennsylvania v. Mid-Atlantic Toyota Distributors, 704 F.2d 125, 134 (1983).

77. Donald G. Gifford, "Impersonating the Legislature: State Attorneys General and *Parens Patriae* Product Litigation," *Boston College Law Review* 49, no. 4 (2008): 913–969.

CHAPTER 3. LAWYERS, DRUGS, AND MONEY: LITIGATING PHARMACEUTICAL PRICING

1. Douglas Jehl, "Pharmacist Helps Clinton Sell His Health Plan," *New York Times,* February 25, 1994.

2. Bill Nichols, "Pitching Health-Care Pathos," *USA Today,* February 25, 1994.

3. Robert Pear, "Drug Company Ads Attack Medicare Coverage of Drugs," *New York Times,* July 29, 1999.

4. Dan Morgan, "Drugmakers Launch Campaign on Medicare; Industry Wary of Prescription Cost Controls," *Washington Post,* July 28, 1999.

5. Patricia M. Danzon and Michael F. Furukawa, "International Prices and Availability of Pharmaceuticals in 2005," *Health Affairs* 27, no. 1 (2008): 221–233.

6. Julie Rovner, "Prescription Drug Prices," *CQ Researcher,* July 17, 1992.

7. For example, see the Prescription Drug Cost Containment Act, S. 2000, 102nd Cong. (1991); Medication Price Control Act, HR 5358, 101st Cong. (1990).

8. Milt Freudenheim, "Drug Companies Feeling Pressure of Clinton's Plan to Keep Their Prices Down," *New York Times,* September 30, 1993.

9. Ibid.

10. See, for example, Prescription Drug Parity Act, S. 1191, 106th Cong. (1999).

11. Until 2003, Medicare provided only a limited number of prescription drugs, mainly for cancer treatments, in its Part B program. Medicaid has long covered a wider range of drugs.

12. Dawn M. Gencarelli, "Average Wholesale Price for Prescription Drugs: Is There a More Appropriate Pricing Mechanism?," *National Health Policy Forum,* Issue Brief 775, June 7, 2002, http://www.nhpf.org.

13. Robert Pear, "Bayer to Pay $14 Million to Settle Charges of Causing Inflated Medicaid Claims," *New York Times,* January 24, 2001.

14. James M. Spears and Jeff Pullman, "Using Litigation to Regulate Drug Prices: The Assault," *Medical Marketing and Media,* June 2002, 72.

15. Ibid., 73.

16. Paul E. Kalb, I. Scott Bass, and Robert Fabrikant, "The Average Wholesale Price: It Ain't What the Government Wants to Pay," *Health Care Fraud Report,* February 21, 2001, 182.

17. Gencarelli, "Average Wholesale Price."

18. Terry Carter, "Drug Wars," *ABA Journal,* December 2002, 44.

19. Balanced Budget Act of 1997, Pub. L. No. 105-33; 111 Stat. 251, 462-63; 42 USC §1395u(o)(1) (2000)).

20. Bill Alpert, "A Drug Bust in the Making?," *Barron's,* October 27, 1997, 14.

21. Julie Appleby, "Drug Pricing Probed," *USA Today,* April 6, 2000.

22. Ibid.

23. Medicare, Medicaid, and SCHIP Benefits Improvement and Protection Act of 2000, Pub. L. No. 106-554 (2000), §429.

24. Julie Appleby, "Drugmakers Accused of 'Unethical' Pricing," *USA Today,* September 27, 2000.

25. Joan H. Krause, "A Conceptual Model of Health Care Fraud Enforcement," *Journal of Law and Policy* 12, no. 1 (2003): 65.

26. Ibid., 67.

27. False Claims Act Amendments of 1986, Pub. L. No. 99-562 (1986), codified at 31 USC §§3729–3733; Jack A. Meyer and Stephanie E. Anthony, "Reducing Health Care Fraud," *Taxpayers Against Fraud,* September 2001, 17–20, 28–31 (on file with author).

28. Christopher D. Zalesky, "Pharmaceutical Marketing Practices: Balancing Public Health and Law Enforcement Interests," *Journal of Health Law* 39, no. 2 (2006): 235–264.

29. David S. Cloud and Laurie McGinley, "US, States, Bayer Start Settlement Talks," *Wall Street Journal,* May 10, 2000.

30. Corporate Integrity Agreement between the Office of Inspector General of the Department of Health and Human Services and Bayer Corporation, January 23, 2001, http://www.oig.hhs.gov (hereafter Bayer Corporate Integrity Agreement).

31. Kalb, Bass, and Fabrikant, "Average Wholesale Price," 4.

32. Pear, "Bayer to Pay $14 Million."

33. Department of Justice, "TAP Pharmaceutical Products Inc. and Seven Others Charged with Health Care Crimes," October 3, 2001, http://www.justice.gov.

34. Corporate Integrity Agreement between the Office of Inspector General of the Department of Health and Human Services and TAP Pharmaceutical Products Inc., September 28, 2001, available at https://oig.hhs.gov (hereafter TAP Corporate Integrity Agreement).

35. "TAP Settlement Redefining Marketing, Relationships between Drug Firms, Doctors," *Pharmaceutical Law and Industry Report,* December 13, 2001.

36. Pamela M. Prah, "Fraud Cops Target Drug Makers, Clinical Trials," *Kiplinger Business Forecasts,* April 9, 2002.

37. Mary Guiden, "States Mull Suit Against Drug Companies," Stateline.org, April 2, 2001.

38. John E. Clark, "Sharp, New Teeth for the State and Cash Rewards for Relators Exposing Wrongdoers," *Texas Bar Journal* 65 (2002): 120, 122.

39. Kimberly A. Yelkin, "States Target Medicaid Fraud in the Pharmaceutical Industry," *Federation of Regulatory Counsel Journal* 18 (Fall 2007), http://www.forc.org.

40. Texas Human Resources Code Annotated §32.039 (2000).

41. "Boehringer Ingelheim to Pay $10 Million to Settle Texas AG's Overcharge Allegations," *Pharmaceutical Law and Industry Report,* December 2, 2005.

42. Andrew Caffrey, Scott Hensley, and Russell Gold, "States Go to Court in Effort to Rein in Costs of Medicine," *Wall Street Journal,* May 21, 2002.

43. Yelkin, "States Target Medicaid Fraud."

44. See, for example, Settlement Agreement and Release, State of Texas v. Roxane Laboratories, No. GV3-03079 (District Court of Travis County, Texas), III(3).

45. The complaint also named 100 "John Doe" pharmaceutical companies as defendants, to be filled in when "the true names and capacities of the defendants" became known. Complaint for Injunctive Relief, Damages, Restitution Disgorgement, Forfeiture, Civil Penalties and Other Relief Exempt from Arbitration, State

of Nevada v. Abbott Laboratories, et al. (2nd Judicial Court for the District Court of Nevada, Washoe County), ¶36.

46. Complaint for Injunctive Relief, State of Nevada v. Abbott Laboratories, counts 1–7.

47. Ibid., count 4. Also see Caffrey, Hensley, and Gold, "States Go to Court."

48. William G. Castagnoli, "Nevada Suit Attacks Rx Firms on AWP System," *Medical Marketing and Media,* June 2002, 78. By my count, the Nevada AG's complaint mentions the defendants' alleged AWP scheme forty-one times.

49. Complaint for Injunctive Relief, State of Nevada v. Abbott Laboratories, count 3.

50. The information in Table 3.1 was collected from a search of the websites of each of the fifty states' attorney generals' offices, which typically contain a listing of legal complaints filed and/or press releases concerning new litigation. This search was supplemented with a search of the "All News" database within Lexis-Nexis, starting with the terms "average wholesale price" and "Alabama" and subsequently continuing through all fifty states.

51. Joyce E. Cutler, "AGs Targeting Pricing, Antitrust Issues in Pharmaceutical Industry, Official Says," *Pharmaceutical Law and Industry Report,* October 3, 2003. I discuss several of these multistate suits in chapter 4.

52. The private plaintiffs' firm was Hagens Berman, which also developed complaints in other state AWP cases.

53. Prescription Access Litigation, "PAL Coalition," http://www.prescription-access.org.

54. Russell Gold and Andrew Caffrey, "States Suing Drug Makers Spurn Former Allies on Tobacco," *Wall Street Journal,* May 29, 2002.

55. In Re Pharmaceutical Industry Average Wholesale Price Litigation, MDL No. 1456 (D. Mass, filed December 2001).

56. Second Amended Master Consolidated Class Action Complaint, In Re Pharmaceutical Industry Average Wholesale Price Litigation, MDL No. 1456 (filed February 24, 2004), 39.

57. In Re Pharmaceutical Industry Average Wholesale Price Litigation, MDL No. 1456 (D. Mass).

58. Jenny Anderson, "New Cops on the Beat," *Institutional Investor,* July 24, 2002, http://www.institutionalinvestor.com.

59. Frederic R. Curtiss, Phillip Lettrich, and Kathleen A. Fairman, "What Is the Price Benchmark to Replace Average Wholesale Price (AWP)?," *Journal of Managed Care Pharmacy* 16, no. 7 (2010): 492–501.

60. Alex Sugerman-Brozan and James Woolman, "Drug Spending and the Average Wholesale Price," *Pharmaceutical Law and Industry Report,* September 9, 2005.

61. Bayer Corporate Integrity Agreement, 11–15.

62. Ibid.

63. Caffrey, Hensley, and Gold, "States Go to Court."

64. Epp, *Making Rights Real.*

65. Ibid., 3.

66. Bayer Corporate Integrity Agreement, 4.

67. Ibid., 29.

68. TAP Corporate Integrity Agreement.

69. Spears and Pullman, "Using Litigation to Regulate Drug Prices," 73.

70. Carter, "Drug Wars," 44.

71. For a typical example, see Office of the Attorney General of Louisiana, "Attorney General Recovers $38 Million from Drug Companies Charged with Fraud," July 25, 2012, http://www.ag.state.la.us.

72. "House Committee Questions Drugmakers in Expanded Medicaid Fraud Investigation," *Pharmaceutical Law and Industry Report,* July 4, 2003; "Grassley Asks DOJ for Confidential Information From Medicaid Investigations," *Pharmaceutical Law and Industry Report,* May 28, 2004.

73. Joint Hearing Before the House Subcommittee on Health and the Subcommittee on Oversight and Investigations of the Committee on Energy and Commerce, "Medicare Drug Reimbursements: A Broken System for Patients and Taxpayers," 107th Cong., September 21, 2001.

74. Ibid., 10.

75. Problems with AWP have been mentioned at least in passing in dozens of congressional hearings beginning in 2001, with major hearings discussing AWP at length occurring nearly every year since.

76. For example, see Hearing Before the Subcommittee on Oversight and Investigations of the House Committee on Energy and Commerce, "Medicaid Prescription Drug Reimbursement: Why the Government Pays Too Much," 108th Cong., December 7, 2004 (testimony of Patrick O'Connell, Texas Attorney General's Office).

77. Medicare Prescription Drug, Improvement, and Modernization Act of 2003, Pub. L. No. 108-173, codified at 42 USC 1395w(3)(a).

78. Congressional Research Service, "Medicaid and SCHIP: The President's FY2006 Budget Proposals," April 1, 2005, 16–17.

79. Deficit Reduction Act of 2005, Pub. L. No. 109-171, at §6031.

80. Ibid., §6032.

81. Finding of Fact and Conclusions of Law, In Re Pharmaceutical Industry Average Wholesale Price Litigation, MDL No. 1456 (D. Mass, June 21, 2007), 144.

82. *Health Care Fraud Report (BNA),* March 12, 2008, 239.

83. Cary O'Reilly and Karen Freifeld, "GlaxoSmithKline to Pay $70 Million to End Drug Suits," *Bloomberg,* August 10, 2006, http://www.bloomberg.com.

84. Office of the New York Attorney General, "Leading Pharmaceutical Company Settles Suit Alleging Illegal Pricing Scheme for Cancer Patient Medications and Other Drugs," August 10, 2006, http://www.ag.ny.gov.

85. Martha Kessler, "GSK Pays $70 Million to Settle Lawsuit Alleging Artificial Inflation of Drug Prices," *Pharmaceutical Law and Industry Report,* August 18, 2006.

86. Office of the New York Attorney General, "Leading Pharmaceutical Company Settles Suit."

87. Nora Lockwood Tooher, "Drug Makers Agree to $125 Million Settlement in US District Court in Boston," *Lawyers USA,* March 12, 2008.

CHAPTER 4. EXPANDING THE NEWEST WAR ON DRUGS: LITIGATING PHARMACEUTICAL MARKETING

1. In 2008 alone, for example, drug companies spent $4.8 billion in direct-to-consumer advertisements. Natasha Singer, "Citing Risks, Lawmakers Seek to Curb Drug Commercials," *New York Times,* July 27, 2009.

2. Les Toop and Dee Richards, "Direct-to-Consumer Advertising (DTCA) of Prescription Medicines in New Zealand: For Health or for Profit?" *New Zealand Medical Journal* 116, no. 1180 (2003): U556.

3. Gardiner Harris, "Group Urges Ban on Medical Giveaways," *New York Times,* April 28, 2008.

4. Ray Moynihan and Alan Cassels, *Selling Sickness: How the World's Biggest Pharmaceutical Companies Are Turning Us All into Patients* (New York: Nation Books, 2006).

5. C. Lee Ventola, "Direct-to-Consumer Pharmaceutical Advertising: Therapeutic or Toxic?," *Pharmacy and Therapeutics* 36, no. 10 (2011): 669–674, 681–684.

6. Pub. L. No. 75-717, 52 Stat. 1040 (1938) (codified as amended 21 USC §§301 et seq.); Memorandum of Understanding between Federal Trade Commission and the Food and Drug Administration, 36 Fed. Reg. 18,539 (September 16, 1971).

7. Steven Woloshin, Lisa M. Schwartz, Jennifer Tremmel, and H. Gilbert Welch, "Direct-to-Consumer Advertisements for Prescription Drugs: What Are Americans Being Sold?," *Lancet* 358, no. 9288 (2001): 1141–1146.

8. Ibid., 1141.

9. Code of Federal Regulations, "Prescription Drug Advertising," title 21, §202.1 (2000).

10. FDA, "Guidance for Industry: Consumer-Directed Broadcast Advertisements," April 18, 2002, http://www.fda.gov.

11. "Spending on Direct-to-Consumer Drug Ads Increased in Spite of Criticism, Study Finds," *Pharmaceutical Law and Industry Report,* August 24, 2007.

12. Amanda Gardner, "Direct-to-Consumer Ads Booming Despite Criticisms," *Healthday Reporter,* August 15, 2007, http://consumer.healthday.com.

13. "Study Says Direct Consumer Ads Play Big Part in Increased Drug Spending," *Pharmaceutical Law and Industry Report,* November 29, 2001.

14. Susan M. Rapp, "Direct-to-Consumer Advertising: Jury is Still Out on the Benefit to Orthopedics," *Orthopedics Today,* June 2007, http://www.healio.com.

15. Dorothy L. Smith, "DTC Ads: Promoting Compliance a Win–Win Prospect," *Pharmaceutical Executive* 19 (December 1999).

16. Dana A. Elfin, "Drug Ads Don't Cause Improper Prescribing, Top FDA Official Tells Senate Subcommittee," *Pharmaceutical Law and Industry Report,* July 26, 2001.

17. "Spending on Direct-to-Consumer Drug Ads Increased."

18. Elfin, "Drug Ads."

19. "Waxman Report Says FDA Enforcement of Misleading Advertising Rules Ineffective," *Pharmaceutical Law and Industry Report,* February 6, 2004.

20. Ziad F. Gellad and Kenneth W. Lyles, "Direct-to-Consumer Advertising of Pharmaceuticals," *American Journal of Medicine* 120, no. 6 (2007): 478.

21. Enhancing Drug Safety and Innovation Act of 2007, S. 484, 110th Cong.; Food and Drug Administration Safety Act of 2007, S. 468, 110th Cong.

22. Responsibility in Drug and Device Advertising Act of 2008, HR 6151, 110th Cong.; Food and Drug Administration Revitalization Act, S. 1082, 110th Cong.

23. Fair Balance Prescription Drug Advertisement Act of 2007, HR 2823, 110th Cong.; Protecting Americans from Drug Marketing Act, S. 1763, 111th Cong.; Say No to Drug Ads Act, HR 722, 112th Cong.

24. Food, Drug, and Cosmetic Act, Pub. L. No. 75-717, 52 Stat. 1040 (codified at 21 USC §355(a)) (2006).

25. Ibid., §321(p).

26. Ibid., §396.

27. David C. Radley, Stan N. Finkelstein, and Randall S. Stafford, "Off-Label Prescribing Among Office-Based Physicians," *Archives of Internal Medicine* 166, no. 9 (2006): 1021–1026.

28. Vicki W. Girard, "Punishing Pharmaceutical Companies for Unlawful Promotion of Approved Drugs: Why the False Claims Act Is the Wrong Rx," *Journal of Health Care Law and Policy* 12 (2009): 131.

29. Radley, Finkelstein, and Stafford, "Off-Label Prescribing."

30. 63 Fed. Reg. 64,556 (November 20, 1998).

31. Pub. L. No. 105-115, 111 Stat. 2330 (1997).

32. Ibid.

33. Fazal Khan and Justin Holloway, "Verify, Then Trust: How to Legalize Off-Label Drug Marketing," *Penn State Law Review* 117, no. 2 (2012): 426–428.

34. Washington Legal Foundation v. Henney, 56 F. Supp. 2d 81, 84, 87 (D.D.C. 1999).

35. The FDA announced this position at oral argument in the government's appeal of the *Henney* case in the DC Circuit. Washington Legal Foundation v. Henney, 202 F. 3d 331 (D.C. Cir. 2000).

36. Food and Drug Administration, "Guidance for Industry on Good Reprint Practices for the Distribution of Medical Journal Articles and Medical or Scientific Reference Publications on Unapproved New Uses of Approved Drugs and Approved or Cleared Medical Devices," 74 Fed. Reg. 1,694 (January 13, 2009), http://www.fda.gov

37. Enhancing Drug Safety and Innovation Act of 2006, S. 3807, 109th Cong.

38. Assurance of Voluntary Compliance, In the Matter of Pfizer Inc. (December 27, 2002), ¶3, http://apps.americanbar.org.

39. Ibid., ¶4.

40. Ibid., footnote 1.

41. Ibid., ¶6; "Pfizer Inc. Enters $6 Million Settlement with 19 States Over Advertising of Antibiotic," *Pharmaceutical Law and Industry Report,* January 9, 2003.

42. Office of the New York Attorney General, "Ads for Leading Antibiotic Found to Be Misleading," January 6, 2003, http://www.ag.ny.gov.

43. Warren Allen, "The Unexpected Regulator: Regulation through Settlement After Vioxx and Bextra," *Brooklyn Journal of Corporate, Financial, and Commercial Law* 6, no. 2 (2012): 565–591.

44. Drew Douglas, "Merck Will Pay $58 Million to Settle States' Probe into Marketing of Vioxx," *Pharmaceutical Law and Industry Report,* May 23, 2008.

45. Office of the New York Attorney General, "Cuomo, Bloomberg Sue Maker of Vioxx for Hiding Drug's Risks," September 17, 2007, http://www.ag.ny.gov; Douglas, "Merck Will Pay."

46. Stipulated General Judgment, State of Oregon v. Merck & Co. (Circuit Court for the County of Marion, Oregon, 2008); Douglas, "Merck Will Pay."

47. Susanne Pagano, "Merck, Schering-Plough Settle With States over Vytorin Study Release," *Pharmaceutical Law and Industry Report,* July 17, 2009.

48. As with a number of these cases, the FDA chose not to investigate Pfizer's alleged off-label marketing of these drugs.

49. Final Consent Judgment, State of New Jersey v. Pfizer Inc. (Superior Court of New Jersey, No. MER-C-134-08), ¶7–¶8.

50. Brian C. Anderson and Michael E. Stamp, "Shooting the Messenger: 'Off-Label Marketing' Attacks against Pharmaceutical Companies by State Attorneys General," American Enterprise Institute, May 22, 2008, http://www.aei.org.

51. "Pfizer Unit Pays $430 Million to Settle Neurontin Off-Label, Medicaid Claims," *Pharmaceutical Law and Industry Report,* May 14, 2004.

52. Anderson and Stamp, "Shooting the Messenger," 9.

53. Ibid., 8–9. This case was heard before Judge Patti Saris of the federal district court in Massachusetts, along with the AWP litigation noted earlier.

54. Order Governing the Administration of the Multistate Grant and Advertising Program, In the Matter of Warner-Lambert Company, LLC (Circuit Court, County of Marion, Oregon, 2004), ¶2.2 and ¶2.3.

55. Ibid., §2; "Pfizer Unit Pays $430 Million to Settle Neurontin Off-Label, Medicaid Claims," *Pharmaceutical Law and Industry Report,* May 14, 2004.

56. Office of the New York Attorney General, "Spitzer Announces $14.9 Million Prescription Drug Education Grant Program Funded by Settlement with Pfizer," August 31, 2005, http://www.ag.ny.gov.

57. Carl Elliott, "Pharmed Out: An Interview with Adriane Fugh-Berman," *Chronicle of Higher Education,* May 22, 2012, http://chronicle.com. The organization's website is available at http://www.pharmedout.org.

58. Order Governing the Administration of the Multistate Grant and Advertising Program, In the Matter of Warner-Lambert Company, §3.

59. Connecticut Attorney General's Office, "Attorney General Demands Action on OxyContin," July 31, 2007, http://www.ct.gov. Blumenthal later sued the FDA in an effort to force them to act on his petition. "Connecticut Attorney General Files Suit over Request to FDA for OxyContin Warning," *Pharmaceutical Law and Industry Report,* April 4, 2008.

60. Connecticut Attorney General's Office, "Attorney General Demands Action."

61. "Purdue Pharma Settles OxyContin Lawsuit with West Virginia Officials for $10 Million," *Pharmaceutical Law and Industry Report,* November 12, 2004.

62. Final Judgment and Agreed Final Injunction, State of Texas v. Purdue Pharma Inc. (District Court of Dallas County, Texas, 2007), ¶5–¶6.

63. Ibid., ¶17.

64. Ibid., ¶20; "OxyContin's Maker, Executives to Pay $600 Million in Drug Misbranding Case," *Pharmaceutical Law and Industry Report,* May 18, 2007.

65. For example, see the Enhancing Drug Safety and Innovation Act of 2006, S. 3807, 109th Cong.

66. Final Judgment and Agreed Permanent Injunction, State of Texas v. Bayer Corporation (District Court of Dallas County, Texas, 2007), ¶15–¶23.

67. See, for example, Maryland Attorney General, "AG Gansler Reaches $90 Million Settlement with GlaxoSmithKline," November 16, 2012, http://www.oag.state.md.us.

68. Andrew Ballard, "Eli Lilly to Pay States $62 Million Under Zyprexa Marketing Settlement," *Pharmaceutical Law and Industry Report,* October 10, 2008.

69. Oregon Department of Justice, "AG Reaches $62 Million Settlement with Eli Lilly Pharmaceutical," October 7, 2008, http://www.doj.state.or.us.

70. Ballard, "Eli Lilly to Pay States."

71. Office of the New York Attorney General, "Attorney General Cuomo Announces Landmark Settlement with Eli Lilly," October 7, 2008, http://www.ag.ny.gov.

72. Ballard, "Eli Lilly to Pay States."

73. Stipulated General Judgment, State of Oregon v. Merck & Co., ¶19.

74. International Committee of Medical Journal Editors, "Uniform Requirements for Manuscripts Submitted to Biomedical Journals: Writing and Editing for Biomedical Publication," October 2008, http://www.icmje.org.

75. Katie Thomas, "Johnson & Johnson Unit Settles State Cases over Risperdal," *New York Times,* August 31, 2012.

76. Gardiner Harris, "Pfizer to Pay $2.3 Billion to Settle Inquiry over Marketing," *New York Times,* September 3, 2009; Katie Thomas and Michael S. Schmidt, "Drug Firm Guilty in Criminal Case," *New York Times,* July 3, 2012; Brady Dennis, "Drug Firm to Pay $2.2 Billion in Fraud Settlement," *Washington Post,* November 5, 2013.

77. The various proposals included several referenced throughout this chapter. Also see Singer, "Citing Risks."

78. "PhRMA Issues Drug Advertising Guidelines, but Some Want Moratorium, Firmer Oversight," *Pharmaceutical Law and Industry Report,* August 5, 2005; "International Pharma Trade Group Adopts New Code Barring Some Marketing Activities," *Pharmaceutical Law and Industry Report,* January 5, 2007; "Rx Industry Group Issues New Guidelines for Companies on Direct-to-Consumer Ads," *Pharmaceutical Law and Industry Report,* December 12, 2008.

79. Matthew Arnold, "Four Agree to Moratorium," *Medical Marketing and Media,* July 1, 2008, 24.

80. 425 US 748 (1976); Central Hudson Gas & Electric Corp. v. Public Service

Commission, 447 US 557 (1980); 44 Liquormart, Inc. v. Rhode Island, 517 US 484 (1996).

81. 535 US 357 (2002).

82. 131 S. Ct. 2653 (2011).

83. For example, see Singer, "Citing Risks," noting Representative Jerrold Nadler's (D-NY) comment that "on First Amendment grounds, I am not going to say we will ban" drug advertising.

84. Gardiner Harris, "Spitzer Sues a Drug Maker, Saying it Hid Negative Data," *New York Times*, June 3, 2004.

85. US v. Caronia, 703 F. 3d 149 (2d Cir. 2012). Shortly after this decision, the FDA announced that it would not appeal the decision to the Supreme Court.

86. Katie Thomas, "J.&J. Fined $1.2 Billion in Drug Case," *New York Times*, April 12, 2012.

87. Natasha Singer, "Maker of Botox Settles Inquiry on Off-Label Use," *New York Times*, September 2, 2010.

88. Searle Civil Justice Institute, "State Consumer Protection Acts: An Empirical Investigation of Private Litigation," December 2009, http://www.masonlec.org.

89. US Department of Health and Human Services, *CDER Handbook* 53 (2010): 53–54, http://www.fda.gov.

90. Tresa Baldas, "FDA Letters Are Key in Deceptive Drug Ad Suits," *National Law Journal*, March 30, 2009.

91. Ibid.

92. "FDA Warns Bayer that Yaz TV Ads Overstate Efficacy, Minimize Risks," *Pharmaceutical Law and Industry Report*, October 17, 2008.

93. Baldas, "FDA Letters Are Key."

94. "Bayer to Submit TV Ads on Yaz Birth Control Pill to FDA Prior to Airing," *Pharmaceutical Law and Industry Report*, February 13, 2009.

CHAPTER 5. STATE LITIGATION AND NATIONAL PHARMACEUTICAL POLICY

1. Sammy Almashat and Sidney Wolfe, "Pharmaceutical Industry Criminal and Civil Penalties: An Update," *Public Citizen*, September 27, 2012, http://www.citizen.org.

2. Office of the New York Attorney General, "AG Schneiderman Announces Over $335 Million in Medicaid Fraud Recoveries for Taxpayers in 2012," January 23, 2013, http://www.ag.ny.gov.

3. Anderson, "New Cops on the Beat."

4. Gardbaum, "New Deal Constitutionalism."

5. Rosenberg, *Hollow Hope;* Alexander Hamilton, "Federalist #78," in *The Federalist Papers*, ed. Clinton Rossiter (New York: New American Library, 1961), 467.

6. Mnookin and Kornhauser, "Bargaining in the Shadow of the Law."

7. George Tsebelis, *Veto Players: How Political Institutions Work* (Princeton, NJ: Princeton University Press, 2002).

8. Administrative Procedures Act of 1946, Pub. L. No. 79-404, codified at 5 USC §553(b)–(c).

9. R. Shep Melnick, *Regulation and the Courts: The Case of the Clean Air Act* (Washington, DC: Brookings Institution Press, 1983).

10. Pharmaceutical Research and Manufacturers of America v. Concannon, 249 F. 3d 66 (1st Cir. 2001).

11. Federal courts eventually invalidated the DC law, known as the Prescription Drugs Excessive Pricing Act. Biotechnology Industry Organization v. District of Columbia, 496 F. 3d 1362 (Fed. Cir. 2007).

12. Washington Legal Foundation v. Henney, 56 F. Supp. 2d 81 (D.D.C. 1999).

13. See, for example, "BMS to Launch Internal Reviews of Sales, Marketing, Pricing Practices," *Pharmaceutical Law and Industry Report,* July 25, 2003; press release, "Lilly Set to Become First Pharmaceutical Research Company to Disclose Physician Payments," September 24, 2008, http://newsroom.lilly.com; press release, "Pfizer to Publicly Disclose Payments to US Physicians, Healthcare Professionals and Clinical Investigators," February 9, 2009, http://press.pfizer.com; press release, "Medtronic to Voluntarily Disclose Payments to US Physicians," February 24, 2009, http://newsroom.medtronic.com.

14. See, for example, "PhRMA Issues Drug Advertising Guidelines, but Some Want Moratorium, Firmer Oversight," *Pharmaceutical Law and Industry Report,* August 5, 2005; "International Pharma Trade Group Adopts New Code Barring Some Marketing Activities," *Pharmaceutical Law and Industry Report,* January 5, 2007, 16; "Rx Industry Group Issues New Guidelines for Companies on Direct-to-Consumer Ads," *Pharmaceutical Law and Industry Report,* December 12, 2008.

15. Finding of Fact and Conclusions of Law, In Re Pharmaceutical Industry Average Wholesale Price Litigation, MDL No. 1456 (D. Mass, June 21, 2007), 144.

16. This included an industry victory following a jury trial in West Virginia and the Alabama supreme court's overturning of a jury verdict against drug companies in 2012 because the AG's effort represented "regulation through litigation." West Virginia v. Johnson & Johnson, 2010 WL 4709084 (W.V. November 18, 2010); Sandoz v. Alabama, 2012 WL 1081402 (Ala. July 13, 2012).

17. For example, after the decision in *Sandoz v. Alabama,* the Alabama Medicaid agency announced that it was going to continue modifying the state prescription drug pricing system regardless of the court's decision.

18. Hacker, *Divided Welfare State.*

19. Elazar, *American Federalism,* 2.

20. Nicole Huberfeld, "Federalizing Medicaid," *University of Pennsylvania Journal of Constitutional Law* 14, no. 2 (2011): 431–484.

21. Jeffrey S. Cahill, "Combating Health Care Fraud and Patient Abuse: The Role of the Medicaid Fraud Unit," *New Hampshire Bar Journal,* Spring 2004, 71.

22. The variations in the federal Medicaid share are the result of a formula based on per capita income in each state relative to the national per capita income. Alison Mitchell and Evelyne P. Baumrucker, "Medicaid's Federal Medical Assistance Percentage, FY2014," *CRS Report for Congress,* January 30, 2013, https://www.fas.org.

23. Center for Medicaid Services, "National Health Expenditures 2012 Highlights," http://www.cms.gov.

24. “Medicare and Medicaid Frauds,” Hearing Before the Senate Special Committee on Aging, Subcommittee in Long-Term Care, 94th Cong., 776 (1976).

25. Myers and Ross, *State Attorneys General,* 324.

26. The federal statutory definition of “state MFCU” in the original 1977 statute encouraged states to place the MFCU under the purview of the state’s AG because AGs already typically possessed the sort of statewide authority to prosecute criminal violations specified as part of the MFCUs’ duties. Medicare–Medicaid Anti-Fraud and Abuse Amendments of 1977, Pub. L. No. 95-142, 91 Stat. 1175 (1977): 1175, codified at 42 USC §1396b(q). Nearly all of the states have done this, with forty-three state MFCUs under the exclusive jurisdiction of the state’s AG. Even in the states with separate MFCUs, all have a close working relationship with AG offices.

27. Myers and Ross, *State Attorneys General,* 328.

28. Office of the Inspector General, “State Medicaid Fraud Control Units, FY2012 Grant Expenditures and Statistics,” http://oig.hhs.gov.

29. Office of the Inspector General, “MFCU Statistical Data for Fiscal Year 2012,” http://oig.hhs.gov.

30. Deficit Reduction Act of 2005, Pub. L. No. 109-171, 120 Stat. 4 (2005): 4, codified at 42 USC 1305.

31. Taxpayers Against Fraud Education Fund, “States with False Claims Acts,” https://www.taf.org.

32. Patient Protection and Affordable Care Act, Pub. L. No. 111-148, 124 Stat. 119 (2010), especially §§1313, 6402, 6408, and 10606.

33. Fraud Enforcement and Recovery Act of 2009, Pub. L. No. 111-21, §4, 123 Stat. 1617, 1621–25; Health Care Fraud Enforcement Act of 2009, S. 1959, 111th Cong. (2009); Affordable Health Choices Act, S. 1679, 111th Cong. §§501–502 (2009).

34. Myers and Ross, *State Attorneys General,* 331.

35. Both organizations are located on the eighth floor of 2030 M Street NW in Washington, DC.

36. Almashat and Wolfe, “Pharmaceutical Industry,” 5.

37. Myers and Ross, *State Attorneys General,* 333.

38. Food and Drug Administration Amendments Act of 2007, Pub. L. No. 110-85, 121 Stat. 823, codified at 42 USC §282(j)(3)(D).

39. Patient Protection and Affordable Care Act, Pub. L. No. 111-148, 124 Stat. 119 (2010), §§6002, 6004, and 6005.

40. Melnick, *Regulation and the Courts;* R. Shep Melnick, *Between the Lines: Interpreting Welfare Rights* (Washington, DC: Brookings Institution Press, 1994).

41. E. E. Schattschneider, *The Semi-Sovereign People* (New York: Holt, Rinehart, and Winston, 1960), 2, 7.

42. Robert Cohen and Ed Silverman, “Drug Makers Face Slew of Lawsuits Extending Beyond Claims of Harm,” *Newhouse News Service,* April 9, 2003 (on file with author).

43. Carter, “Drug Wars,” 43.

44. Gold and Caffrey, “States Suing Drug Makers Spurn Former Allies.”

45. This quote is from W. Dee Miles at Beasley Allen, a plaintiffs’ firm in Mont-

gomery, Alabama. Tooher, "Plaintiffs' Lawyers Tackle Drug Price-Fixing Litigation."

46. A listing of the various cases in which the Hagens Berman law firm has been involved is available on the firm's website (http://www.hbsslaw.com).

47. Prescription Access Litigation, "PAL Coalition," http://web.archive.org/web/20130430105917/http://www.prescriptionaccess.org/lawsuitssettlements?id=0005.

48. Guiden, "States Mull Suit."

49. According to PAL's website, the coalition has retained several private firms as part of their litigation, including Hagens Berman, which also worked closely with AGs on AWP issues. Prescription Access Litigation, "PAL Coalition."

50. Eugene Lewis, *Public Entrepreneurship: Toward a Theory of Bureaucratic Political Power* (Bloomington: Indiana University Press, 1980), 17–18.

51. Sen. Grassley (IA), Congressional Record, 109th Cong., 1st Sess., 2005, pt. 12069.

52. Sen. McCain (AZ), Congressional Record, 109th Cong., 1st Sess., 2005, pt. 14073.

53. As chapter 2 indicated, these participation rates are nearly identical (70.28 percent and 69.76 percent, respectively).

54. Rich Thomaselli, "FDA Orders Company to Correct Earlier Claims about Yaz Birth Control," *Advertising Age,* February 16, 2009, 2.

CHAPTER 6. FIGHTING A GUERRILLA WAR IN THE COURTS: LITIGATING ACID RAIN

1. Rachel Carson, *Silent Spring* (New York: Houghton Mifflin, 1962); Albert Gore, *Earth in the Balance: Ecology and the Human Spirit* (New York: Houghton Mifflin, 1992).

2. "Forest Service Chief McGuire Asks Extent of Acid Precipitation Risk," *Environment Reporter,* May 23, 1975, 207.

3. "Acid Precipitation Increasing in Northeast, EPA Official Says," *Environment Reporter,* July 25, 1975, 517; "Pipes Corroded from Acid Rain Could Contaminate Drinking Water," *Environment Reporter,* September 14, 1979, 1168–1169.

4. "National Academy of Sciences Report Says No Sulfur Dioxide Rule Change Justified," *Environment Reporter,* January 26, 1979, 1772.

5. Thomas F. P. Sullivan, ed., *Environmental Law Handbook,* 12th ed. (Rockville, MD: Government Institutes, 1993), 244.

6. "EPA Responds to Carter by Earmarking $4 Million for Acid Rain Study This Year," *Environment Reporter,* August 17, 1979, 1016; Pub. L. No. 96-294, 94 Stat. 770 (1980), codified at 42 USC §§8901–8905, 8911–8912.

7. "Control of Acid Rain Major Change in Act Sought by Environmentalists," *Environment Reporter,* December 5, 1980, 1179.

8. "EPA Official Says Amending Act Only Way Now to Control Acid Rain," *Environment Reporter,* October 12, 1979, 1342.

9. "'Environmental Decade is Indeed Over,' Conservation Foundation President Says," *Environment Reporter,* November 28, 1980, 1109.

10. "Reagan's Proposed Fiscal 1982 Budget Would Cut EPA Funding to $1.39 Billion," *Environment Reporter,* March 13, 1981, 2083–2085.

11. "EPA Draft Proposal for Clean Air Act Would Give States Greater Authority," *Environment Reporter,* June 26, 1981, 275–276.

12. Ibid.

13. "Mitchell Plans to Introduce Senate Bill Amending Air Act for Control of Acid Rain," *Environment Reporter,* August 31, 1981, 560; "Three Bills Introduced in Senate to Abate Acid Rain, Long-Range Pollution Transport," *Environment Reporter,* October 16, 1981, 745–746; "Scheuer Offers Acid Rain Bill Calling for 36 Percent Sulfur Emission Cuts in East," *Environment Reporter,* November 27, 1981, 937.

14. "Senate Panel Told Acid Rain Proposals Put Unfair Burden on Midwestern States," *Environment Reporter,* November 6, 1981, 836–837.

15. "Senate, House Staff Members Say Acid Rain Inseparable from Clean Air Act Legislation," *Environment Reporter,* May 6, 1983, 8.

16. Ibid.

17. "Waxman Offers 48-State Acid Rain Bill Requiring 14 Million Tons of Reductions," *Environment Reporter,* July 1, 1983, 333.

18. "Senate Panel Approves Air Act Amendment to Control Acid Rain through Emissions Cut," *Environment Reporter,* July 30, 1982, 419. The Senate committee ended up approving this plan in March 1984, though it again died before reaching the floor.

19. "Stafford Introduces Air Act Amendments, Including Proposals for Acid Rain Control," *Environment Reporter,* March 18, 1983, 2079–2080.

20. Frank Lynn, "Abrams Is Seeking Lefkowitz's Post," *New York Times,* May 8, 1974; "Abrams Tried Four Years Ago against Lefkowitz," *New York Times,* November 8, 1978.

21. Clean Air Act Amendments of 1970, Pub. L. No. 91-604, 84 Stat. 1676, §304.

22. "Abrams Says He May Sue EPA in Clean Air Dispute," *New York Times,* December 11, 1980.

23. Mike Clancy, "Maine Opposes Air Standards Relaxation," *United Press International,* September 22, 1981.

24. The three states were Pennsylvania, Vermont, and Massachusetts.

25. "Senate Acid Rain Amendment Labeled 'Excessive,' 'Premature,' by EPA Official," *Environment Reporter,* August 20, 1982, 530.

26. "Researcher Say Data Still Lacking for Government to Regulate Acid Rain," *Environment Reporter,* June 26, 1981, 282–283.

27. "Five States Notify EPA of Intent to Sue over Transboundary Pollution, Acid Rain," *Environment Reporter,* January 27, 1984, 1644.

28. New York v. Ruckelshaus, 1984 US Dist. Lexis 22953 (D.D.C. 1984), *8–*12.

29. Stuart Taylor Jr., "Judge Orders EPA to Act on Acid Rain," *New York Times,* October 11, 1984.

30. "Northeastern States Allege EPA Failed to Order Midwest States to Reduce Emissions," *Environment Reporter,* April 29, 1988, 2552.

31. "EPA Denies Northeast States' Petitions Asking for Action on Emissions in Midwest," *Environment Reporter,* December 7, 1984, 1326–1327.

32. New York v. EPA, 852 F.2d 574, 578 (D.C. Cir. 1988).

33. "EPA Decision Not to Review Midwestern SIPs, NEPA Leasing Ruling Denied Court Review," *Environment Reporter,* March 10, 1989, 2373.

34. "Northeast States Lose Battle to Force EPA to Address Acid Rain from Midwest Sources," *Environment Reporter,* July 29, 1988, 426.

35. David R. Wooley, "Acid Rain: Canadian Litigation Options in US Court and Agency Proceedings," *University of Toledo Law Review* 17, no. 1 (1985): 139–152.

36. New York v. Thomas, 613 F. Supp. 1472, 1482 (D.D.C. 1985).

37. Wooley, "Acid Rain," 150.

38. Ibid.

39. "Five States Notify EPA of Intent to Sue over Transboundary Pollution, Acid Rain," *Environment Reporter,* January 27, 1984, 1644.

40. "Bid to Use Transboundary Sections of Law for Acid Rain Draws Ruckelshaus' Opposition," *Environment Reporter,* February 3, 1984, 30.

41. New York v. Thomas, 613 F. Supp. 1472 (D.D.C. 1985).

42. Wooley, "Acid Rain," 139; "EPA Must Order States to Cut Emissions to Reduce Acid Rain in Canada, Court Says," *Environment Reporter,* August 2, 1985, 541.

43. Wooley, "Acid Rain," 139.

44. "EPA Appeals Federal District Court Decision Requiring Acid Rain Control, Seeks More Time," *Environment Reporter,* September 27, 1985, 940.

45. "Federal Court Told Costle Acid Rain Letters Do Not Require EPA to Order Emissions Cuts," *Environment Reporter,* May 23, 1986, 90–91.

46. Thomas v. New York, 802 F.2d 1443 (D.C. Cir. 1986).

47. "EPA Petitioned to Control Acid Rain Under International Provision of Air Act," *Environment Reporter,* April 22, 1988, 2526–2527.

48. "New York Petition to Cut Midwest Emissions Gets Negative Reaction from High EPA Official," *Environment Reporter,* October 21, 1988, 1205–1206.

49. Her Majesty the Queen v. EPA, 912 F.2d. 1525, 1533–34 (D.C. Cir. 1990).

50. "Acid Rain Control Measure Too Expensive, Not Backed by Science, Thomas Tells Panel," *Environment Reporter,* May 2, 1986, 4.

51. "Bush Tells GOP Governors He Will Act on Acid Rain, Wetlands, Global Warming," *Environment Reporter,* December 2, 1988, 1564–1565.

52. "Bush Air Bill Gets Good Initial Reviews, but Questions Remain on Details of Proposal," *Environment Reporter,* June 16, 1989, 429–431.

53. Reitze, *Air Pollution Control Law,* 22.

54. Clean Air Act Amendments of 1990, Pub. L. No. 101-549, 104 Stat. 2468 (codified as amended at 42 USC §§7401–7671q).

55. Matthew L. Wald, "States Sue EPA over Lack of Clean Air Rules," *New York Times,* April 14, 1992; Matthew L. Wald, "Suit Attacks Swap Plan on Pollution," *New York Times,* March 14, 1992.

56. Tom Kenworthy, "Activist Ex-Aide to Gore Tapped to Direct EPA," *Washington Post,* December 12, 1992, A10.

57. "SO2 Trading Program Offers Answers for Other Pollution Problems, Group Says," *Environment Reporter,* November 21, 1997, 1408.

58. Virginia v. EPA, 108 F. 3d 1397 (D.C. Cir. 1997).

59. "Northeast States, EPA Reach Agreement On Petitions Addressing Ozone Transport," *Environment Reporter,* January 2, 1998, 1645.

60. "Northeast States File Consent Decree to Enforce Agreement over NOx Petitions," *Environment Reporter,* February 27, 1998, 2288.

61. "Initial Analysis of Section 126 Petitions Implicates 16 States, District of Columbia," *Environment Reporter,* May 1, 1998, 5; Reitze, *Air Pollution Control Law,* 241.

62. "Documents Prove Northeastern States Aware Problems Mostly Local, Group Says," *Environment Reporter,* February 6, 1998, 2007.

63. Environmental Protection Agency, "Basic Information: New Source Review," http://www.epa.gov.

64. Clean Air Act, 42 USC §7411(a)(4).

65. US Environmental Protection Agency, "Prevention of Significant Deterioration of Air Quality," 40 CFR 52.21(b)(2)(i).

66. Matthew H. Snell, "Major Modifications and Routine Maintenance: Does the EPA's New Exclusion Equal More Pollution?," *New England Law Review* 39, no. 1 (2004): 208.

67. "New York State Announces Intent to Sue 17 Power Plants over Transported Pollution," *Environment Reporter,* September 17, 1999, 901.

68. Office of the New York Attorney General, "Spitzer Takes on Midwestern Power Plants over Acid Rain, Smog," September 15, 1999, http://www.ag.ny.gov.

69. Richard Perez-Pena, "Power Plants to Cut Emissions Faulted in Northeast Smog," *New York Times,* November 16, 2000.

70. William B. Eimicke, "Eliot Spitzer: The People's Lawyer," *Public Integrity* 7, no. 4 (2005): 361.

71. Brooke Masters, *Spoiling for a Fight: The Rise of Eliot Spitzer* (New York: Times Books, 2006), 55–56.

72. Elizabeth Kolbert, "The Pollution Buster," *OnEarth Magazine,* September 22, 2004, 8.

73. "Government Sues Electric Companies over New Source Review at 17 Power Plants," *Environment Reporter,* November 12, 1999, 1269.

74. "EPA Amends Suits against Utilities to Allege Violations at 12 More Plants," *Environment Reporter,* March 3, 2000, 375.

75. Richard Perez-Pena, "Possible Federal Pullout Clouds Northeast States' Pollution Suits," *New York Times,* August 20, 2001.

76. "Connecticut Announces Intent to Sue 16 Power Plants over Transported Pollution," *Environment Reporter,* November 26, 1999, 1357.

77. "New York, Connecticut Sue Power Firm, Allege New Source Violations at 10 Plants," *Environment Reporter,* December 3, 1999, 1399.

78. "New York State Announces Intent to Sue."

79. "Claims in NSR Lawsuits Are Without Merit, Ohio-Based Power Company Asserts in Filing," *Environment Reporter,* May 12, 2000, 921.

80. Julie R. Domike and Alec C. Zacaroli, "Reinterpretation of NSR Regulations

Could Have Costly Implications for Businesses," *Environment Reporter,* March 3, 2000, 407.

81. "EPA Ignored Procedures in Redefining New Source Review, Industry Petition Says," *Environment Reporter,* January 14, 2000, 61.

82. "Enforcement against Utilities Seen as Shift Away from Rules to Achieve Pollution Cuts," *Environment Reporter,* February 18, 2000, 278.

83. Domike and Zacaroli, "Reinterpretation of NSR Regulations."

84. "Trials Set for New Source Review Cases Against Electric Utilities in Indiana, Ohio," *Environment Reporter,* April 19, 2002, 846.

85. Randal C. Archibald, "Tentative Deal on Acid Rain Is Reached with Third Utility," *New York Times,* December 22, 2000; Perez-Pena, "Power Plants to Cut Emissions Faulted."

86. Archibald, "Tentative Deal."

87. Ibid.

88. Cinergy Corporation, "Cinergy, EPA, Other Parties Reach Agreement on Power Plant Lawsuit," December 21, 2000, http://www.sec.gov.

89. J. R. Pegg, "AEP to Pay $4.6 Billion: Largest Clean Air Settlement in US History," *Environment News Service,* October 9, 2007.

90. Masters, *Spoiling for a Fight,* 57.

91. Perez-Pena, "Possible Federal Pullout."

92. "White House Plan Offers Possible Relief to Power Companies in Pollution Lawsuits," *Environment Reporter,* May 18, 2001, 950.

93. "Utility, Refinery Lawsuits Going Ahead Despite Bush-Mandated Policy Review," *Environment Reporter,* September 14, 2001, 1794.

94. "Utility Groups, State Officials Disagree on Enforcement of Program by Agency," *Environment Reporter,* July 20, 2001, 1401.

95. Connecticut Attorney General, "Attorney General Denounces Bush Administration's Back Room Deals Designed to Eviscerate the Clean Air Act," December 19, 2001, http://www.ct.gov.

96. Press release, "President Announces Clear Skies and Global Climate Change Initiatives," February 14, 2002, http://georgewbush-whitehouse.archives.gov.

97. "'Clear Skies' Legislation to Cut Emissions from Power Plants Introduced in Congress," *Environment Reporter,* August 8, 2002, 1693.

98. "Long-Awaited Administration Reforms Seek Relaxed Requirements for Power Plants," *Environment Reporter,* June 14, 2002, 1309.

99. US Department of Justice, Office of Legal Policy, "New Source Review: An Analysis of the Consistency of Enforcement Actions with the Clean Air Act and Implementing Regulations," January 15, 2002, http://www.envinfo.com.

100. "DOJ Announces New Source Review Cases May Proceed, Asserting Law Supports Them," *Environment Reporter,* January 18, 2002, 117.

101. Office of the New York Attorney General, "Statement by Attorney General Eliot Spitzer Regarding the Federal Department of Justice Clean Air Act Report," January 15, 2002, http://www.ag.ny.gov.

102. "US Settles with Three Refineries over New Source Review Violations," *Environment Reporter,* January 4, 2002, 8.

103. "Trials Set for New Source Review Cases against Electric Utilities in Indiana, Ohio," *Environment Reporter,* April 19, 2002, 846.

104. "EPA Reportedly to Drop New Cases in Enforcement against Major Sources," *Environment Reporter,* November 7, 2003, 2429.

105. "Departing EPA Official Issues Broadside at Bush Administration's Clean Air Programs," *Environment Reporter,* March 1, 2002, 462.

106. "GAO Report Shows Concern by EPA Staff over Effect of Plant Modification Exemptions," *Environment Reporter,* October 24, 2003, 2325.

107. "EPA Enforcement 'Seriously Hampered' By 2003 Revisions, Inspector General Says," *Environment Reporter,* October 8, 2004, 2095.

108. Jennifer 8. Lee, "Utility to Spend $1.2 Billion to Cut Emissions," *New York Times,* April 19, 2003.

109. Jennifer 8. Lee, "Vowing to Enforce the Clean Air Act, While Also Trying to Change It," *New York Times,* April 22, 2003.

110. "Modifications at Ohio Edison Plant Violated Clean Air Act Provisions, Federal Court Says," *Environment Reporter,* August 8, 2003, 1757.

111. "Decision against Ohio Power Company Will Boost Other Pending Cases, Officials Say," *Environment Reporter,* August 15, 2003, 1819.

112. "Ohio Edison Argues Its Plant Modifications Comply with Revised New Source Review," *Environment Reporter,* March 19, 2004, 585. The company eventually settled, agreeing to implement more than $1.1B in new pollution-control equipment. "Ohio Edison Co. Agrees to Pay $1.1 Billion to Cut Emissions 212,000 Tons from Plants," *Environment Reporter,* March 25, 2005, 573.

113. Office of the New York Attorney General, "Spitzer Urges EPA to Hand Over Information on Clean Air Act Cases," November 6, 2003, http://www.ag.ny.gov.

114. Anthony DePalma, "New York and 3 Other States Join Against Air Pollution," *New York Times,* May 21, 2004.

115. Darren Samuelsohn, "States, Enviros Seek End Run Around Bush NSR Strategy with New Lawsuits," *Greenwire,* July 29, 2004.

116. Ibid.

117. "Tie Vote in Senate Environment Committee Kills President's Clear Skies Bill in Congress," *Environment Reporter,* March 11, 2005, 462.

118. "Bush Administration Completes Rules Easing Pollution Controls for Power Plants, Factories," *Environment Reporter,* November 29, 2002, 2557.

119. EPA, "Supplemental Analysis of the Environmental Impact of the 2002 Final NSR Improvement Rules," November 21, 2002, http://www.epa.gov.

120. "Agency Receives Thousands of Comments on Proposed Revisions to New Source Review," *Environment Reporter,* May 9, 2003, 1045.

121. John Herzfeld, "Nine State Attorneys General Announce Plans to Fight EPA's Revisions to Rules," *Environment Reporter,* November 29, 2002, 2559; Steve Cook, "EPA Issues Changes to Enforcement Program; Nine States File Lawsuit to Block Final Rule," *Environment Reporter,* January 3, 2003, 5.

122. Complaint, New York v. EPA, Case 02-1387 (D.C. Cir., filed December 31, 2002).

123. Steve Cook, "Kerry Joins Brief Supporting Challenge to Revisions in Plant Modification Rules," *Environment Reporter,* May 21, 2004, 1097.

124. "Manufacturers Group Mobilizes to Defend EPA's New Regulations from State Lawsuit," *Environment Reporter,* January 10, 2003, 79.

125. Steve Cook, Michael Bologna, and Carolyn Whetzel, "Court Denies Request to Block Revisions; Advocacy Groups, More States Sue Agency," *Environment Reporter,* March 7, 2003, 517.

126. New York v. EPA, 413 F. 3d 3 (D.C. Cir. 2005).

127. Office of the New York Attorney General, "Federal Court Decision Upholds Clean Air Effort," June 24, 2005, http://www.ag.ny.gov.

128. Equipment Replacement Provision of the Routine Maintenance, Repair and Replacement Exclusion, 68 Fed. Reg. 61,248, 61,270 (October 27, 2003).

129. Pamela Najor, Martha Kessler, and Carolyn Whetzel, "Revised Rule on Equipment Replacement to Exempt Thousands of Industrial Facilities," *Environment Reporter,* September 5, 2003, 1919.

130. New York v. EPA, 443. F. 3d 880 (D.C. Cir. 2006); Steve Cook, "14 States, 29 Municipalities Ask Court to Block EPA Rules on Facility Modifications," *Environment Reporter,* November 21, 2003, 2542.

131. Final Reply Brief of Government Petitioners the States of New York, et al., New York v. EPA, 443. F. 3d 880 (D.C. Cir. 2006).

132. Steve Cook, "Virginia, Eight Other States Back EPA in Suit over Exemptions for Major Facilities," *Environment Reporter,* December 5, 2003, 2640.

133. Steve Cook, "Appeals Court Blocks EPA Implementation of Rule on Routine Maintenance Exemptions," *Environment Reporter,* January 2, 2004, 5.

134. New York v. EPA, 443. F. 3d at 11–13.

135. For example, see Pamela Najor, "Seven States Notify EPA They Will Sue over Failure to Regulate Carbon Emissions," *Environment Reporter,* February 28, 2003, 459.

CHAPTER 7. FROM SO_2 TO CO_2: LITIGATING CLIMATE CHANGE

1. White House, Office of the Press Secretary, "Remarks by the President on Climate Change," June 25, 2013, http://www.whitehouse.gov.

2. Ibid. See also Justin Gillis, "Not Even Close: 2012 Was Hottest Ever in US," *New York Times,* January 9, 2013.

3. White House, "Remarks by the President on Climate Change."

4. Senator James M. Inhofe, "Obama Again Declares War on Affordable Energy," June 25, 2013, http://www.inhofe.senate.gov.

5. James Salzman and J. B. Ruhl, "Who's Number One?," *Environmental Forum* 26, no. 6 (2009): 36–40.

6. "Carbon Dioxide Could Double in Atmosphere by 2025, NOAA Says," *Environment Reporter,* June 1, 1979, 159.

7. "Limits on Total Fossil Fuel Use Seen One Answer to 'Greenhouse Effect,'" *Environment Reporter,* August 3, 1979, 895–896.

8. "EPA Outlook Examines Future Changes in World Climate Due to Carbon Dioxide," *Environment Reporter,* February 29, 1980, 2060.

9. "Higher Temperatures, Rising Seas Seen Unless Greenhouse Gas Emissions Lowered," *Environment Reporter,* June 10, 1988, 206–207.

10. "Rise in Sea Level from Greenhouse Effect Could Mean Major Wetland Losses, EPA Says," *Environment Reporter,* August 19, 1988, 692.

11. "Wirth, Stafford Introduce Legislation to Control Emissions of Greenhouse Gases," *Environment Reporter,* August 5, 1988, 461.

12. Barry Rabe, *Statehouse and Greenhouse: The Emerging Politics of American Climate Policy* (Washington, DC: Brookings Institution Press, 2004), 9.

13. Pub. L. No. 101-606, 104 Stat. 3096 (1990).

14. Clean Air Act Amendments of 1990, Pub. L. No. 101-549, 104 Stat. 2399 (codified as amended at 42 USC §§7401–7671q), §602(e).

15. "Bush Signing to Cap US Successes on Treaty, but Europeans Still Press for Stronger Action," *Environment Reporter,* June 12, 1992, 646.

16. "Clinton Commits US to Reduce Emissions of Greenhouse Gases to 1990 Level by 2000," *Environment Reporter,* April 23, 1993, 3187.

17. "Administration Preparing Options to Meet Clinton's Greenhouse Gas Goal, Official Says," *Environment Reporter,* June 18, 1993, 317–318; "Bill to Create Tradable Allowance System for Greenhouse Gases Planned by House Members," *Environment Reporter,* June 4, 1993, 239.

18. "Greenhouse Effect Gases Biggest Threat to Environment, Gore Says at Conference," *Environment Reporter,* April 29, 1994, 2227.

19. "House Majority Whip Introduces Legislation to Repeal Several Portions of Clean Air Act," *Environment Reporter,* January 20, 1995, 1787–1788.

20. President Clinton later vetoed this legislation. "Conferees Approve EPA Funding of $5.7 Billion; Temporary Spending, Reconciliation Bills Passed," *Environment Reporter,* November 24, 1995, 1265.

21. "Agency Furloughs Nonessential Workers as Government Shuts Down in Budget Dispute," *Environment Reporter,* November 17, 1995, 1210.

22. Rabe, *Statehouse and Greenhouse,* 12.

23. "Climate Change Report Says Action Needed to Curb Harmful Effects of Greenhouse Gases," *Environment Reporter,* January 5, 1996, 1574.

24. "Global Trading of Greenhouse Gases Sought in US Proposal for Climate Treaty Amendment," *Environment Reporter,* January 24, 1997, 1926.

25. "Climate Change Protocol Must Not Impose Economic Hardship, Senator Tells Conference," *Environment Reporter,* September 22, 1995, 935.

26. "Senators Criticize Clinton Administration on 'Binding' Accord to Cut Greenhouse Gases," *Environment Reporter,* September 20, 1996, 1144.

27. Byrd-Hagel Resolution, S. Res. 98, 105th Cong., July 25, 1997.

28. "Senate Committee Adopts Resolution Backing Commitments by Developing Nations," *Environment Reporter,* July 25, 1997, 586.

29. "Last-Minute Move by US Led to Pact, Some Delegates to Negotiations Assert," *Environment Reporter,* December 12, 1997, 1567.

30. "Negotiators in Japan Reach Agreement for 6 Percent Emission Cut by

2008–2012," *Environment Reporter*, December 12, 1997, 1565; Rabe, *Statehouse and Greenhouse*, 11.

31. "Administration 'Rushing into Deal' that Will Hurt Economy, GOP Senators Say," *Environment Reporter*, December 12, 1997, 1566.

32. "Chafee, 10 Others Introduce Bill to Credit Voluntary Greenhouse Gas Emission Cuts," *Environment Reporter*, March 12, 1999, 2214.

33. Rabe, *Statehouse and Greenhouse*, 15.

34. "Democrats Ask President to Veto Bills with 'Anti-Environmental' Riders," *Environment Reporter*, October 2, 1998, 1118.

35. Memorandum from Jonathan Z. Cannon to Carol M. Browner, "EPA's Authority to Regulate Pollutants Emitted by Electric Power Generation Sources," April 10, 1998 (on file with author).

36. Clean Air Act, 42 USC §7602(g) (as amended by the Clean Air Act Amendments of 1977, Pub. L. No. 95-95, 91 Stat. 685).

37. Memorandum from Cannon.

38. Joint Hearings before the Subcommittee on National Economic Growth, Natural Resources, and Regulatory Affairs of the House Committee on Government Reform, and the Subcommittee on Energy and Environment of the House Committee on Science, 106th Cong., 1st Sess., October 6, 1999.

39. Ibid. (testimony of Gary S. Guzy, general counsel of the EPA).

40. Ibid.; "No Plans to Regulate Carbon Dioxide, Although Legal Authority Exists, EPA Says," *Environment Reporter*, October 15, 1999, 1085.

41. International Center for Technology Assessment et al., Petition for Rulemaking and Collateral Relief Seeking the Regulation of Greenhouse Gas Emissions from New Motor Vehicles under §202 of the Clean Air Act, October 20, 1999, http://www.ciel.org.

42. Ibid., 29; "Groups Urge EPA to Limit Automotive CO_2, Vow Suit Unless Tailpipe Gases Regulated," *Environment Reporter*, October 22, 1999, 1127.

43. "Groups Urge EPA to Limit Automotive CO_2."

44. "Bush Will Not Negotiate Kyoto Pact, Calls for Cabinet Review of CO_2 Issues," *Environment Reporter*, March 30, 2001, 581.

45. Douglas Jehl and Andrew C. Revkin, "Bush, in Reversal, Won't Seek Cut in Emissions of Carbon Dioxide," *New York Times*, March 14, 2001; "Bush Refuses to Support Mandatory Cuts of Carbon Dioxide from Electric Power Plants," *Environment Reporter*, March 16, 2001, 477.

46. Rabe, *Statehouse and Greenhouse*, 14–15.

47. "Lieberman, McCain Announce Intent to Draft Legislation Creating Cap-and-Trade System," *Environment Reporter*, 1574.

48. Rabe, *Statehouse and Greenhouse*, 15.

49. Ibid.; Eric Pianin, "On Global Warming, States Act Locally," *Washington Post*, November 11, 2002.

50. Letter from 11 State Attorneys General to President Bush, July 17, 2002, http://www.ag.ny.gov.

51. "11 Attorneys General Prod White House, Threaten Legal Action to Force Policy Change," *Environment Reporter*, July 19, 2002, 1599.

52. Pianin, "On Global Warming."

53. International Center for Technology Assessment v. Whitman, Docket No. DC-1:02 CV 2376 (D.D.C., filed December 5, 2002).

54. "Lawsuit Filed to Force EPA to Regulate Greenhouse Gases from Mobile Sources," *Environment Reporter,* December 13, 2002, 2681.

55. Ibid.

56. Clean Air Act, 42 USC §7408(a)(1).

57. Massachusetts v. Whitman, No. 03-1361 (D. Conn., filed June 4, 2003).

58. Complaint, Massachusetts v. Whitman, No. 03–1361, at 29–30 (D. Conn., filed June 4, 2003).

59. Nicholas Zamiska, "EPA Is Sued Over Carbon Dioxide: 3 NE States Charge Violation," *Boston Globe,* June 5, 2003.

60. Ibid.

61. Notice of Denial of Petition for Rulemaking, 68 Fed. Reg. 52,922 (September 8, 2003).

62. "EPA Says It Does Not Have Authority to Regulate Carbon Dioxide from Vehicles," *Environment Reporter*, September 5, 2003, 1925.

63. Ibid.

64. "States, Cities, Advocacy Groups File Lawsuit Saying EPA Has Authority to Regulate Gases," *Environment Reporter*, October 31, 2003, 2381.

65. Final Brief for Petitioners in Consolidated Cases, Massachusetts v. EPA, 415 F. 3d 50 (D.C. Cir. 2005).

66. Ibid., 36–37.

67. "Forum: The Role of State Attorneys General in National Environmental Policy," *Columbia Journal of Environmental Law* 30, no. 2 (2005): 342.

68. Ibid., 344.

69. Tom Nugent, "Mother Earth's Counsel," *University of Chicago Magazine,* September–October 2007.

70. The ten AGs represented Alaska, Idaho, Kansas, Michigan, North Dakota, Nebraska, Ohio, South Dakota, Texas, and Utah. Indiana's AG also participated as an amici.

71. 467 US 837, 842–843 (1984).

72. Final Brief for the Intervenor States of Michigan, et al., Massachusetts v. EPA, No. 03-1361 (D.C. Cir. 2005).

73. Massachusetts v. EPA, 415 F. 3d 50 (D.C. Cir. 2005), 58.

74. Ibid., 59–60 (Judge Sentelle dissenting in part and concurring in the judgment).

75. Ibid., 64–68, 81 (Judge Tatel dissenting).

76. The DC circuit court rejected en banc review by a 7–3 vote. "Court Denies Request to Rehear Petition Seeking EPA Rule on Auto Greenhouse Gases," *Environment Reporter*, December 9, 2005, 2498.

77. "States Brief to High Court Says EPA Has Authority to Regulate Greenhouse Gases," *Environment Reporter*, September 8, 2006, 1818.

78. Sierra Club, "Powerful Coalition Petitions Supreme Court to Order EPA to Obey the Law," August 31, 2006, http://www.florida.sierraclub.org.

79. Massachusetts v. EPA, 549 US 497, 518–520 (2007).

80. Ibid., 531.

81. Ibid., 533–534.

82. Office of the New York Attorney General, "Attorney General Andrew Cuomo Issues Statement on Historic Global Warming Decision," April 2, 2007, http://www.ag.ny.gov.

83. Massachusetts v. EPA, 549 US 497 at 532.

84. Ron Scherer and Alexandra Marks, "New Environmental Cops: State Attorneys General," *Christian Science Monitor*, July 22, 2004, quoting California attorney general Bill Lockyer.

85. New York City's counsel also joined the lawsuit. Office of the New York Attorney General, "Eight States and NYC Sue Top Five US Global Warming Polluters," July 21, 2004, http://www.ag.ny.gov.

86. Complaint, Connecticut v. American Electric Power, No. 04-CV-05669, at 49 (S.D.N.Y., filed July 21, 2004).

87. "Utilities Argue that States Lack Standing to Sue over Control of Greenhouse Gases," *Environment Reporter*, August 19, 2005, 1713.

88. Office of the New York Attorney General, "Eight States and NYC Sue."

89. Complaint, Connecticut v. American Electric Power, No. 04-CV-05669, at 43–49.

90. "8 States to Sue Power Companies," *CBS News*, July 21, 2004, http://www.cbsnews.com.

91. US Chamber of Commerce, "US Chamber Calls Global Warming Lawsuit an End-Run Around Congress and Regulatory Agencies," July 20, 2004, https://www.uschamber.com.

92. Vincent S. Oleszkiewicz and Douglas B. Sanders, "The Advent of Climate Change Litigation against Corporate Defendants," *Environment Reporter*, November 12, 2004, 2365.

93. Office of the New York Attorney General, "Eight States and NYC Sue."

94. Complaint, Connecticut v. American Electric Power, No. 04-CV-05669, at 39, 44.

95. "The Role of State Attorneys General in Environmental Policy," *Columbia Journal of Environmental Law* 30, no. 2 (2005): 340.

96. Larry Neumeister, "Five Large Power Companies Sued over Global Warming," *Associated Press*, July 21, 2004.

97. "Conservation Groups File Separate Lawsuit against Utilities over CO_2," *Environment Reporter*, July 23, 2004, 1567.

98. Connecticut v. American Electric Power, 406 F. Supp. 2d 265, 272–274 (S.D.N.Y. 2005).

99. "Judge Dismisses Greenhouse Gases Lawsuit, Says Other Branches Control Policy Decision," *Environment Reporter*, September 23, 2005, 1945.

100. Marcia Coyle, "Questions Arise about Long Delay by Sotomayor-Led Panel in Climate Case," *National Law Journal*, May 28, 2009, http://www.alm.law.com.

101. The importance of the *parens patriae* doctrine to AG litigation is also noted in chapter 2.

102. Connecticut v. American Electric Power Company, 582 F. 3d 309 (2nd Cir. 2009).

103. Ibid., 325, 332.

104. Ibid., 325.

105. Ibid., 337–338, 356, 392.

106. Connecticut Attorney General's Office, "Attorney General Praises Appeals Court Ruling Reinstating Global Warming Lawsuit," September 21, 2009, http://www.ct.gov.

107. Ibid.

108. Chris Rizo, "State AGs Hail Ruling in Greenhouse Gas Case," *Legal Newsline*, September 21, 2009, http://legalnewsline.com.

109. "Strategies for Reducing Greenhouse Gases Help Profitability, Corporate Executives Say," *Environment Reporter*, May 14, 2004, 1078.

110. John Schwartz, "Courts Emerging as Battlefield for Fights over Climate Change," *New York Times*, January 27, 2010.

111. Brief of the States of Indiana, et al., American Electric Power, et al. v. State of Connecticut, et al., No. 10-174 (September 3, 2010), 2.

112. Brief of Unions for Jobs and the Environment, American Electric Power, et al. v. State of Connecticut, et al., No. 10-174 (September 1, 2010), 2.

113. Steven D. Cook, "Administration Asks Supreme Court to Vacate Ruling Allowing Nuisance Claims on Climate," *Environment Reporter*, August 27, 2010, 1934.

114. Brief for the Tennessee Valley Authority in Support of Petitioners, American Electric Power v. State of Connecticut, No. 10-174 (filed August 2010); Steven Mufson, "Administration Backs Utilities in Climate Case," *Washington Post*, August 27, 2010.

115. Cook, "Administration Asks Supreme Court to Vacate Ruling."

116. American Electric Power v. Connecticut, 131 S. Ct. 2527 (2011).

117. Ibid., at §3. The decision on this standing ground was 4 to 4 because Justice Sotomayor did not participate in this case, the result of her participation on the Second Circuit panel that had decided the case below.

118. Ibid., at §5.

CHAPTER 8. STATE LITIGATION AND NATIONAL ENVIRONMENTAL POLICY

1. The quotations are from an influential document by William Safire (writing as Publius) and distributed among Nixon presidential assistants. Publius, "New Federalist Paper No. 1," *Publius: The Journal of Federalism* 2, no. 1 (1972): 111–112.

2. For example, see "EPA to Give States Main Responsibility for Stopping Significant Deterioration," *Environment Reporter*, April 19, 1974, 2091.

3. Farhang, *Litigation State*.

4. Reitze, *Air Pollution Control Law*, 599–600.

5. Clean Air Act, Pub. L. No. 91-604, 84 Stat. 1676, §304(a)(1)–(2) (codified at 42 USC §7604(a)(1)–(2)).

6. Clean Air Act Amendments of 1990, Pub. L. No. 101-549, 104 Stat. 2399, §707 (adding a new §304(g) to the CAA and amending the existing §304(a)).

7. See, for example, Adam J. Sulkowski, "Ultra Vires Statutes: Alive, Kicking,

and a Means of Circumventing the Scalia Standing Gauntlet in Environmental Litigation," *Journal of Environmental Law and Litigation* 24, no. 1 (2009): 75–118.

8. Massachusetts v. EPA, 549 US 497, 520 (2007).

9. Lujan v. Defenders of Wildlife, 504 US 555 (1992).

10. Natural Resources Defense Council v. EPA, 542 F. 3d 1235 (2008), 1248n8; California Resources Agency, et al. v. US Department of Agriculture, 2009 US Dist. Lexis 89991 (N.D. Cal. 2009), *24–*25; Southeastern Federal Power Customers, Inc. v. Geren, 514 F. 3d 1316 (2008), 1322; North Carolina v. EPA, 587 F. 3d 422, 427 (D.C. Cir. 2009).

11. Coalition for Responsible Regulation v. EPA, 684 F. 3d 102 (D.C. Cir. 2012); Wyoming v. US Department of the Interior, 674 F. 3d 1220, 1238 (10th Cir. 2012).

12. Masters, *Spoiling for a Fight,* 57.

13. "Documents Prove Northeastern States Aware Problems Mostly Local, Group Says," *Environment Reporter,* February 6, 1998, 2007.

14. One prominent example was a settlement between the Obama administration's EPA and AG plaintiffs requiring the EPA to limit the amount of greenhouse gas emissions from new fossil fuel power plants. Office of the New York Attorney General, "AG Schneiderman Commends EPA for Taking Actions to Limit Greenhouse Gas Pollution from New Power Plants," March 27, 2012, http://www.ag.ny.gov.

15. Chris Casteel, "Correspondence with Groups is Sought," *Oklahoman,* August 11, 2012; Oklahoma Office of the Attorney General, "Attorney General Pruitt Leads Multi-State Lawsuit Demanding Transparency in EPA's Sweetheart Settlements with Environmental Groups," July 16, 2013, http://www.oag.state.ok.us.

16. Melnick, *Regulation and the Courts.*

17. Examples of courts' skepticism of private party standing in climate change lawsuits, even after Massachusetts v. EPA, include Comer v. Murphy Oil, 839 F. Supp. 2d 849, 861 (S.D. Miss. 2012), and Washington Environmental Council v. Bellon, 732 F. 3d 1131 (9th Cir. 2013), request for en banc review denied, 741 F. 3d 1075 (9th Cir. 2014) (M. Smith, circuit judge, concurring).

18. See "Litigating Climate Change Policy" in chapter 9.

19. Specifically, in the eight multistate acid rain cases before the CAA of 1990, Democratic AGs made thirty-six appearances in favor of stricter air pollution regulations and Republican AGs made twenty appearances. Two of the cases involved AGs supporting the EPA's less strict regulatory approach, and both cases involved three Democratic AGs and one Republican AG.

20. Richard L. Madden, "State Bands with 6 Others in the Battle on Acid Rain," *New York Times,* August 11, 1985.

21. "GOP Delegates Favor Acid Rain Controls; Platform Differs with Some Reagan Policies," *Environment Reporter,* August 19, 1988, 691.

22. Rabe, *Statehouse and Greenhouse,* 165.

23. John M. Broder, "EPA Expected to Regulate Carbon Dioxide and Other Heat-Trapping Gases," *New York Times,* February 19, 2009.

24. "Bid to Use Transboundary Sections of Law for Acid Rain Draws Ruckelshaus' Opposition," *Environment Reporter,* February 3, 1984, 30.

25. These regulations state that the EPA has authority to regulate stationary source emissions involving "any pollutant that otherwise is subject to regulation under the Act." US Environmental Protection Agency, "Prevention of Significant Deterioration of Air Quality," 40 Code of Federal Regulations 52.21(b)(50)(iv); Requirements for Preparation, Adoption, and Submittal of Implementation Plans; Approval and Promulgation of Implementation Plans, 45 Fed. Reg. 52,676 (August 7, 1980). Because *Massachusetts v. EPA* triggered regulation of greenhouse gases under the Clean Air Act, greenhouse gases became pollutants "subject to regulation under the Act" and thereby covered by these stationary source provisions.

26. "EPA Working on Climate Regulations Affecting Mobile, Stationary Sources," *Environment Reporter*, January 22, 2010, S-11.

27. "Despite EPA Concerns, Permit Alternatives May Be Possible if Emissions Are Regulated," *Environment Reporter*, April 11, 2008, 698.

28. "Prospect of EPA Regulation of Emissions Should Spur Congress to Act, Supporters Say," *Environment Reporter*, April 24, 2009, 909.

29. The major effort is the US Climate Action Partnership, which includes among its members Duke Energy, General Electric, PG&E Corporation, and several other Fortune 500 firms. US Climate Action Partnership, "About Us," http://www.us-cap.org.

30. For example, American Electric Power, the largest and most prominent defendant in the *Connecticut* suit, supported the House cap-and-trade legislation. John Schwartz, "Courts Emerging as Battlefield for Fights over Climate Change," *New York Times*, January 27, 2010.

31. "Proposed Endangerment and Cause or Contribute Findings for Greenhouse Gases under Section 202(a) of the Clean Air Act." 74 Fed. Reg. 18,885 (April 24, 2009); "Standard on Vehicle Carbon Emissions Announced in EPA Greenhouse Gas Limits," *Environment Reporter*, April 2, 2010, 723.

32. "House Bill Would Amend Clean Air Act to Bar EPA Greenhouse Gas Emissions Rules," *Environment Reporter*, August 8, 2008, 1576; "Senate Climate Bill Goes Down to Defeat, Falling 12 Votes Short on Cloture Motion," *Environment Reporter*, June 13, 2008, 1146; Steven D. Cook, "Senate Rejects Murkowski Resolution Aimed at Halting Greenhouse Gas Rules," *Environment Reporter*, June 11, 2010, 1291.

33. Donald L. Horowitz, *Courts and Social Policy* (Washington, DC: Brookings Institution Press, 1977), especially chapter 2.

CHAPTER 9. THE RISE OF CONSERVATIVE STATE LITIGATION AND THE CHANGING SHAPE OF AG ACTIVISM

1. Will Weissert, "Texas Spends Big Bucks Suing Federal Government on State Issues," Associated Press, September 9, 2012, http://m.lubbockonline.com; Manny Fernandez, "Texas Attorney General to New Yorkers: Come on Down, with Guns," *New York Times*, January 20, 2013.

2. I discuss climate change litigation later in this chapter. Challenges to financial regulations included an Oklahoma-led effort against the Dodd-Frank financial

regulations enacted in 2009. Oklahoma Office of the Attorney General, "Oklahoma, 10 Other States File Appeal of Lawsuit against Dodd-Frank Financial Law," February 12, 2014, http://www.oag.state.ok.us. For other examples of litigation involving Republican AGs, see Paul Nolette, "State Litigation during the Obama Administration: Diverging Agendas in an Era of Polarized Politics," *Publius: The Journal of Federalism* 44, no. 3 (2014): 451–474.

3. Massachusetts v. Mellon, 262 US 447 (1923); South Carolina v. Katzenbach, 383 US 301 (1966).

4. Scott Wilson, "With a Signature, Obama Seals His Health-Care Victory," *Washington Post,* March 24, 2010.

5. Patient Protection and Affordable Care Act of 2010, Pub. L. No. 111-148, 124 Stat. 199 (2010).

6. Statement of Douglas W. Elmendorf, "CBO's Analysis of the Major Health Care Legislation Enacted in March 2010," Subcommittee on Health, Committee on Energy and Commerce, March 30, 2011, http://www.cbo.gov.

7. Sheryl Gay Stolberg and Robert Pear, "Obama Signs Health Care Overhaul Bill, with a Flourish," *New York Times,* March 24, 2010.

8. Peter Slevin and Rosalind S. Helderman, "GOP State Leaders Say They'll Fight Health-Care Legislation," *Washington Post,* March 23, 2010, A8.

9. David B. Rivkin Jr. and Lee A. Casey, "Mandatory Insurance Is Unconstitutional," *Wall Street Journal,* September 18, 2009.

10. Chris Frates, "Payoffs for States Get Harry Reid to 60 Votes," *Politico,* December 19, 2009, http://www.politico.com.

11. Letter from 13 Attorneys General to Speaker Nancy Pelosi and Majority Leader Harry Reid, December 30, 2009, http://thehill.com.

12. Kevin Sack and Eric Lichtblau, "For Attorneys General, a Long Shot on Health Care Law Brings Payoffs," *New York Times,* July 1, 2012.

13. Letter from 13 Attorneys General.

14. Michael C. Bender, "McCollum Questions Health Reforms," *Palm Beach Post (FL),* December 30, 2009, A2.

15. Two additions included Nebraska's AG as well as Louisiana's Buddy Caldwell, who served as the only Democratic AG to join the health care litigation—albeit only for a short time before he switched to the Republican Party a few months later. Two AGs had signed the letter but did not appear as plaintiffs on the original ACA complaint. This included North Dakota's AG, who later joined the suit, and the acting Virginia AG whom Cuccinelli replaced after his election in 2009.

16. The three judges in Pensacola were Margaret Catherine Rodgers (G. W. Bush), Lacey Collier (G. H. W. Bush), and Roger Vinson (Reagan). The Tallahassee judges included Robert Hinkle (Clinton), William Stafford Jr. (Ford), and Stephan Mickle (Clinton).

17. Kevin Sack, "Florida Suit Rated Best as Challenge to Care Law," *New York Times,* May 11, 2010.

18. Neil A. Lewis, "Bush Is Not Expected to Feel Need to Pick Woman Again," *New York Times,* October 28, 2005.

19. Complaint, Florida v. Health and Human Services, No. 3:10-cv-91 (N.D. Fla., filed March 23, 2010), 4, 16.

20. Rosalind S. Helderman, "Virginia Assembly Approves Bill to Bar Health-Insurance Mandate," *Washington Post,* March 11, 2010.

21. Complaint for Declaratory and Injunctive Relief, Virginia v. Sebelius, No. 3:10-cv-188 (E.D. Va., filed March 23, 2010), 5.

22. Office of the Virginia Attorney General, "Federal Government Responds to Virginia's Lawsuit over Health Care Law," May 24, 2010, http://www.oag.state.va.us.

23. Cost Share Agreement, Florida v. HHS (No. 3:10-cv-91, N.D. FL) (signed April 2, 2010) (document available from author).

24. Complaint, Thomas More Law Center v. Obama, No. 2:10-cv-11156 (E.D. Mich., filed March 23, 2010).

25. N. C. Aizenman, "An Outbreak of Battles for Health-Care Law," *Washington Post,* May 12, 2010.

26. Katie Kerwin McKrimmon, "Court Fight over Health Law Escalates," *Health News Colorado,* December 8, 2010, http://www.healthnewscolorado.org.

27. "Health Care Reform Is Constitutional," *Politico,* October 23, 2009, http://www.politico.com.

28. Simon Lazarus and Alan Morrison, "Lawsuit Abuse, GOP Style," *Slate,* May 5, 2010, http://www.slate.com.

29. Aizenman, "Outbreak of Battles."

30. Fried made the comments on Fox News on April 14, 2010. A transcript of the exchange is available online (http://www.foxnews.com).

31. Virginia v. Sebelius, 702 F. Supp. 2d 768 (E.D. Va. 2010).

32. Florida v. Health and Human Services, 780 F. Supp. 2d 1256 (N.D. Fla. 2011).

33. Repealing the Job-Killing Health Care Law Act, HR 2, 112th Cong. (2011).

34. Testimony of Kenneth T. Cuccinelli II before the House Judiciary Committee, February 16, 2011, http://judiciary.house.gov.

35. Aizenman, "Outbreak of Battles."

36. California Attorney General, "Attorney General Kamala D. Harris Files Brief in Defense of Health Care Reform," April 12, 2011, http://oag.ca.gov.

37. Brief of the States of Oregon, et al., Florida v. HHS, Nos. 11-11021-HH and 11-11067-HH (11th Cir., filed April 8, 2011), 4, 26.

38. Alexander Bolton, "Lawmakers Press Supreme Court for Verdict on Health-care Law," *The Hill,* February 2, 2011, http://thehill.com.

39. Joan Biskupic, "Behind the Health-Care Law Case: The Challengers' Tale," Reuters, March 13, 2012, http://www.reuters.com.

40. Sarah E. Needleman and Angus Loten, "A Small-Business Lobby's Million-Dollar Legal Assault," *Wall Street Journal,* March 27, 2012.

41. Charles Elmore, "Lobbying Group Picks up Costs of Florida's Health-Care Challenge," *Palm Beach Post (FL),* February 19, 2011, http://www.palmbeachpost.com.

42. The eight US district court cases were Thomas More Law Center v. Obama,

720 F. Supp. 2d 882 (E.D. Mich. 2010); Liberty University v. Geithner, 753 F. Supp. 2d 611 (W.D. Va. 2010); New Jersey Physicians, Inc. v. Obama, 757 F.Supp. 2d 502 (D.N.J. 2010); Bryant v. Holder, 809 F. Supp. 2d 563 (S.D. Miss. 2011); Mead v. Holder, 766 F. Supp. 2d 16 (D.D.C. 2011); Peterson v. Obama, 1:10-CV-00170 (D.N.H. 2011); Purpura v. Sebelius, 2011 WL 1547768 (D.N.J. 2011); Kinder v. Department of Treasury, 1:10-CV-00101 (E.D. Mo. 2011).

43. Thomas More Law Center v. Obama, 651 F. 3d 529 (6th Cir. 2011).

44. New Jersey Physicians Inc. v. Obama, No. 10-4600 (3rd Cir. 2011).

45. Florida v. Health and Human Services, 648 F. 3d 1235 (11th Cir. 2011).

46. Virginia v. Sebelius, 656 F. 3d 253 (4th Cir. 2011).

47. The NFIB filed its cert petition on the morning of September 28, 2011, with the states filing theirs just before noon and the DOJ later that afternoon. Because it was filed first, the NFIB petition received a lower case number than either the states' or the DOJ's appeal. The appellant with the lowest case number appears in the title of consolidated cases, explaining why the case will forever carry the title *NFIB v. Sebelius.*

48. Adam Serwer, "Obamacare's Supreme Court Disaster," *Mother Jones,* March 27, 2012, http://www.motherjones.com.

49. NFIB v. Sebelius, 132 S. Ct. 2566, 2600 (2012).

50. Ibid., at 2608.

51. John Rossomando, "Florida Atty. Gen. Pam Bondi Calls Obamacare Decision a Partial Victory for Limited Gov't," August 4, 2012, http://redalertpolitics.com.

52. Sack and Lichtblau, "For Attorneys General, a Long Shot."

53. As of June 2014, twenty-one states had declined to accept the Medicaid expansion. Kaiser Family Foundation, "Status of State Action on the Medicaid Expansion Decision," June 10, 2014, http://kff.org.

54. Jonathan Weisman and Ashley Parker, "Shutdown Is Over," *New York Times,* October 17, 2013; John Parkinson, "House Takes 50th Vote to Change 'Obamacare,'" *ABC News,* March 5, 2014, http://abcnews.go.com.

55. Kaiser Family Foundation, "Kaiser Health Tracking Poll: April 2013," April 30, 2013, http://kff.org.

56. Complaint, Nebraska v. Health and Human Services, No. 4:12-CV-3035 (D. Neb., filed February 23, 2012).

57. Brief of Amicus Curiae States of Michigan, et al., Sebelius v. Hobby Lobby Stores, Inc., Nos. 13-354 and 13-356 (filed January 27, 2014); Brief of California, et al., Sebelius v. Hobby Lobby Stores, Inc., Nos. 13-354 and 13-356 (filed January 28, 2014).

58. Burwell v. Hobby Lobby Stores, Inc., 573 US ____ (2014).

59. Amended Complaint for Declaratory and Injunctive Relief, Pruitt v. Sebelius, No. CIV-11-030-RAW (filed September 19, 2012).

60. Complaint for Declaratory and Injunctive Relief and Judicial Estoppel, State of Indiana v. IRS, No. 1:13-cv-1612 (S.D. Ind., filed October 8, 2013); Complaint, King v. Burwell, No. 13-CV-630 (E.D. Va., filed September 16, 2013); Complaint, Halbig v. Sebelius, No. 13-623 (D.D.C., filed May 2, 2013).

61. Halbig v. Burwell, 2014 US App. LEXIS 13880 (DC Cir. July 22, 2014).

62. Brief of Texas, et al., Hotze v. Sebelius, No. 14–20039 (5th Cir., filed May 15, 2014).

63. Massachusetts v. EPA, 549 US 497 (2007).

64. In a memorandum to EPA employees issued on her first day as administrator, Jackson mentioned reducing greenhouse gas emissions as the first of her top five priorities. Lisa P. Jackson, "Opening Memo to EPA Employees," January 23, 2009, http://blog.epa.gov.

65. "Light Duty Vehicle Greenhouse Gas Emission Standards and Corporate Average Fuel Economy Standards," 75 Fed. Reg. 25,324 (May 7, 2010).

66. Clean Air Act, 42 USC §7479(1).

67. Requirements for Preparation, Adoption, and Submittal of Implementation Plans; Approval and Promulgation of Implementation Plans, 45 Fed. Reg. 52,676 (August 7, 1980).

68. "Reconsideration of Interpretation of Regulations that Determine Pollutants Covered by Clean Air Act Permitting Programs," 75 Fed. Reg. 17,004 (April 2, 2010).

69. "Prevention of Significant Deterioration and Title V Greenhouse Gas Tailoring Rule," 74 Fed. Reg. 55,291 (October 27, 2009).

70. "Prevention of Significant Deterioration and Title V Greenhouse Gas Tailoring Rule," 75 Fed. Reg. 31,514 (June 3, 2010).

71. John M. Broder, "Greenhouse Gases Imperil Health, EPA Announces," *New York Times,* December 8, 2009.

72. Steven D. Cook and Carolyn Whetzel, "EPA Proposal Would Require Large Sources to Control Their Greenhouse Gas Emissions," *Environment Reporter,* October 2, 2009, 2281.

73. Jim Snyder, "EPA Head Blasts Efforts to Block Regs," *The Hill,* March 4, 2010, 12, http://thehill.com.

74. Cook, "Senate Rejects Murkowski Resolution."

75. National Conference of State Legislatures, "Climate Change: State Policy Update 2011," August 2011, http://www.ncsl.org.

76. Jim Snyder, "Big Business Plots to Block EPA," *The Hill,* January 20, 2010, http://thehill.com.

77. Robin Bravender, "Lawsuits Roll In as 'Endangerment' Deadline Looms," *New York Times,* February 16, 2010.

78. Neela Banerjee, "Texas Challenges the EPA over Climate Change Rules," *Washington Post,* November 28, 2010, A9.

79. Asher Price, "State Files Federal Lawsuit to Prevent EPA from Regulating Greenhouse Gases," *Austin American-Statesman,* February 17, 2010, A1.

80. Mark Clayton, "Texas, Virginia Challenge EPA Greenhouse Gas Finding," *Christian Science Monitor,* February 17, 2010.

81. Attorney General of Virginia, "Statement Regarding the University of Virginia's Challenge of the Attorney General's Civil Investigative Demand," May 28, 2010, http://www.oag.state.va.us.

82. Cuccinelli v. University of Virginia, No. 102359 (Va. March 2, 2012).

83. John M. Broder, "EPA Won't Require Pollution Permits This Year," *New York Times,* March 30, 2010.

84. Congressman Jim Moran, "Memo to Cuccinelli: Stop Harassment and Intimidation of UVA Scientist," May 13, 2010, http://moran.house.gov; Bryan McKenzie, "Senators Target Cuccinelli's UVA Probe," *Daily Progress (VA),* January 18, 2011.

85. Massachusetts AG's Office, "Attorney General Martha Coakley's Office Moves to Intervene in Lawsuit to Block Federal Emissions Regulations," January 22, 2010, http://www.mass.gov.

86. Asher Price, "Lawyer Representing Texas in Environment and Health Suits Has Ties to Industries," *Austin American-Statesman,* February 27, 2011, http://www.statesman.com.

87. Brief of Texas for State Petitioners and Supporting Intervenors, Coalition for Responsible Regulation v. EPA, No. 10-1073 (D.C. Cir., filed May 20, 2011).

88. Brief of State Petitioners and Supporting Intervenors, Coalition for Responsible Regulation v. EPA, No. 10-1073 (D.C. Cir., filed June 20, 2011), 18.

89. Brief for State and Environmental Intervenors in Support of Respondents, Coalition for Responsible Regulation v. EPA, No. 10-1131 (D.C. Cir., filed October 17, 2011).

90. Coalition for Responsible Regulation v. EPA, 684 F. 3d 102 (D.C. Cir. 2012), 28, 77.

91. Utility Air Regulatory Group v. EPA, 573 US ___ (2014).

92. Office of the Texas Attorney General, "US Supreme Court Overturns EPA's Illegal Greenhouse Gas Permitting Scheme," June 23, 2014, https://www.texasattorneygeneral.gov.

93. Massachusetts Attorney General's Office, "Supreme Court Upholds EPA's Regulation of Greenhouse Gas Pollution from Large Stationary Sources," June 23, 2014, http://www.mass.gov/ago.

94. Joan Biskupic, "State Attorneys General: New Republican Power," Reuters, April 24, 2012, http://www.reuters.com.

95. See Reno v. Condon, 528 US 141 (2000).

96. Republican governors such as George Allen (VA), Jim Edgar (IL), and Pete Wilson (CA) were leaders of the effort against the motor-voter law. Peter Baker, "Allen to Join Motor Voter Rebellion," *Washington Post,* March 30, 1995.

97. Of the AGs supporting Abrams's challenge, thirteen were Democrats and only four were Republican. Two Democratic and one Republican AG supported the federal government's position.

98. Brief of the States of Ohio, et al., United States v. Lopez, 514 US 549 (1995) (filed June 2, 1994).

99. Supporting the federal government's position were thirty-two Democratic and four Republican AGs.

100. Petition for a Writ of Certiorari Before Judgment, Virginia v. Sebelius (filed February 8, 2011).

101. Waltenburg and Swinford, *Litigating Federalism*, 57–65; Michael Solimine, "State Amici, Collective Action, and the Development of the Federalism Doctrine," *Georgia Law Review* 46 (2012): 355–406.

102. Nolette, "State Litigation."

103. Michael E. Solimine, "The Solicitor General Unbound: Amicus Curiae Activism and Deference in the Supreme Court," *Arizona State Law Journal* 45, no. 2 (2013): 1183–1225.

104. Information about how these data were collected is available in the Appendix.

105. I chose this 80 percent threshold because it provides the best balance between cases attracting significant bipartisan support and cases that might have attracted the support of one or two AGs from the opposite party but were nevertheless clearly partisan in nature. However, I also examined the data using a 70, 90, and 100 percent threshold to determine partisanship, and the trends were similar.

106. The five cases were Romer v. Evans, 517 US 620 (1996) (gay rights), United States v. Virginia, 518 US 515 (1996) (sex discrimination), Printz v. United States, 521 US 898 (1997) (whether Congress can require state officials to regulate handgun purchases), Norfolk Southern Railway Co. v. Shanklin, 529 US 344 (2000) (whether federal law preempts state-level private tort claims), and Bush v. Palm Beach County Canvassing Board, 531 US 70 (2000) (involving the contested 2000 presidential election).

107. Bowers v. Hardwick, 478 US 186 (1986); Edwards v. Aguillard, 482 US 578 (1987).

108. Pew Research Center, "Partisan Polarization Surges in Bush, Obama Years," June 4, 2012, http://www.people-press.org.

109. Dale Krane, "The Middle Tier in American Federalism," *Publius: The Journal of Federalism* 37 (2007): 453–477.

110. Karl Kurtz, "These Unified States," *State Legislatures* 24 (May 2013), http://www.ncsl.org.

111. Between 1980 and 1994, Democrats controlled no fewer than thirty-one of the fifty state AG positions. Apart from dropping to twenty-nine seats for two years after the 1994 elections, Democrats continued to control at least thirty seats every year until 2005.

112. William H. Pryor Jr., "State Attorney General Litigation: Regulation through Litigation and the Separation of Powers," *Seton Hall Law Review* 31 (2007): 604–611.

113. See the website of the Democratic Attorneys General Association (http://www.democraticags.org).

114. Mark Curriden, "Republican AG Group Creates Friction; Stated Goal Is to Battle Trend of Making Policy via Litigation," *Dallas Morning News*, July 10, 1999.

115. Dan Balz, "Red, Blue States Move in Opposite Directions in a New Era of Single-Party Control," *Washington Post*, December 28, 2013.

116. Barbara Sinclair, *Party Wars* (University of Oklahoma Press, 2006), chapter 4.

117. Teles, *Rise of the Conservative Legal Movement*.

118. Nugent, "Mother Earth's Counsel."

119. In addition to chapters 3 through 5 of this book, see Paul Nolette's forthcoming "Law Enforcement as Legal Mobilization: Reforming the Pharmaceutical Industry through Government Litigation" in *Law and Social Inquiry.*

120. Jack Balkin, "*Bush v. Gore* and the Boundary between Law and Politics," *Yale Law Journal* 110, no. 8 (2001): 1407–1458.

121. Gregory A. Caldeira and John R. Wright, "Organized Interests and Agenda-Setting in the US Supreme Court," *American Political Science Review* 82, no. 4 (1988): 1109–1128.

122. Virginia v. Sebelius, 702 F. Supp. 2d 598 (E.D. Va. 2010), 606n5.

123. Massachusetts Attorney General's Office, "AG Coakley Leads Multistate Effort Urging Supreme Court to Strike Down California's Proposition 8 and DOMA as Unconstitutional," February 28, 2013, http://www.mass.gov.

124. Brief of Indiana, et al., Hollingsworth v. Perry, 133 S. Ct. 2652 (2013); Brief of Indiana, et al. United States v. Windsor, 133 S. Ct. 2675 (2013).

125. Brief of Michigan, et al., McCullen v. Coakley, No. 1168 (cert. granted June 24, 2013).

126. Brief of Texas, et al., McDonald v. Chicago, 561 US 3025 (2010).

127. Brief of California, et al., Schuette v. Coalition to Defend Affirmative Action, 133 S. Ct. 1633 (2014).

128. Nolette, "State Litigation," 10.

CHAPTER 10. STATE ATTORNEYS GENERAL AND THE NATIONALIZATION OF STATE LITIGATION

1. See, for example, Weaver and Rockman, "Assessing the Effects of Institutions," 26.

2. Madison, "Federalist #51," 322.

3. See, for example, Sanford Levinson, *Our Undemocratic Constitution: Where the Constitution Goes Wrong* (New York: Oxford University Press, 2006); Daniel Lazare, *The Frozen Republic: How the Constitution Is Paralyzing Democracy* (New York: Harcourt Brace, 1997).

4. Silverstein, *Law's Allure.*

5. Farhang, *Litigation State.*

6. Amended Complaint, Florida v. Health and Human Services, No. 3:10-cv-91 (N.D. Fla., filed May 14, 2010), 4.

7. For more on AGs' increasingly polarized amicus brief filings, see Nolette, "State Litigation."

8. As noted in earlier chapters, Alabama AG William Pryor founded the Republican Attorneys General Association in response to perceived regulatory overreaches by his liberal colleagues in the tobacco litigation. A more recent example includes Republican Oklahoma AG Scott Pruitt's initial criticism of the 2012 national foreclosure settlement as "greatly overreach[ing] the authority of state attorneys general." Oklahoma Office of the Attorney General, "Attorney General Scott Pruitt."

9. Hans Von Spakovsky, "The University of Texas Will Have to Fight Its Own Battle," *National Review,* August 2, 2013, http://www.nationalreview.com.

10. Jan Murphy, "Attorney General Kathleen Kane Says Appeal of Voter ID Ruling Rests with Gov. Tom Corbett," *Patriot-News (PA)*, January 20, 2014, http://www.pennlive.com; Office of the California Attorney General, "Attorney General Kamala D. Harris Issues Statements on Prop. 8 Arguments," March 26, 2013, http://oag.ca.gov.

11. Timothy Williams and Trip Gabriel, "Virginia's New Attorney General Opposes Ban on Gay Marriage," *New York Times*, January 24, 2014.

12. John Suthers, "A 'Veto' Attorneys General Shouldn't Wield," *Wall Street Journal*, February 2, 2014.

13. John Miller, "Idaho First to Sign Law against Health Care Reform," *Associated Press*, March 18, 2010; Robbie Brown, "Georgia Attorney General Spurns Suit on Health Care," *New York Times*, March 31, 2010.

14. "Gibbons Will Join Lawsuit over Health Care Reform," *Las Vegas Sun*, April 2, 2010, http://www.lasvegassun.com; Kevin Wheeler, "Barbour Bypasses Hood, Will Join Obamacare Challenge," *WDAM (MS)*, April 13, 2010, http://www.wdam.com.

15. Jim Brunner, "Democrats May Go After McKenna's Budget," *Seattle Times*, March 23, 2010, http://seattletimes.com; Rachel La Corte, "State Attorney General Rob McKenna's Power Questioned in Lawsuits," *Seattle Times*, November 17, 2010, http://seattletimes.com.

16. Myriam Gilles and Gary Friedman, "After Class: Aggregate Litigation in the Wake of *AT&T Mobility v. Concepcion*," *University of Chicago Law Review* 79, no. 2 (2012): 623–675.

17. Schapiro, "From Dualism to Polyphony," 42.

18. Schapiro, *Polyphonic Federalism*.

19. Ibid., 98.

20. Thomas O. McGarity, "The Regulation–Common Law Feedback Loop in Nonpreemptive Regimes," in Buzbee, *Preemption Choice*, 236.

21. Schapiro, *Polyphonic Federalism*, 99.

22. David L. Shapiro, *Federalism: A Dialogue* (Chicago: Northwestern University Press, 1995), 140.

23. Pietro S. Nivola, "Does Federalism Have a Future?," *Public Interest* 142 (2001), 55.

24. Kagan, *Adversarial Legalism*, 9.

25. Silverstein, *Law's Allure*, 4.

26. Deborah Solomon and Ian McDonald, "Spitzer Decries Lax Regulation over Insurance," *Wall Street Journal*, November 17, 2004.

27. See, for example, Clayton, "Law, Politics, and the New Federalism."

28. Schapiro, *Polyphonic Federalism*, 100.

29. Judith Resnick, "Foreign as Domestic: Rethinking Horizontal Federalism and Foreign Affairs Preemption in Light of Translocal Internationalism," *Emory Law Journal* 57, no. 1 (2007): 41.

30. Schapiro, *Polyphonic Federalism*, 101.

31. David C. Vladeck, "Preemption and Regulatory Failure Risks," in Buzbee, *Preemption Choice*, 56.

32. James Madison, "Federalist #46," in *The Federalist Papers*, ed. Clinton Rossiter (New York: New American Library, 1961), 296. Also see Martha Derthick, *Keeping the Compound Republic: Essays on American Federalism* (Washington, DC: Brookings Institution Press, 2001), 94–96.

33. Terry Calvani, "Advertising Regulation: The States v. FTC," *Antitrust Law Journal* 58, no. 2 (1989).

34. Frank B. Cross, "Pragmatic Pathologies of Judicial Review of Administrative Rulemaking," *North Carolina Law Review* 78, no. 4 (2000): 1027–1036.

35. New State Ice Co. v. Liebmann, 285 US 262, 311 (1932) (J. Brandeis, dissenting).

36. Schapiro, *Polyphonic Federalism*, 98. Also see Erwin Chemerinsky, *Enhancing Government: Federalism for the 21st Century* (Stanford, CA: Stanford University Press, 2008); J. B. Ruhl and James Salzman, "Climate Change, Dead Zones, and Massive Problems in the Administrative State: A Guide for Whittling Away," *California Law Review* 98, no. 1 (2010): 59–120.

37. Masters, *Spoiling for a Fight*, 273.

38. Chemerinsky, *Enhancing Government*, 119.

39. David Vogel, *Trading Up: Consumer and Environmental Regulation in a Global Economy* (Cambridge, MA: Harvard University Press, 1995), 5–6.

40. Ibid., 147.

41. Samuel Issacharoff and Catherine Sharkey, "Backdoor Federalization," *UCLA Law Review* 53, no. 6 (2006): 1431.

42. Alexander Hamilton, "Federalist #70," in *The Federalist Papers*, ed. Clinton Rossiter (New York: New American Library, 1961).

43. Suzanne Mettler, *The Submerged State: How Invisible Government Policies Undermine American Democracy* (Chicago: University of Chicago Press, 2011).

44. Louis D. Brandeis, *Other People's Money* (New York: Stokes, 1914), 92.

45. Dean Baker, "Mortgage Settlement Lets Banks Off the Hook, Again," *CNN*, February 13, 2012, http://www.cnn.com.

46. Stephan Paul Mahinka and Kathleen M. Sanzo, "Multistate Antitrust and Consumer Protection Investigations: Practical Concerns," *Antitrust Law Journal* 63, no. 1 (1994): 234.

47. See, for example, J. G. March and J. P. Olsen, eds., *Ambiguity and Choice in Organizations* (Bergen, Norway: Universitetsforlaget, 1979); Frank R. Baumgartner and Bryan D. Jones, *Policy Dynamics* (Chicago: University of Chicago Press, 2002).

48. Bryan D. Jones and Frank R. Baumgartner, *The Politics of Attention: How Government Prioritizes Problems* (Chicago: University of Chicago Press, 2005), 139.

49. Gary Taylor, "AGs Police Environmental Ads," *National Law Journal*, January 28, 1991, 3.

50. Alan Greenblatt, "The Avengers General," *Governing Magazine*, May 2003, 52.

51. Howard M. Erichson, "A Typology of Aggregate Settlements," *Notre Dame Law Review* 80, no. 5 (2005): 1775–1780.

52. Scott Barclay and Shauna Fisher, "Cause Lawyers in the First Wave of the

Same-Sex Marriage Litigation," in *Cause Lawyers and Social Movements*, ed. Austin Sarat and Stuart Scheingold (Stanford: Stanford University Press, 2006), 91.

53. Balkin, "*Bush v. Gore.*"

54. Lewis, *Public Entrepreneurship*, 17–18.

55. Jonathan Simon, *Governing through Crime: How the War on Crime Transformed American Democracy and Created a Culture of Fear* (New York: Oxford University Press, 2008); Michael McCann, William Haltom, and Shauna Fisher, "Criminalizing Big Tobacco: Legal Mobilization and the Politics of Responsibility for Health Risks in the United States," *Law and Social Inquiry* 38, no. 2 (2013): 288–321.

56. McCann, Haltom, and Fisher, "Criminalizing Big Tobacco," 299.

57. Michael Greve, "Why 'Defunding the Left' Failed," *Public Interest* 89 (1987): 91–106.

58. Class Action Fairness Act of 2005, Pub. L. No. 109-2, 119 Stat. 4 (codified at 28 USC §§1332(d), 1453, 1711–15 (2006)).

59. AT&T Mobility v. Concepcion, 131 S. Ct. 1740 (2011); Wal-Mart v. Dukes, 131 S. Ct. 2541 (2011).

60. Lujan v. Defenders of Wildlife, 504 US 555 (1992); Summers v. Earth Island Institute, 129 S. Ct. 1142 (2009); Ledbetter v. Goodyear Tire & Rubber, 550 US 618 (2007); CompuCredit Corp. v. Greenwood, 132 S. Ct. 665 (2012).

61. Ashley L Taylor Jr., Anthony F. Troy, and Katherine W. Tanner Smith, "State Attorneys General: The Robust Use of Previously Ignored State Powers," *Urban Lawyer* 40, no. 3 (2008): 516.

62. Massachusetts v. EPA, 549 US 497 (2007); Cuomo v. Clearing House Association, 557 US 519 (2009); Mississippi ex rel. Jim Hood v. AU Optronics Corp., 134 S. Ct. 736 (2014).

63. Farhang, *Litigation State.*

64. Kenneth A. Shepsle, "Congress Is a 'They,' Not an 'It': Legislative Intent as Oxymoron," *International Review of Law and Economics* 12, no. 2 (1992): 239–256.

65. Masters, *Spoiling for a Fight*, 57.

66. Andersen, "Power of the State," 40.

APPENDIX

1. Alfonso Serrano, "'Cocaine' Pulled from Shelves Nationwide," *CBS News*, May 7, 2007, http://www.cbsnews.com.

2. The five AGs with jurisdiction over securities laws include those in Delaware, New Jersey, New York, Maryland, and South Carolina. Myers and Ross, *State Attorneys General*, 265–268.

3. From approximately 2004 to 2006, Spitzer reached civil settlements against Marsh & McLennan, American International Group, Merrill Lynch, and other major insurance and securities firms. He conducted some of his investigations on a multistate basis but conducted others entirely in New York.

4. Patrick McGreevy, "Pepsi Agrees to Get the Lead Out of Labels," *Los Angeles Times*, April 22, 2006, http://articles.latimes.com.

5. In the summer of 2009, for example, Minnesota AG Lori Swanson reached a single-state settlement with the Minnesota-based National Arbitration Forum (NAF), the nation's largest arbitration firm, which resulted in NAF altering their practices nationally. Robert Berner, "Big Arbitration Firm Pulls Out of Credit Card Business," *Business Week,* July 19, 2009, 1.

INDEX